TOEFL® MAP Listening

New TOEFL® Edition

Listening

Basic

DARAKWON

TOEFL® MAP New TOEFL® Edition
Listening Basic

Publisher Chung Kyudo
Editors Cho Sangik, Zong Ziin
Authors Michael A. Putlack, Stephen Poirier, Angela Maas, Maximilian Tolochko
Proofreader Talib Din
Designers Park Narae, Lee Seunghyun

First published in June 2022
By Darakwon, Inc.
Darakwon Bldg., 211, Munbal-ro, Paju-si, Gyeonggi-do 10881
Republic of Korea
Tel: 82-2-736-2031 (Ext. 250)
Fax: 82-2-732-2037

ISBN 978-89-277-8027-4 14740
978-89-277-8025-0 14740 (set)

www.darakwon.co.kr

Photo Credits
Shutterstock.com

Components Main Book / Answers, Explanations, and Scripts
10 9 8 7 6 5 4   24 25 26 27 28

Introduction

Studying for the TOEFL® iBT is no easy task and is not one that is to be undertaken lightly. It requires a great deal of effort as well as dedication on the part of the student. It is our hope that, by using *TOEFL® Map Listening Basic* as either a textbook or a study guide, the task of studying for the TOEFL® iBT will become somewhat easier for the student and less of a burden.

Students who wish to excel on the TOEFL® iBT must attain a solid grasp of the four important skills in the English language: reading, listening, speaking, and writing. The Darakwon *TOEFL® Map* series covers all four of these skills in separate books. There are also three different levels in all four topics. This book, *TOEFL® Map Listening Basic*, covers the listening aspect of the test at the basic level. Students who want to listen to lectures and conversations, learn vocabulary terms, and study topics that appear on the TOEFL® iBT will have their wishes granted by using this book.

TOEFL® Map Listening Basic has been designed for use both in a classroom setting and as a study guide for individual learners. For this reason, it offers a comprehensive overview of the TOEFL® iBT Listening section. In Part A, the different types of questions that are found on the TOEFL® iBT Listening section are explained, and hints on how to answer these questions properly are also provided. In Part B, learners have the opportunity to build their background knowledge of the topics that appear on the TOEFL® iBT by listening to the lectures and conversations of varying lengths that are found in each chapter. Each lecture and conversation is followed by the types of questions that appear on the TOEFL® iBT. Each chapter also has a vocabulary section, which enables learners to test their knowledge of vocabulary that is specific to the particular topics covered in each chapter. Finally, in Part C, students can take two TOEFL® iBT practice tests. These are lectures and conversations that have the same numbers and types of questions that appear on actual TOEFL® iBT Listening section passages. Combined, all of these should be able to help learners prepare themselves to take and, more importantly, to excel on the TOEFL® iBT.

TOEFL® Map Listening Basic has a great amount of information and should prove to be invaluable as a study guide for learners who are preparing for the TOEFL® iBT. However, while this book is comprehensive, it is up to each person to do the actual work. In order for *TOEFL® Map Listening Basic* to be of any use, the individual learner must dedicate him or herself to studying the information found within its pages. While we have strived to make this book as user friendly and as full of crucial information as possible, ultimately, it is up to each person to make the best of the material in the book. We wish you luck in your study of both English and the TOEFL® iBT, and we hope that you are able to use *TOEFL® Map Listening Basic* to improve your abilities in both of them.

Michael A. Putlack
Stephen Poirier
Angela Maas
Maximilian Tolochko

TABLE
OF
CONTENTS

How Is This Book Different?   6
How to Use This Book   7

Part A | Understanding Listening Question Types

Question Type 01   Gist-Content   10
Question Type 02   Gist-Purpose   14
Question Type 03   Detail   18
Question Type 04   Understanding the Function of What Is Said   22
Question Type 05   Understanding the Speaker's Attitude   26
Question Type 06   Understanding Organization   30
Question Type 07   Connecting Content   34
Question Type 08   Making Inferences   38

Part B | Building Background Knowledge of TOEFL Topics

Chapter 01 Life Sciences 1 & Conversations
Mastering Question Types with Lectures & Conversations A   44
Mastering Topics with Lectures B1, B2   47
Mastering Topics with Conversations B3   49
TOEFL Practice Tests C1   50
TOEFL Practice Tests C2   52
Star Performer Word Files   54
Vocabulary Review   56

Chapter 02 Life Sciences 2 & Conversations
Mastering Question Types with Lectures & Conversations A   58
Mastering Topics with Lectures B1, B2   61
Mastering Topics with Conversations B3   63
TOEFL Practice Tests C1   64
TOEFL Practice Tests C2   66
Star Performer Word Files   68
Vocabulary Review   70

Chapter 03 Social Sciences 1 & Conversations
Mastering Question Types with Lectures & Conversations A   72
Mastering Topics with Lectures B1, B2   75
Mastering Topics with Conversations B3   77
TOEFL Practice Tests C1   78
TOEFL Practice Tests C2   80

Star Performer Word Files   82

Vocabulary Review   84

Chapter 04 Social Sciences 2 & Conversations

Mastering Question Types with Lectures & Conversations A   86

Mastering Topics with Lectures B1, B2   89

Mastering Topics with Conversations B3   91

TOEFL Practice Tests C1   92

TOEFL Practice Tests C2   94

Star Performer Word Files   96

Vocabulary Review   98

Chapter 05 Physical Sciences 1 & Conversations

Mastering Question Types with Lectures & Conversations A   100

Mastering Topics with Lectures B1, B2   103

Mastering Topics with Conversations B3   105

TOEFL Practice Tests C1   106

TOEFL Practice Tests C2   108

Star Performer Word Files   110

Vocabulary Review   112

Chapter 06 Physical Sciences 2 & Conversations

Mastering Question Types with Lectures & Conversations A   114

Mastering Topics with Lectures B1, B2   117

Mastering Topics with Conversations B3   119

TOEFL Practice Tests C1   120

TOEFL Practice Tests C2   122

Star Performer Word Files   124

Vocabulary Review   126

Chapter 07 Arts 1 & Conversations

Mastering Question Types with Lectures & Conversations A   128

Mastering Topics with Lectures B1, B2   131

Mastering Topics with Conversations B3   133

TOEFL Practice Tests C1   134

TOEFL Practice Tests C2   136

Star Performer Word Files   138

Vocabulary Review   140

Chapter 08 Arts 2 & Conversations

Mastering Question Types with Lectures & Conversations A   142

Mastering Topics with Lectures B1, B2   145

Mastering Topics with Conversations B3   147

TOEFL Practice Tests C1   148

TOEFL Practice Tests C2   150

Star Performer Word Files   152

Vocabulary Review   154

Part C | Experiencing the TOEFL iBT Actual Tests

Actual Test 01   156

Actual Test 02   166

How Is This Book Different?

When searching for the ideal book to use to study for the TOEFL® iBT, it is often difficult to differentiate between the numerous books available on a bookstore's shelves. However, *TOEFL® Map Listening Basic* differs from many other TOEFL® iBT books and study guides in several important ways.

Many TOEFL® iBT books arrange the material according to the types of questions on the test. This often results in learners listening to a lecture on astronomy, followed by a lecture on history, followed by a conversation between a student and a professor, and so on. Simply put, there is little cohesion except for the questions. However, *TOEFL® Map Listening Basic* is arranged by subject. This book has eight chapters, all of which cover subjects that appear on the TOEFL® iBT. For instance, there are two chapters on life sciences, two chapters on social sciences, two chapters on physical sciences, and two chapters on the arts. By arranging the chapters according to subjects, learners can listen to lectures related to one another all throughout each chapter. This enables them to build upon their knowledge as they progress through each chapter. Additionally, since many vocabulary terms are used in certain subjects, learners can more easily recognize these specialized terms, understand how they are used, and retain the knowledge of what these terms mean. Finally, by arranging the chapters according to subjects, learners can cover and become familiar with every TOEFL® iBT question type in each chapter rather than just focus on a single type of question.

TOEFL® Map Listening Basic, unlike many other TOEFL® iBT books and study guides, does not have any translations into foreign languages within its pages. All too often, learners rely on translations in their native language. They use these translations to help them get through the material. However, the actual TOEFL® iBT has no translations, so neither does this book. This will better prepare learners to take the test the test by encouraging them to learn difficult terms and expressions through context, just as native speakers of English do when they encounter unfamiliar terms and expressions. Additionally, learners will find that their fluency in English will improve more rapidly when they use *TOEFL® Map Listening Basic* without relying on any translations.

Finally, the lectures and conversations in *TOEFL® Map Listening Basic* are based on topics that have appeared on the actual TOEFL® iBT in the past. Therefore, learners can see what kinds of topics appear on the TOEFL® iBT. This will enable them to recognize the difficulty level, the style of TOEFL® iBT lectures and conversations, and the difficulty of the vocabulary on the test. Second, learners can enhance their knowledge of topics that have appeared on the TOEFL® iBT. By knowing more about these topics when they take the actual test, test takers will be sure to improve their scores. Third, learners will also gain knowledge of the specialized vocabulary in particular topics, which will help them more easily understand lectures and conversations on the actual test. Finally, many topics appear multiple times on the TOEFL® iBT. Thus, students who study some of these topics may be pleasantly surprised to find the same topic when they take the actual TOEFL® iBT. That will no doubt help them improve their test scores.

How to Use
This Book

TOEFL® Map Listening Basic is designed for use either as a textbook in a classroom in a TOEFL® iBT preparation course or as a study guide for individuals who are studying for the TOEFL® iBT on their own. *TOEFL® Map Listening Basic* has been divided into three sections: Part A, Part B, and Part C. All three sections offer information which is important to learners preparing for the TOEFL® iBT. Part A is divided into 8 sections, each of which explains one of the question types that appear on the TOEFL® iBT Listening section. Part B is divided into 8 chapters. There are two chapters that cover each of the four subjects that appear on the TOEFL® iBT. Part C has 2 compete practice tests that resemble those which appear on the TOEFL® iBT.

Part A Understanding Listening Question Types

This section is designed to acquaint learners with each question type on the TOEFL® iBT Listening section. Therefore there are 8 sections in this chapter—one for each question type. Each section is divided into 5 parts. The first part offers a short explanation of the question type. The second part shows the ways in which questions of that particular type often appear on the test. The third part provides helpful hints on how to answer these questions correctly. The fourth part has either a lecture or a conversation followed by one question. The fifth part has a combination of four short lectures and conversations followed by one question each.

Part B Building Background Knowledge of TOEFL Topics

The purpose of this section is to introduce the various subjects that most frequently appear on the TOEFL® iBT. There are 8 chapters in Part B. Each chapter covers a single subject and contains 5 Listening lectures and 3 Listening conversations of various lengths as well as vocabulary words and exercises. Each chapter is divided into several parts.

Mastering Question Types with Lectures & Conversations

This section contains 2 Listening lectures that are between 200 and 250 words in length and 1 Listening conversation that is 100-150 words long. Following each lecture, there are 4 Listening questions. Each question is identified by type. The first and third Listening lectures always ask the same types of questions while the second lecture asks different types of questions. This ensures that all 8 question types are covered in this section. In addition, there are four true/false questions about the lecture for learners to answer. Following each conversation, there are 4 Listening questions. Each question is identified by type. The most common types of questions that appear after TOEFL® iBT Listening conversations are asked here. In addition, there are four true-false questions about the conversation for learners to answer.

Mastering Topics with Lectures and Conversations

This section contains 2 Listening lectures that are between 300 and 350 words in length and 1 Listening conversation that is 200-250 words long. There is a graphic organizer for learners to fill out as they listen to each lecture and conversation. This will help learners improve their organizational skills. Following each lecture, there are 3 Listening questions. These questions may be from any of the 8 types of Listening questions. Then, there are four fill-in-the-blank sentences about the lecture for learners to complete. Following each conversation, there are 3 Listening questions. These questions may be from any of the 8 types of Listening questions. Then, there are four fill-in-the-blank sentences about the conversation for learners to complete.

TOEFL Practice Tests

This section contains 1 Listening lecture that is between 500 and 550 words in length and 1 Listening conversation that is 350-400 words in length. The lecture has 6 Listening questions of any type while the conversation has 5 Listening questions of any type. The purpose of this section is to acquaint learners with the types of lectures and conversations they will encounter when they take the TOEFL® iBT.

Star Performer Word Files and Vocabulary Review

This section contains around 40 vocabulary words that were used in the lectures in each chapter. The words include nouns, verbs, adjectives, and adverbs. Definitions and sample sentences are provided for each word. There are also 12 questions that review the vocabulary words that learners cover in each chapter. The purpose of this section is to teach learners specific words that often appear in lectures on certain subjects and to make sure that learners know the meanings of these words and how to use them properly.

Part C Experiencing the TOEFL Actual Tests

This section contains 4 long TOEFL® iBT Listening lectures and questions and 2 long TOEFL® iBT Listening conversations and questions. The purpose of this section is to let learners experience long Listening lectures and conversations and to see if they can apply the knowledge they have learned in the course of studying *TOEFL® Map Listening Basic*.

Part A

Understanding Listening Question Types

Exercises with Gist-Content Questions

Exercise 1   Listen to part of a lecture in a sociology class.

M Professor: So the Industrial Revolution totally changed the Western world. How . . . ? There were many ways. For example, manufacturing became more industrialized. People began building products in factories. In addition, transportation methods improved. They became faster and more efficient. Society changed as well. Not every change was positive. Still, there were lots of changes. Let me tell you about them.

01-02

Q What aspect of the Industrial Revolution does the professor mainly discuss?

    Ⓐ When it began and ended

    Ⓑ The new inventions made during it

    Ⓒ The changes that it caused

    Ⓓ How transportation methods got better

Exercise 2   Listen to part of a conversation between a student and a professor.

W Student: Hi, Professor Gordon. I want to talk to you about my class grade for a minute.

M Professor: Sure, Sarah. Ah, your grade. It's not so good. Your test score was a little low.

01-03

W: Yes, I know. So I was wondering . . . Is it possible to do an extra assignment? You know, to, uh, earn some extra credit. I really need to get a good grade in your class.

M: Well . . . I suppose that's possible. Let me think about it for a moment.

Q What are the speakers mainly discussing?

    Ⓐ How the student can improve her grade

    Ⓑ A recent test that the student took

    Ⓒ An assignment that the student turned in

    Ⓓ The student's grades in all of her classes

Listen to part of a lecture in an art history class.

W Professor: There were numerous art movements in the twentieth century. Pop Art was one. The most famous artist in this movement was Andy Warhol. You probably know him for one thing: his painting of the Campbell's Soup can. But he did much more than that. He was quite an influential artist. Let me show you some of his best works.

01-04

Q What is the main topic of the lecture?

Ⓐ Pop Art

Ⓑ Campbell's Soup cans

Ⓒ Andy Warhol

Ⓓ Famous artists

Exercise 4   Listen to part of a conversation between a student and a student housing office employee.

M Student: Pardon me. I've got a big problem with my dorm room. Uh . . . Are you the person I should talk to?

W Student Housing Office Employee: That's right. What's the matter with your room? No key?

01-05

M: No. I have a key. But there's no bed in my room. And I don't enjoy sleeping on the floor.

W: Yeah. That would be uncomfortable. Okay. Can you give me your information? I'll take care of your problem immediately.

Q What problem does the student have?

Ⓐ His dormitory room is missing a bed.

Ⓑ He cannot afford his dormitory room.

Ⓒ He lost the key to his dormitory room.

Ⓓ He dislikes his new dormitory room.

Gist-Purpose questions focus on the theme of the passage. They usually appear after conversations. They sometimes appear after lectures. These questions ask about the purpose or theme of the passage. They always begin with "why." They ask about the entire passage, not specific details.

Gist-Purpose questions often look like this:

▸ Why does the student visit the professor?

▸ Why did the professor ask to see the student?

▸ Why does the professor explain X?

Tips for answering the questions:

■ Listen carefully for the reason for the conversation or lecture. In a conversation, the student often states why he or she is visiting a person. Or the professor may explain why he or she wants to see the student.

■ In a service encounter, the student often has a specific problem. This problem is always the student's purpose in visiting in a certain office.

■ The reason why the speakers are having the conversation is usually mentioned at the beginning of the passage.

■ The speakers may sum up the conversation at the end. The professor may also explain the purpose of his or her lecture at the end.

Example of a Gist-Purpose Question

Listen to part of a conversation between a student and a professor.

M Student: Hello, Professor Taylor. Sue Parker said you wanted to speak with me. Is there something you need?

01-06

W Professor: Actually, Tom, yes, there is. I noticed you didn't turn in your essay today. All of the other students submitted their papers. But you didn't. What happened?

M: Oh, yeah. The paper. Well, uh, I need some more time to finish it.

W: Why didn't you ask me for more time during class?

M: Uh . . . I was too embarrassed to ask you in front of everyone else. I really wanted to talk to you then. But I just couldn't. So, um . . . Can I get some more time for this assignment?

W: Why do you need more time?

M: I've got two other papers to write in my other classes. That's why I'm not finished yet.

W: All right. You have twenty-four hours. Turn in your paper by this time tomorrow.

Q Why did the professor ask to see the student?

   Ⓐ To talk about the topic of his report

   Ⓑ To assign him a paper to write

   Ⓒ To give him the results of his test

   Ⓓ To inquire about his essay

⊘ Answer Explanation

Choice Ⓓ is the reason why the professor asked to see the student. The professor mentions that everyone except for the student turned in their essays. She then asks the student why he did not submit his paper. Choices Ⓐ, Ⓑ, and Ⓒ are not mentioned in the conversation.

Exercises with Gist-Purpose Questions

Exercise 1 Listen to part of a conversation between a student and a professor.

01-07

M Student: Professor Travolta, can I talk to you about today's lecture?

W Professor: Sure, Kevin. What do you want to know?

M: Well, I didn't understand much of the class. I thought the part about the Earth's core was particularly difficult.

W: Yeah, that was hard. Okay. Let me explain a few things to you. Then, I'm sure you'll understand.

Q Why does the student visit the professor?

    Ⓐ To apologize for missing a class

    Ⓑ To complain about his grade

    Ⓒ To ask about the previous lecture

    Ⓓ To explain something to the professor

Exercise 2 Listen to part of a lecture in a zoology class.

01-08

M Student: So, um, do all snakes rely on venom?

W Professor: Not at all. Some kill their prey in other ways. The most common is by constriction. The boa constrictor and the anaconda use this method. They wrap themselves around their prey. Then, they squeeze the animal until it suffocates and dies. After that, they eat the animal, uh, by swallowing it whole.

Q Why does the professor explain the constriction method snakes use?

    Ⓐ To show how some snakes kill their prey

    Ⓑ To compare it to the use of venom

    Ⓒ To prove it is more efficient than using venom

    Ⓓ To say where the snakes that use it live

Listen to part of a conversation between a student and a professor.

W1 Student: Good morning. I got your message, ma'am. You wanted me to visit your office for something. Is, uh, everything all right?

W2 Professor: Not really, Stephanie. It's about your midterm exam.

W1: What? Did I fail the test? I sure hope not.

W2: No, you didn't fail it. But, um, it wasn't your best work. Did something happen? Did you forget to study for the exam?

01-09

Q Why did the professor ask to see the student?

   Ⓐ To prepare the student for a test

   Ⓑ To tell the student she failed a test

   Ⓒ To give the student the date of an upcoming test

   Ⓓ To discuss the student's midterm exam

Exercise 4 Listen to part of a conversation between a student and a housing office employee.

M Housing Office Employee: Yes? You're waiting to see me, right? How can I help you today?

W Student: I'm here to change rooms. I can't stand my roommate. So, uh, I want a new dorm room.

01-10

M: Okay. Today is the last day you can change rooms. Are you sure you want to do this?

W: Totally. My roommate and I simply don't get along.

Q Why does the student visit the housing office?

   Ⓐ To pay her student housing bill

   Ⓑ To file a complaint about her roommate

   Ⓒ To ask for a new dormitory room

   Ⓓ To attend a meeting with her roommate

Detail questions focus on the facts and the data that appear in the passage. They appear after both lectures and conversations. The test taker must listen for and remember details from the passage. Most Detail questions ask for information about major topics, not minor ones.

Detail questions often look like this:

❶ Most Detail questions are multiple-choice questions with four answer choices and one correct answer. One-answer questions usually appear like this:

▶ According to the professor, what is one way that X can affect Y?

▶ What are X?

▶ What resulted from the invention of the X?

❷ Some detail questions have two or more correct answers. These questions either require you to click on two answers or to indicate whether a number of statements are true or not. Two-answer questions usually appear like this:

▶ According to the professor, what information should the student include in her statement of purpose? [Click on 2 answers.]

▶ In the lecture, the professor describes a number of facts about earthquakes. Indicate whether each of the following is a fact about earthquakes. [Click in the correct box for each sentence.]

Tips for answering the questions:

- Determine the main topic of the passage. Then, focus on the facts and the details that are related to the main topic.

- Ignore the facts and the details that are related to minor topics or ideas.

- Take notes on the facts and the details that concern the main topic. Correct answer choices often use words and phrases that do not appear in the passage. Look for words and phrases similar to those used in the passage.

Example of a Detail Question

Listen to part of a lecture in an art history class.

M Professor: The art created today owes a lot to artistic advances made during the Renaissance. This was a period in Europe from around, uh, let's say 1400 to 1600. However, prior to the Renaissance, art was much, much different.

01-11

The Middle Ages came before the Renaissance. Art from this period—from medieval times—had three main characteristics. First, it was mostly religious in nature. Next, many of the surviving works of art were made of durable materials such as gold, silver, and gems. Third, medieval art was two dimensional in appearance.

During the Middle Ages, religion . . . that is, uh, Christianity . . . dominated life. In addition, artwork was expensive to make then. The Catholic Church, which was wealthy, could afford to pay for art. But most private individuals could not. This explains why religious themes dominated medieval art. Most artwork was made for the insides of churches—for the walls, the ceilings, and even the windows. Artists also illustrated Bibles and other religious books by drawing pictures in them.

Many works of art made in the Middle Ages didn't last very long. The ones that have survived were mostly made of precious metals and gems, stone, wood, and glass. In addition, some paintings have survived. These paintings—and those on church walls and stained-glass windows and in books—depict two-dimensional scenes. The pictures lack depth and appear flat. It wasn't until the Renaissance that artists learned about perspective. Perspective, by the way, is the ability to give paintings depth and to make them look three dimensional.

Q In the lecture, the professor describes a number of facts about art in the Middle Ages. Indicate whether each of the following is a fact about art in the Middle Ages.
Click in the correct box for each sentence.

	Fact	Not a Fact
1 Most medieval art has religious themes.		
2 Artists often drew pictures in Bibles.		
3 Many medieval paintings contained gems.		
4 Medieval art looks three dimensional.		

⊘ **Answer Explanation**

Choices 1 and 2 are both facts. For Choice 1, the professor says, "This explains why religious themes dominated medieval art." For Choice 2, the professor states, "Artists also illustrated Bibles and other religious books by drawing pictures in them." Choice 3 is incorrect because the professor does not mention that medieval paintings had gems in them. And Choice 4 is incorrect because Renaissance art, not medieval art, looks three dimensional. Medieval art looks two dimensional.

Exercises with Detail Questions

Exercise 1 Listen to part of a conversation between a student and a professor.

01-12

W1 Professor: Tina, what happened to you in class? You were thirty minutes late today.

W2 Student: I'm sorry, Professor Gibbs. I had some problems with my car. It wouldn't start this morning.

W1: Okay, but you need to be on time from now on. That's the third class you've been late to.

W2: Yes, ma'am. I won't let that happen again.

Q What resulted from the student's car problems?

(A) She missed an exam.

(B) She did not attend class.

(C) She was late for class.

(D) She could not give her presentation.

Exercise 2 Listen to part of a lecture in an art class.

01-13

W Professor: Most pottery has two basic functions. It can be used to hold various items or for display purposes. You can see the difference here . . . This pot isn't decorated at all. It's plain and ordinary. Yet this one here is. The first pot was made to be used, uh, probably for cooking. The second is rather ornate. It's for decoration.

Q According to the professor, what is a function of pottery?
Click on 2 answers.

(A) To be displayed

(B) To transport items

(C) To hold objects

(D) To hide items

Exercise 3   Listen to part of a conversation between a student and a professor.

M Professor: So, Janet . . . Are you going to apply for the scholarship?

W Student: I think so. Can you tell me one more time . . . Uh, what exactly do I need to do?

M: Okay. First, you have to write an essay. Then, you need to fill out a form. And you need a recommendation from a professor. I'll do that. That's all there is to it.

W: Really? That's easy. Okay. I'll get to work on the essay.

01-14

Q What must the student do first to apply for a scholarship?

    Ⓐ Fill out a form

    Ⓑ Write an essay

    Ⓒ Have an interview

    Ⓓ Get a recommendation

Exercise 4   Listen to part of a lecture in a zoology class.

M Professor: Now, what about animals with stripes? Let's see . . . There's the zebra. There's also the tiger. The zebra is a prey animal while the tiger is a predator. Yet they both have stripes. Interestingly, it's for the same reason: camouflage. Both hunters and the hunted need camouflage. They use it to hide from one another.

01-15

Q According to the professor, why do animals have stripes?

    Ⓐ To attract possible mates

    Ⓑ To be able to avoid tigers

    Ⓒ To make themselves more attractive

    Ⓓ To hide from other animals

Understanding the Function of What Is Said questions focus on what is said in the passage. They appear after both lectures and conversations. These questions often replay a part of the passage. For some of these questions, the test taker must infer the meaning of a phrase or sentence. For other questions, the test taker must infer the purpose of a statement a person makes.

Understanding the Function of What Is Said questions often look like this:

❶ Some Understanding the Function of What Is Said questions ask about what the speaker is inferring. These are usually replay questions. They may appear like this:

▸ What does the professor imply when he says this: (replay)

▸ What can be inferred from the professor's response to the student? (replay)

❷ Other Understanding the Function of What Is Said questions ask about the purpose of a statement or a topic in the lecture or conversation. These can be regular questions or replay questions. They may appear like this:

▸ What is the purpose of the woman's response? (replay)

▸ Why does the student say this: (replay)

▸ Why does the professor ask the student about his grades?

Tips for answering the questions:

- People do not always speak literally. Their statements often have hidden meanings. Learn to understand what people are implying when they speak.

- Listen to the tone of voice the speaker uses. This can help you understand what a person is implying.

- In lectures, there is sometimes dialogue between a student and a professor. The student may ask or answer a question. These parts often appear in replay questions.

- For replay questions, listen to the entire part that is replayed. This will help you understand what the speaker means or is implying.

Example of an Understanding the Function of What Is Said Question

Listen to part of a conversation between a student and a professor.

01-16

W1 Student: Good morning, Professor Johnson. Can I talk to you for a bit?

W2 Professor: Of course you can. What's on your mind today, Denise?

W1: Yesterday's lecture. To tell you the truth, well, uh . . . A lot of it went over my head. I just didn't get it.

W2: These things happen. Tell me . . . What part of it did you have trouble with?

W1: All of it. It was just really confusing for me.

W2: Okay. Did you do the assigned reading? How did you feel about the material in the book?

W1: Yes, I did the reading. It wasn't too bad. But I still couldn't understand most of your lecture. What should I do?

W2: Hmm . . . I've got a couple of articles for you to read. They should help you figure out the material. Hold on while I try to find them.

Q Listen again to part of the conversation. Then answer the question.

    W1: Yesterday's lecture. To tell you the truth, well, uh . . . A lot of it went over my head. I just didn't get it.

    W2: These things happen.

What can be inferred from the professor's response to the student?

    W2: These things happen.

    Ⓐ She understands the student's situation.
    Ⓑ She thinks the student should try harder.
    Ⓒ She is upset with the student's behavior.
    Ⓓ She believes the student should drop the class.

⊘ Answer Explanation

Choice Ⓐ best describes what the professor is implying. When the professor says, "These things happen," she indicates that she understands that students sometimes have a hard time with the material. Her tone of voice also indicates her sympathy toward the student. Choices Ⓑ, Ⓒ, and Ⓓ are not mentioned in the conversation.

Exercises with Understanding the Function of What Is Said Questions

Exercise 1   Listen to part of a lecture in an art history class.

> **W Student**: But wasn't medieval art fairly advanced?
>
> **M Professor**: **Not really.** Medieval artists weren't able to make very sophisticated paintings. In fact, take a look at some medieval artwork sometime. In some cases, it's, uh, well, quite simplistic. Then, compare it with Renaissance art. You'll see that Renaissance artists knew many advanced techniques that medieval artists simply didn't know.

01-17

Q Listen again to part of the lecture. Then answer the question.
What is the purpose of the professor's response?

(A) To consider the student's comment

(B) To disagree with the student

(C) To ask the student for more information

(D) To bring up a new topic

Exercise 2   Listen to part of a conversation between a student and a Registrar's office employee.

> **W Registrar's Office Employee**: How may I help you this morning?
>
> **M Student**: Hi. I'd like to get some copies of my transcript. And I need them today if that's possible.
>
> **W**: Today? **That's going to be hard to manage.**
>
> **M**: Please. I really need them. I have to send them to some graduate schools by today.

01-18

Q Listen again to part of the conversation. Then answer the question.
What does the woman imply when she says this:

(A) It will be expensive to make copies of the student's transcript.

(B) The student is unlikely to get his transcript that day.

(C) Students can have instant access to their transcripts.

(D) The woman no longer manages the Registrar's office.

Listen to part of a conversation between a student and a professor.

W Student: Is there anything I can do to improve my grade in this class? I just can't get a C.

M Professor: Well, you could join one of the class study groups.

W: Study groups? Would they really help my grade?

M: I think so. A lot of students are very pleased with them. Here's the schedule for when they meet.

01-19

Q Why does the student ask the professor about study groups?

   Ⓐ She forgot who the leader of her group is.

   Ⓑ She lost her study group schedule.

   Ⓒ She wants to find a way to improve her grade.

   Ⓓ She would like to lead a study group.

Listen to part of a lecture in a paleontology class.

W Professor: We know so much about dinosaurs thanks to fossils. You know, the, uh, petrified remains of animals. We can tell a lot about the past just by studying fossils. **But I don't want to talk about what we can learn from fossils yet**. Instead, I want to talk about how fossils get formed right now. All right?

01-20

Q Listen again to part of the lecture. Then answer the question.
Why does the professor say this:

   Ⓐ To note that she wants to discuss a different topic

   Ⓑ To admit that she does not know much about fossils

   Ⓒ To tell the students that the class is almost over

   Ⓓ To find out what the students want to learn

Understanding the Speaker's Attitude

Understanding the Speaker's Attitude questions focus on a speaker's attitude or opinion toward something. They appear after both lectures and conversations. These questions often replay a part of the passage. For some of these questions, the test taker is asked how the speaker feels about something or if the speaker likes or dislikes something. For other questions, the test taker is asked to make an inference concerning what a speaker says.

Understanding the Speaker's Attitude questions often look like this:

❶ Some Understanding Attitude questions ask about the speaker's feelings. These can be regular questions or replay questions. They may appear like this:

▸ What is the professor's attitude toward X?

▸ What is the professor's opinion of X?

▸ What does the woman mean when she says this: (replay)

❷ Other Understanding the Speaker's Attitude questions ask about the speaker's opinions. These can be regular questions or replay questions. They may appear like this:

▸ What can be inferred about the student?

▸ What can be inferred about the student when she says this: (replay)

Tips for answering the questions:

▪ Listen to the tone of voice the speaker uses. This can help you determine the speaker's opinion about something.

▪ The speaker will sometimes give his or her opinion about a topic. Listen carefully to determine how the speaker feels about that topic. Focus on the speaker's opinion of main topics or themes, not minor ones.

▪ Notice when people are speaking literally and when they are making inferences. Learn how to read between the lines concerning what people are saying.

▪ For replay questions, listen to the entire part that is replayed. This will help you understand what the speaker means or is implying.

Example of an Understanding the Speaker's Attitude Question

Listen to part of a conversation between a student and a librarian.

W Student: Excuse me. Can I borrow a moment of your time?

M Librarian: Sure. What can I do for you?

01-21

W: I'm looking for a past issue of a journal. But it doesn't seem to be in the library though. The name of the journal is *Scientific American*.

M: Oh, yes. That's a well-known journal. We definitely have it. What year is the article that you're looking for?

W: It's from, um . . . uh, 1978. So it's kind of old.

M: Ah. I can tell you exactly why it's not on the shelves. You see, all issues of *Scientific American* from before 1980 are on microfilm. So we don't have physical copies of those old issues anymore.

W: I see . . . So, uh, where do I find the microfilm?

M: It's in another section. Follow me, and I'll show you.

Q Listen again to part of the conversation. Then answer the question.

M: Ah. I can tell you exactly why it's not on the shelves. You see, all issues of *Scientific American* from before 1980 are on microfilm. So we don't have physical copies of those old issues anymore.

W: I see . . . So, uh, where do I find the microfilm?

What can be inferred about the student when she says this: 🎧

W: So, uh, where do I find the microfilm?

- Ⓐ She dislikes having to work with microfilm.
- Ⓑ She has not used the library's microfilm collection before.
- Ⓒ She believes that the article is not important to her work.
- Ⓓ She wants the librarian to copy the article for her.

⊘ Answer Explanation

Choice Ⓑ can be inferred about the student. She asks where the microfilm is. So she implies that she has not used the library's microfilm collection before. Choice Ⓐ may be true, but the student does not imply that. Choice Ⓒ is unlikely to be true since the student wants to find the article. So it is probably important to her. In addition, the student does not mention or imply anything about photocopying the article, so Choice Ⓓ is not correct.

Exercises with Understanding the Speaker's Attitude Questions

Exercise 1   Listen to part of a lecture in an environmental studies class.

01-22

W Professor: Eventually, the supply of fossil fuels on the Earth will run out. That's one reason why people are using alternative energy. Solar, wind, geothermal, and nuclear are forms of alternative energy. They have many advantages. But they aren't perfect. Each type of alternative energy has drawbacks as well. For instance, wind energy is unreliable. It's only good when the wind blows.

Q What is the professor's opinion of alternative energy?

    Ⓐ It is much better than using fossil fuels.

    Ⓑ It has advantages and disadvantages.

    Ⓒ It is always too unreliable.

    Ⓓ It is the best type of energy.

Exercise 2   Listen to part of a lecture in an archaeology class.

01-23

M Professor: The Anasazi were a Native American tribe. They lived in the area that's the Southwest United States today. They created a widespread civilization over several centuries. They also traded with cultures near the Mississippi River. Impressive, isn't it? After all, the Mississippi was quite distant from where the Anasazi mainly lived. Yet the Anasazi still traded many items with the people there.

Q What does the professor imply about the Anasazi?

    Ⓐ They were defeated in war by other tribes.

    Ⓑ They were the most cultured tribe in their region.

    Ⓒ The Mississippi River was of no interest to them.

    Ⓓ The distances they traveled were remarkable.

Exercise 3   Listen to part of a conversation between a student and a student employment office employee.

M Student: Hi. I'm looking for a part-time job. Is this the right office?

W Student Employment Office Employee: It sure is. I'd be glad to help you. What kind of job are you looking for?

M: Hmm . . . I'd like to work indoors in an office. And I'd like a job that pays decent money.

W: Yeah. That's what everyone says. Let me show you some jobs that are available.

01-24

Q What is the woman's attitude toward the student?

   Ⓐ She is helpful.

   Ⓑ She is impolite.

   Ⓒ She is nervous.

   Ⓓ She is uncooperative.

Exercise 4   Listen to part of a conversation between a student and a professor.

M1 Professor: Stuart, you didn't turn in your homework again. What's going on?

M2 Student: I'm sorry about that, sir. I'll turn it in tomorrow.

M1: That's not good enough. I want your homework one hour from now.

M2: Yes, sir. I'll do my best to get it to you then. I'll be back by three.

01-25

Q Listen again to part of the conversation. Then answer the question.
What does the professor mean when he says this: 🎧

   Ⓐ He dislikes the student's suggestion.

   Ⓑ The student will lose points on his homework.

   Ⓒ The student is going to fail the class.

   Ⓓ He wants the student to do better.

Understanding Organization

Understanding Organization questions focus on the organization of the passage. They almost always appear after lectures. They seldom appear after conversations. Some of these questions ask about how the professor organizes the information and presents the lecture. Other questions ask about individual information presented in the lecture.

Understanding Organization questions often look like this:

❶ Some Understanding Organization questions ask about the organization of the material in the professor's lecture. They may appear like this:

▸ How does the professor organize the information about X that he presents to the class?

▸ How is the discussion organized?

❷ Other Understanding Organization questions ask about specific information in the lecture. They ask about why the professor discusses or mentions certain pieces of information. They may appear like this:

▸ Why does the professor discuss X?

▸ Why does the professor mention X?

Tips for answering the questions:

■ Focus on how the lecture is organized. Lectures are often organized as follows: by chronology, by complexity, by comparing or contrasting, by giving examples, by classifying, by categorizing, by describing a problem and a solution, and by describing a cause and an effect.

■ The professor often explains how he or she will present the information at the beginning of the lecture. The professor may also explain why he or she presented the information in a certain way at the end of the lecture.

■ Professors often use specific words or phrases to indicate how they plan to organize their lectures. For instance, a professor might say, "In today's class, I'm going to show you some slides of famous buildings," or, "Let's compare and contrast the different types of stars."

Example of an Understanding Organization Question

Listen to part of a lecture in an archaeology class.

M Professor: Tutankhamen was an Egyptian pharaoh, or king. You probably know him by a different name though: King Tut. In 1922, a research team led by Howard Carter discovered King Tut's tomb. Inside were, as Carter said, "Wonderful things." There were more than 5,000 items in his tomb. Most were well preserved. This included some of the most famous treasures found there. I'm talking about King Tut's mummified remains and his burial mask. The mask was made of gold. And King Tut's coffin was solid gold. Yeah . . . Can you imagine that? Anyway, tens of thousands of people around the world have seen King Tut's treasures. This makes him one of the most recognizable figures in Egyptian history.

01-26

Despite his fame, we knew little about King Tut until recently. After all, he only ruled for a decade. He reigned from about 1333 B.C. to 1323 B.C. He died while young at, uh, around nineteen years of age. For many years, people believed he had been assassinated. Yet experts now think he died from a combination of medical problems. An examination of his mummy showed he was born with a clubbed foot. This made it difficult for him to walk. He also had some bone diseases in his foot. His bones were, well, uh, literally dying. The same study took some DNA samples from his mummy. They showed that King Tut had malaria. Experts have concluded that the combination of these problems made him too weak to fight off other infections. That was what ultimately killed him.

Q Why does the professor mention Howard Carter?

Ⓐ To accuse him of robbing King Tut's grave

Ⓑ To mention that he conducted DNA studies on King Tut

Ⓒ To say that he found King Tut's tomb

Ⓓ To name him as a world-famous archaeologist

⊘ Answer Explanation

Choice Ⓒ best describes why the professor mentions Howard Carter. The professor states, "In 1922, a research team led by Howard Carter discovered King Tut's tomb." So he is focusing on Carter's discovery. Choice Ⓐ is incorrect since the professor mentions nothing about grave robbing. Choice Ⓑ is incorrect since Howard Carter did not conduct any DNA studies. And Choice Ⓓ is incorrect because the professor says nothing about how famous Carter was.

Exercises with Understanding Organization Questions

Exercise 1   Listen to part of a lecture in a history class.

M Professor: We all know that Christopher Columbus discovered the New World. That was in 1492. But what about some other explorers from Spain . . . ? Well, in 1502, Rodrigo de Bastidas sailed to Panama. In 1513, Vasco Nunez de Balboa crossed Panama and reached the Pacific Ocean. And in 1518 . . . No. Wait. In 1519, Hernan Cortez landed in Mexico, where he fought the Aztecs.

01-27

Q How is the discussion organized?

   Ⓐ According to the explorers' nationalities

   Ⓑ In chronological order

   Ⓒ In alphabetical order

   Ⓓ According to the sizes of the expeditions

Exercise 2   Listen to part of a lecture in a linguistics class.

M Professor: Ancient civilizations utilized many different types of writing systems. For example, the Egyptians used hieroglyphics. See here . . . And look at the slide here . . . Other cultures relied on pictograms, too. Here is one such ancient writing system . . . And here's another . . . The Greeks, however, developed an alphabet. Here . . . is what it looked like. Greek looks more like a modern-day alphabet, doesn't it?

01-28

Q How does the professor organize the information about writing systems that he presents to the class?

   Ⓐ By quoting parts of the textbook

   Ⓑ By encouraging the students to ask questions

   Ⓒ By focusing on a single civilization

   Ⓓ By showing the students slides

Exercise 3 Listen to part of a conversation between a student and a housing office employee.

W Housing Office Employee: So, um, you want a new dorm room. How come?

M Student: Well, I live in a triple. I can't have two roommates. That's too many. And my room is so tiny. There's just no space for all of my stuff. We're too crowded in there.

W: I see. Is there anything else?

M: Yes. I need silence to study, but both of my roommates are too noisy.

01-29

Q Why does the student discuss his dormitory room?

    Ⓐ To complain about how messy his roommates are

    Ⓑ To say that he is satisfied with the room he has

    Ⓒ To explain why he wants to move to another one

    Ⓓ To mention why he wants to get a smaller room

Exercise 4 Listen to part of a lecture in a geology class.

W Professor: Gold is one of the most precious of all metals. Of course, people have used it as money for thousands of years. But gold has many important properties. First, it's an excellent conductor of electricity. This makes it incredibly valuable to various industries. It's also possible to beat gold into a very thin sheet.

01-30

Q Why does the professor mention electricity?

    Ⓐ To explain why it is so precious

    Ⓑ To state that gold conducts it well

    Ⓒ To note how industries utilize it

    Ⓓ To focus on its important properties

Question Type | 07 | Connecting Content

Connecting Content questions focus on how the ideas in the passage relate to one another. They usually appear after lectures. They seldom appear after conversations. The test taker needs to recognize the major relationships in the passage. These questions frequently appear after lectures when a professor discusses two or more themes, ideas, objects, or individuals.

Connecting Content questions often look like this:

❶ Many Connecting Content questions appear as charts or tables. There are four sentences or phrases. The test taker must match them with a theme, idea, cause, effect, object, or individual. They may appear like this:

▶ Based on the information in the lecture, do the following sentences refer to X or Y? [Click in the correct box for each sentence.]

	X	Y
1 [a statement]		
2 [a statement]		
3 [a statement]		
4 [a statement]		

❷ Other Connecting Content questions ask the test taker to make inferences from the relationships that are mentioned in the passage. They may appear like this:

▶ What does the professor imply about X?

▶ What comparison does the professor make between X and Y?

Tips for answering the questions:

■ These questions are frequently charts or tables. You might have to put sentences or phrases in the correct order. Take notes when the professor mentions certain steps in a procedure.

■ Focus on the relationships between the facts, concepts, or ideas that a professor discusses. These questions often appear after a professor mentions some similarities and differences between two or more things he or she discusses.

■ These questions often require you to make comparisons, recognize cause and effect, follow a sequence, or identify a contradiction or agreement.

Example of a Connecting Content Question

Listen to part of a lecture in a biology class.

W Professor: There are countless tiny organisms in the world. Some of them are dangerous to other living things. We call them pathogens. There are four main pathogens. They are bacteria, fungi, viruses, and prions. All of them can be harmful to living organisms. Some, however, can be, uh, be helpful. This is true of many types of bacteria. But for the most part, these microorganisms are killers. Throughout history, they've killed untold millions of people. They do this by spreading through living organisms. This makes them very difficult to destroy.

01-31

The first, bacteria, are found everywhere. They're even inside our bodies. But the human body has many defenses against them. As a result, bacteria are less harmful than other pathogens. However, some bacteria, such as those that cause tuberculosis and pneumonia, are killers. Bacteria can also cause food to spoil. So I suppose they harm humans indirectly as well. As for fungi, despite killing plants, they're not too harmful to people. They mostly cause minor problems for humans.

Viruses, on the other hand, are deadlier. They cause diseases such as smallpox, polio, and influenza. Malaria, a deadly virus, kills more than one million people every year. Finally, what about prions? They're rare yet deadly. Prions cause diseases that attack the brain and nervous system. Mad Cow disease is caused by prions. The human form of this disease is rare, but it's always fatal. Now that you know a little about each type of pathogen, let's go into detail on them. First, bacteria.

Q Based on the information in the lecture, indicate which statements refer to bacteria or viruses. Click in the correct box for each sentence.

	Bacteria	Viruses
1 Can make food spoil		
2 Cause malaria and polio		
3 Are not as harmful as other pathogens		
4 Cause tuberculosis		

⊘ Answer Explanation

Choices 1, 3, and 4 refer to bacteria. According to the professor, bacteria "can also cause food to spoil." In addition, the professor says, "Bacteria are less harmful than other pathogens," and, "Some bacteria, such as those that cause tuberculosis and pneumonia, are killers." Choice 2 refers to viruses. The professor mentions several diseases caused by viruses, including malaria and polio.

Exercises with Connecting Content Questions

Exercise 1   Listen to part of a lecture in an astronomy class.

M Professor: We call our galaxy the Milky Way. It's a spiral galaxy. Take a look at the shape of it up here. Our solar system is about right here . . . There are countless spiral galaxies throughout the universe. However, there are other shapes that galaxies commonly take. Let me show a few more of them to you right now.

01-32

Q What does the professor imply about the Milky Way Galaxy?

  (A) It has a small number of stars.
  (B) It is larger than most galaxies.
  (C) Its shape is not unusual.
  (D) It is located far from other galaxies.

Exercise 2   Listen to part of a lecture in a botany class.

M Professor: In the desert, it doesn't rain much. So plants have evolved ways to get water. The cactus has long roots. These extend far beneath the ground. They help absorb water from the soil. The mesquite tree has roots that can extend more than twenty-five meters. That's incredibly long. As for other desert plants, some store excess water in their leaves.

01-33

Q What comparison does the professor make between the cactus and the mesquite tree?

  (A) How they get water
  (B) What size they grow to
  (C) Why people use them
  (D) Where they grow best

Exercise 3 Listen to part of a conversation between a student and a professor.

W Professor: Jeff, I really think you should apply for the scholarship. It would be a great opportunity for you.

M Student: But what are the chances of me winning it? Are they big or small?

W: They're pretty good. I know all of the students applying. And you're the most qualified.

M: I see. In that case, I guess that I could fill out the application.

01-34

Q What is the likely outcome of the student applying for the scholarship?

    Ⓐ His application will be rejected.

    Ⓑ He will have to sit for an interview.

    Ⓒ His desire to study abroad will be fulfilled.

    Ⓓ He will receive the scholarship.

Exercise 4 Listen to part of a lecture in an art history class.

W Professor: The ancient Greeks made many vases. Fortunately, thousands of them have survived to the present day. That should tell you about the quality of those vases. Anyway, because there are so many vases from ancient Greece, we have learned a lot about them. Now, um, the Greeks used different methods to make the vases. And they decorated them in many ways.

01-35

Q What can be inferred about ancient Greek vases?

    Ⓐ They cost a lot of money today.

    Ⓑ They have few decorations.

    Ⓒ They were very well made.

    Ⓓ They are simple in their styles.

Making Inferences questions focus on implications made in the passage and what they mean. They appear after both lectures and conversations. The test taker needs to listen to information in the passage and then make a conclusion about what it means or what is going to happen as a result of that information.

Making Inferences questions often look like this:

▸ What does the professor imply about X?

▸ What will the student probably do next?

▸ What can be inferred about X?

▸ What does the professor imply when he says this: (replay)

Tips for answering the questions:

■ At the end of the lecture or conversation, a speaker often indicates what he or she will do next.

■ Notice when people are speaking literally and when they are making inferences. Learn how to understand what these inferences mean.

■ For replay questions, listen to the entire part that is replayed. This will help you understand what the speaker means or is implying.

Example of a Making Inferences Question

Listen to part of a lecture in an astronomy class.

M Professor: Between Mars and Jupiter lies a strange region in our solar system. It's called the asteroid belt. Millions of rocky asteroids make up the asteroid belt. Some of these asteroids are large. These large asteroids average around 400 kilometers in width. The largest, Ceres, is even considered a dwarf planet. But most of the asteroids are tiny. In addition, the exact number of asteroids is unknown.

01-36

W Student: Why is that, Professor Gleason?

M: Mostly because the asteroids are in constant motion around the sun. So they, uh, often collide with one another. This sometimes makes them break up, which forms more asteroids. I suppose you could say that the number of asteroids is constantly increasing. But, um, please note that the asteroids don't form a solid wall of matter. Various satellites have easily passed through the asteroid belt and not suffered any damage.

Now, why does the asteroid belt exist? In the past, astronomers commonly believed that the asteroid belt was once a planet. However, for some unknown reason, it broke up. Nowadays, this theory has few followers. Instead, most astronomers believe that the asteroid belt is material that tried to become a planet yet failed. These astronomers believe that the strength of Jupiter's gravity kept a planet from forming there. Basically, we don't really know what happened. More research needs to be done before we can totally understand why the asteroid belt exists.

Q What does the professor imply about the asteroid belt?

(A) A few of the asteroids in it are bigger than Mars.
(B) Some parts of it are safe to travel through.
(C) Its asteroids may combine to form a planet someday.
(D) It is expanding in the direction of Jupiter.

⊘ **Answer Explanation**

Choice (B) best describes what the professor implies about the asteroid belt. The professor states, "But, um, please note that the asteroids don't form a solid wall of matter. Various satellites have easily passed through the asteroid belt and not suffered any damage." Therefore, it can be implied that places in it are safe to travel through. Choice (A) is incorrect because the professor mentions nothing about the size of Mars. The professor states that the asteroid belt might be the remains of a planet that tried to form a long time ago. So Choice (C) is incorrect. Choice (D) is incorrect because the professor does not say anything about where the asteroid belt is expanding toward.

Exercises with Making Inferences Questions

Exercise 1 Listen to part of a lecture in a history class.

W Professor: From 264 B.C. to 146 B.C., Rome fought three wars against Carthage. These wars are called the Punic Wars. Carthage was a city-state in Northern Africa. It had a powerful navy. So it challenged the Romans for dominance on the Mediterranean Sea. After the Third Punic War, Rome was the only remaining major power in the Mediterranean region.

01-37

Q What can be inferred about the Punic Wars?

- Ⓐ Thousands of men were killed during them.
- Ⓑ They mostly involved naval battles.
- Ⓒ The wars were started by the Romans.
- Ⓓ They ended with the defeat of Carthage.

Exercise 2 Listen to part of a conversation between a student and a gym employee.

W1 Student: Here's my completed application for gym membership. Can you take a look at it?

W2 Gym Employee: Sure . . . Hmm . . . Everything looks good. You're all ready to become a member now.

01-38

W1: Great. So, uh . . . Is there anything else I need to do before I start working out?

W2: Ah, there's one more thing. It costs twenty-five dollars per semester to join the gym.

Q What will the student probably do next?

- Ⓐ Start working out at the gym
- Ⓑ Pay her membership fee
- Ⓒ Return to her dormitory
- Ⓓ Go to the gym's dressing room

Listen to part of a lecture in an art history class.

M Professor: A lot of art critics really disliked the Impressionists. In fact, they didn't think that the Impressionists' works were real art. I totally disagree with them. But I understand why the critics felt that way. After all, the Impressionists were abstract artists. And abstract art was fairly new in the 1800s. No one was used to seeing art like they made.

01-39

Q What does the professor imply about Impressionist art?

(A) People should consider it real art.

(B) It was made by some art critics.

(C) It is inferior to other art forms.

(D) It looks better than abstract art.

Exercise 4   Listen to part of a conversation between a student and a professor.

M Professor: Yes, Tina. You wanted to talk to me?

W Student: Yes, sir. It's about my test. I think that you, uh . . . you made a mistake on my test. Sec . . . Um, I only missed seven points. But, er . . . the grade you wrote down was an 87.

01-40

M: Let me see . . . Hmm . . . **Tina, I sincerely apologize.** Thank you for showing me this.

W: No problem, sir.

Q Listen again to part of the conversation. Then answer the question.
What does the professor imply when he says this: 🎧

(A) He will change the student's test grade.

(B) The student can take the test again.

(C) He often makes mistakes on tests.

(D) There is nothing he can do for the student.

Part B

Building Background Knowledge of TOEFL Topics

Chapter 01 | Life Sciences 1 | **Conversations**

zoology • biology • marine biology • medicine • virology • ecology • biochemistry •
botany • public health

02-01

Listen to part of a lecture in a zoology class.

TYPE 1   What is the lecture mainly about?

Ⓐ Why monarch butterflies go through diapause

Ⓑ The routes migrating monarch butterflies take

Ⓒ The life cycle of the monarch butterfly

Ⓓ The migration of the monarch butterfly

TYPE 2   What comparison does the professor make between monarch butterflies and birds?

Ⓐ The places where they migrate

Ⓑ The distances that they migrate

Ⓒ The routes they take when they migrate

Ⓓ The times when they migrate

TYPE 3   Why does the professor mention diapause?

Ⓐ To explain how some monarch butterflies can live very long

Ⓑ To state which kinds of butterflies typically reproduce

Ⓒ To tell the students about an important phase in a butterfly's life

Ⓓ To answer a question that a student asks about butterflies

TYPE 4   What is the professor's attitude toward butterflies migrating long distances?

Ⓐ He considers it to be normal.

Ⓑ He is impressed by their abilities.

Ⓒ He thinks they do not migrate far.

Ⓓ He believes they could fly farther.

✐ Checking Listening Accuracy   Mark the following statements T (true) or F (false).

	T	F	
1	☐	☐	Monarch butterflies may migrate to Mexico.
2	☐	☐	It may take a monarch butterfly three months to migrate.
3	☐	☐	Monarch butterflies always migrate along the same routes.
4	☐	☐	Diapause lets monarch butterflies live a long time.

02-02

Listen to part of a lecture in a botany class.

TYPE 5 Why does the professor explain stratification?

  Ⓐ To describe a process for planting some trees

  Ⓑ To explain a way to water certain plants

  Ⓒ To discuss a factor involving tropical plants

  Ⓓ To state how some seeds can germinate

TYPE 6 According to the professor, what do apple, peach, and pear seeds need to germinate?

  Ⓐ A long time buried in the ground

  Ⓑ A great amount of heat

  Ⓒ Exposure to cold temperatures

  Ⓓ More water than most plants

TYPE 7 What does the professor imply about eucalyptus trees?

  Ⓐ They live in areas that have dry conditions.

  Ⓑ They produce seeds a few times during their lives.

  Ⓒ Their life cycle takes many years to complete.

  Ⓓ Their seeds are able to be burned easily.

TYPE 8 What does the professor tell the students about heat stratification?

  Ⓐ To say it is the best way to make seeds germinate

  Ⓑ To contrast it with another type of stratification

  Ⓒ To claim that the seeds of many fruit trees need it

  Ⓓ To argue that it can harm certain kinds of trees

Checking Listening Accuracy   Mark the following statements T (true) or F (false).

	T	F	
1	☐	☐	Plants need oxygen, soil, and sunlight to grow.
2	☐	☐	Dormant seeds need special care before they germinate.
3	☐	☐	People put some seeds in the freezer for a month.
4	☐	☐	Eucalyptus tree seeds often grow after forest fires.

Listen to part of a conversation between a student and a professor.

02-03

TYPE 9   Why does the student visit the professor?

    Ⓐ   To discuss his next semester's schedule

    Ⓑ   To complain about a change at the school

    Ⓒ   To ask about taking a new science class

    Ⓓ   To find out when he is going to graduate

TYPE 10   What does the professor say about the new graduation requirements?

    Ⓐ   They are for juniors and seniors.

    Ⓑ   She made them up by herself.

    Ⓒ   They do not apply to all students.

    Ⓓ   They affect students majoring in languages.

TYPE 11   What can be inferred about the professor?

    Ⓐ   She recently met the student.

    Ⓑ   The student is taking her class this semester.

    Ⓒ   She is the student's advisor.

    Ⓓ   She is a language instructor.

TYPE 12   Listen again to part of the conversation. Then answer the question.
Why does the student say this: 🎧

    Ⓐ   To complain about his grade

    Ⓑ   To make the professor agree with him

    Ⓒ   To express that he is trying hard

    Ⓓ   To show how upset he is

✎ Checking Listening Accuracy   Mark the following statements T (true) or F (false).

	T	F	
1	☐	☐	The professor knows about the changes for graduation.
2	☐	☐	The student is pleased with the changes for graduation.
3	☐	☐	The student has to take some new classes.
4	☐	☐	Freshmen and sophomores must take the new classes.

Mastering **Topics** with Lectures

Listen to part of a lecture in a marine biology class.

02-04

Coral

Characteristics:	Zooxanthellae:
	What Kills Coral Reefs:

1 Based on the information in the lecture, indicate which statements refer to coral or zooxanthellae. Click in the correct box for each sentence.

	Coral	Zooxanthellae
1 May turn white when starting to die		
2 Able to create nourishment through photosynthesis		
3 Can only live in shallow water		
4 Made up of a single cell		

2 What will the professor probably do next?

- Ⓐ Continue describing coral
- Ⓑ Discuss El Nino's effects on coral reefs
- Ⓒ Give the class a short break
- Ⓓ Ask the class some questions

3 Listen again to part of the lecture. Then answer the question.
What can be inferred about the professor when she says this: 🎧

- Ⓐ She feels that the students need help spelling that word.
- Ⓑ She likes to teach the students long and difficult words.
- Ⓒ She wants the students to learn a lot about coral.
- Ⓓ She believes that the students need to take better notes.

Listening Comprehension Complete the following sentences. Use the words in the box.

a. the calcium carbonate	b. pollution	c. tropical waters	d. the nutrients

1 Coral mostly grows in _____ that are very warm.

2 Coral reefs expand because of _____ they secrete.

3 Zooxanthellae create _____ that let coral survive.

4 _____ is a major reason why some coral reefs die.

Mastering **Topics** with Lectures B2

Listen to part of a lecture in a biology class.

02-05

Fungi

Characteristics:	How They Benefit People:
	How They Harm People:

1 What is the main topic of the lecture?

- Ⓐ How fungi and plants are different
- Ⓑ The primary benefits of fungi
- Ⓒ The ways in which fungi can harm people
- Ⓓ The various characteristics of fungi

2 According to the professor, where do fungi usually grow?

- Ⓐ On tree branches
- Ⓑ In dark and wet places
- Ⓒ Inside caves
- Ⓓ In places that get sunlight

3 Why does the professor discuss athlete's foot?

- Ⓐ To give an example of how fungi are harmful
- Ⓑ To explain why his feet are hurting him
- Ⓒ To talk about a side effect of eating mushrooms
- Ⓓ To ask if any of the students have ever had it

✎ Listening Comprehension   Complete the following sentences. Use the words in the box.

a. cause diseases	b. grows underground	c. the ecosystem	d. photosynthesis

1 Plants undergo _____, but fungi do not.

2 Much of a fungus such as a mushroom _____.

3 Fungi are often beneficial to _____ they live in.

4 Some fungi are poisonous and may _____ in humans.

Mastering **Topics** with Conversations

Listen to part of a conversation between a student and a dining services employee.

02-06

Service Encounter

Reason for Visiting:	➡	Result:
Student's Request:	➡	Man's Response:

1 Why does the student visit the dining services office?

Ⓐ To complain about the food in the cafeteria

Ⓑ To say that her meal plan is too expensive

Ⓒ To compare the cafeteria food with her mother's cooking

Ⓓ To ask about getting a different meal plan

2 Why did the student purchase the plan for twenty meals a week?

Ⓐ She expected to eat all of her meals on campus.

Ⓑ The school makes all freshmen purchase that plan.

Ⓒ The price of that meal plan was inexpensive.

Ⓓ She purchased that meal plan by mistake.

3 Listen again to part of the conversation. Then answer the question.
Why does the student say this: 🎧

Ⓐ To give a compliment

Ⓑ To file a complaint

Ⓒ To answer a question

Ⓓ To make a joke

Listening Comprehension Complete the following sentences. Use the words in the box.

a. her meal plan	b. the man agrees	c. twenty meals a week	d. a waste of money

1 The student wants to talk about _____ with the man.

2 The student's current meal plan gives her _____ .

3 The student believes her meal plan is _____ .

4 _____ to let the student change her meal plan.

02-07

Listen to part of a lecture in a zoology class.

Zoology

1   What aspect of symbiosis does the professor mainly discuss?

    Ⓐ The ways in which it harms some organisms

    Ⓑ The different types of symbiotic relationships

    Ⓒ How it affects ants and other organisms

    Ⓓ The types of organisms that rely on it

2   What kind of relationship is facultative symbiosis?

    Ⓐ One in which both of the organisms get some kind of benefit

    Ⓑ One in which one of the organisms harms or kills the other one

    Ⓒ One in which one organism's survival does not depend the other

    Ⓓ One in which three organisms have a relationship with one another

3   How is the lecture organized?

    Ⓐ The professor describes symbiosis and then provides some examples of it.

    Ⓑ The professor shows slides of some symbiotic relationships and explains them.

    Ⓒ The professor answers questions from the students to cover the material.

    Ⓓ The professor asks questions and then proceeds to provide his own answers.

4   Based on the information in the lecture, indicate which statements refer to ants' relationships with bullhorn acacia trees or aphids.
Click in the correct box for each statement.

	Bullhorn Acacia Trees	Aphids
1 Provide the ants with certain nutrients		
2 Are protected from beetles by the ants		
3 Produce honeydew that the ants eat		
4 Are a relationship that takes place in Central America		

5   Listen again to part of the lecture. Then answer the question.
What does the professor imply when he says this: 🎧

    Ⓐ Organisms have no choice in their symbiotic relationships.

    Ⓑ Almost all organisms have symbiotic relationships.

    Ⓒ The most beneficial relationships are symbiotic ones.

    Ⓓ Some symbiotic relationships can cause harm.

6   Listen again to part of the lecture. Then answer the question.
What does the professor mean when he says this: 🎧

    Ⓐ He is happy the student asked a question.

    Ⓑ He intends to explain what the student asked.

    Ⓒ He thinks the student asked a good question.

    Ⓓ He wants the student to answer her own question.

02-08

Listen to part of a conversation between a student and a professor.

1 Why does the student visit the professor?

    (A) To ask about changing a research topic

    (B) To tell the professor about her internship

    (C) To find out what her next assignment is

    (D) To describe a new class that she is taking

2 What was the student originally planning to do her work on?

    (A) Snakes

    (B) Parrots

    (C) Zoos

    (D) Reptiles

3 What can be inferred about the student?

    (A) She is not a senior.

    (B) She gets good grades.

    (C) Her major is biology.

    (D) She works to make money.

4 What is the professor's opinion of the student's new topic?

    (A) She thinks it is fine.

    (B) She dislikes it.

    (C) She offers no opinion.

    (D) She wants more time to think about it.

5 Listen again to part of the conversation. Then answer the question.
What is the purpose of the professor's response?

    (A) To get the student to apologize

    (B) To ask the student to leave her office

    (C) To show she is not interested in that topic

    (D) To encourage the student to keep talking

Star Performer Word Files

- **absent** (adj) away; not present

  Several people are currently **absent** from the room.

- **cluster** (v) to gather together in a group

  The animals are **clustering** around one another to keep warm.

- **competitor** (n) something that competes with another person or thing; an opponent

  They are **competitors** who often play against each other.

- **comprise** (v) to make up; to consist of

  Many plants are **comprised** of roots, a stem, and leaves.

- **dormant** (adj) inactive; asleep

  The **dormant** volcano has not erupted for more than 200 years.

- **ecosystem** (n) a unique environment

  Deserts and jungles are two types of **ecosystems**.

- **eliminate** (v) to kill; to destroy

  The farmers are trying to **eliminate** the pests.

- **expand** (v) to become bigger; to increase in size

  The population is **expanding** as more animals reproduce.

- **forest fire** (n) a fire that burns a large number of trees in a wooded area

  This region gets lots of **forest fires** whenever it does not rain much.

- **generation** (n) a group of organisms that are roughly the same age

  The current **generation** knows a lot about technology.

- **harden** (v) to become hard

  Glue **hardens** quickly, so it can join two objects.

- **hidden** (adj) unable to be seen

  The trap is **hidden** somewhere in the forest.

- **hollow** (adj) having a hole in the middle

  Part of the tree is **hollow**, so some birds live in it.

- **impressive** (adj) remarkable

  Your performance on the recent test was **impressive**.

- **infection** (n) a disease; an illness

  Mary got an **infection** after she swam in the dirty water.

- **journey** (n) a long trip

  They are going to take a **journey** of 1,000 miles.

- **lifespan** (n) the length of time that an organism lives

  The average **lifespan** for most humans is over seventy.

- **mate** (v) to reproduce; to make offspring

  When two animals **mate**, they can create babies.

- **migration** (n) a trip an animal takes from one place to another

  Every year, people see the **migration** of birds to the south.

- **nutrient** (n) something that provides nourishment

  Plants get some of their **nutrients** from the ground.

- **organism** (n) a living creature

  Trees, humans, and lions are all kinds of **organisms**.

- **oxygen** (n) a gas that living creatures must breathe to survive

  Astronauts breathe **oxygen** in tanks when they go on spacewalks.

- **parasite** (n) an organism that lives on or in another and causes it harm

  Some **parasites** eventually kill their hosts.

- **pest** (n) an annoying animal; an animal that destroys crops and other plants

  Rats and mice are two **pests** that often eat farmers' crops.

- **phase** (n) a period; a stage

  The moon goes through several **phases** as it orbits Earth.

- **poisonous** (adj) having poison; using poison to harm others

  There are some **poisonous** spiders that can harm people.

- **pollution** (n) dirt; something that causes harm to the environment

  There is too much air **pollution** in big cities.

- **process** (n) a method; a way of doing something

  What is the **process** for making this chemical?

- **range** (n) an area

  Deer live in a wide **range** of areas.

- **rapidly** (adv) quickly; swiftly

  The fish are swimming **rapidly** to escape from the shark.

- **reproduce** (v) to make offspring

  Many animals **reproduce** only once a year.

- **route** (n) a path

  There is a small **route** you can take to go up the mountain.

- **sap** (n) a juice that flows through a tree or plant

  If you cut the branch, some **sap** will come out.

- **secrete** (v) to emit; to ooze; to produce

  This animal **secretes** a very sticky substance.

- **seedling** (n) a very small plant that has just started growing

  Be careful with the **seedlings** because they are fragile.

- **simultaneously** (adv) at the same time

  The runners appeared to finish the race **simultaneously**.

- **thorn** (n) a small, sharp branch on a tree, bush, or plant

  Watch out for the **thorns** on that bush; they are sharp.

- **thrive** (v) to do well; to expand

  Some species **thrive** when they go to another ecosystem.

- **treat** (v) to take care of; to tend to

  A doctor needs to **treat** that wound for it to get better.

- **undergo** (v) to experience

  Many insects **undergo** great changes throughout their lives.

■ Choose the word with the closest meaning to each highlighted word or phrase.

1　Sharks are the most dangerous predators in the oceans.

   Ⓐ hunters
   Ⓑ fish
   Ⓒ animals
   Ⓓ organisms

2　Few animals are able to live in very cold regions.

   Ⓐ conditions
   Ⓑ sources
   Ⓒ areas
   Ⓓ temperatures

3　What is the destination of those migrating animals?

   Ⓐ objective
   Ⓑ home
   Ⓒ route
   Ⓓ vision

4　They will transport this package to another location.

   Ⓐ send
   Ⓑ create
   Ⓒ carry
   Ⓓ manufacture

5　Their calculations were erroneous, so they made a mistake.

   Ⓐ precise
   Ⓑ wrong
   Ⓒ crucial
   Ⓓ fascinating

6　The police are trying to protect that man.

   Ⓐ arrest
   Ⓑ watch
   Ⓒ question
   Ⓓ guard

■ Match each word with the correct definition.

7　beverage　•　　•　Ⓐ a drink

8　painful　•　　•　Ⓑ a person who digs for minerals in the ground

9　germinate　•　　•　Ⓒ a use

10　miner　•　　•　Ⓓ hurting badly; sore

11　function　•　　•　Ⓔ to sprout; to start to grow

12　mature　•　　•　Ⓕ adult; fully developed

Part B

Chapter 02 | Life Sciences 2 | Conversations

zoology • biology • marine biology • medicine • virology • ecology • biochemistry • botany • public health

Mastering **the Question Types**
with Lectures & Conversations

TYPE • 1 Gist-Content   TYPE • 2 Connecting Content   TYPE • 3 Understanding Organization   TYPE • 4 Speaker's Attitude

Listen to part of a lecture in a pathology class.

02-09

TYPE 1 What aspect of immune systems does the professor mainly discuss?

- Ⓐ What white blood cells do for the body
- Ⓑ The two major types of immune systems
- Ⓒ How the innate immune system works
- Ⓓ The ways that animals fight off diseases

TYPE 2 Based on the information in the lecture, indicate which statements refer to skin or white blood cells.
Click in the correct box for each statement.

	Skin	White Blood Cells
1 Can keep foreign objects out of the body		
2 Can fight pathogens in the body		
3 May act like soldiers fighting invaders		
4 May be the first line of defense		

TYPE 3 Why does the professor discuss white blood cells?

- Ⓐ To mention that they are found in the stomach
- Ⓑ To compare their effects with those of mucus
- Ⓒ To state that they can fight acids in the body
- Ⓓ To describe a defense found inside the body

TYPE 4 What is the professor's opinion of white blood cells?

- Ⓐ They are not always effective.
- Ⓑ They benefit the body.
- Ⓒ They could work faster.
- Ⓓ They do very little good.

Checking Listening Accuracy Mark the following statements T (true) or F (false).

    T   **F**

1 ☐ / ☐ Pathogens can enter bodies and cause them to become sick.

2 ☐ / ☐ There are two types of immune systems that organisms have.

3 ☐ / ☐ The skin and mucus are part of the adaptive immune system.

4 ☐ / ☐ White blood cells fight pathogens inside the body.

Listen to part of a lecture in a zoology class.

02-10

TYPE 5 What is the main topic of the lecture?

    (A) The problems that mosquitoes cause

    (B) The places where mosquitoes live

    (C) The best ways to kill mosquitoes

    (D) The method in which mosquitoes suck blood

TYPE 6 According to the professor, why do mosquitoes suck animals' blood?

    (A) To provide them with nourishment

    (B) To help them kill their prey

    (C) To let them reproduce

    (D) To lay their eggs inside a host

TYPE 7 What does the professor imply about DDT?

    (A) It is easily available for people to purchase.

    (B) It kills many mosquitoes that carry diseases.

    (C) It is somewhat difficult to manufacture.

    (D) It must be used many times to be successful.

TYPE 8 Listen again to part of the lecture. Then answer the question.
Why does the professor say this: 🎧

    (A) To ask the students an important question

    (B) To emphasize a number he just mentioned

    (C) To repeat something he told the students

    (D) To make sure the students understand him

Checking Listening Accuracy **Mark the following statements T (true) or F (false).**

	T	F	
1	☐	☐	The only mosquitoes that suck blood are males.
2	☐	☐	Mosquitoes get their nourishment from plant nectar.
3	☐	☐	Mosquitoes carry a number of deadly diseases.
4	☐	☐	DDT is legal to use in every country in the world.

02-11

Listen to part of a conversation between a student and a computer services office employee.

TYPE 9   Why does the student visit the computer services office?

    Ⓐ   To get her computer repaired

    Ⓑ   To sign up for an email account

    Ⓒ   To ask the man for help changing her password

    Ⓓ   To find out why she cannot log into her account

TYPE 10   What does the man say the woman failed to do?

    Ⓐ   Change her password

    Ⓑ   Register her account

    Ⓒ   Log in every three months

    Ⓓ   Pay a required fee

TYPE 11   What will the man probably do next?

    Ⓐ   Fix the student's problem

    Ⓑ   Help another student

    Ⓒ   Give the student a new account

    Ⓓ   Send the student an email

TYPE 12   Listen again to part of the conversation. Then answer the question.
What does the student mean when she says this: 🎧

    Ⓐ   She is confused by what the man said.

    Ⓑ   She thinks the man told a good joke.

    Ⓒ   She disagrees with the new policy.

    Ⓓ   She wants the man to be more serious.

Checking Listening Accuracy   **Mark the following statements T (true) or F (false).**

    T   F

1   ☐ / ☐   The student's computer broke down.

2   ☐ / ☐   The student cannot log into her email account.

3   ☐ / ☐   The student has not changed her password in a year.

4   ☐ / ☐   Students must change their passwords every three months.

Mastering **Topics** with Lectures

Listen to part of a lecture in a biology class.

02-12

Spider Webs

Characteristics:		Orb Webs:
	➡	Sheet Webs:
		Tangled Webs:

1 How does the professor organize the information on different types of spider webs?

- Ⓐ By focusing on the most common webs
- Ⓑ By showing pictures as she discusses each type of web
- Ⓒ By mentioning spider species and then saying which webs they make
- Ⓓ By explaining the ways in which spiders decorate their webs

2 What will the professor probably do next?

- Ⓐ Talk about spider web decorations
- Ⓑ Describe some species of spiders
- Ⓒ Explain more about orb webs
- Ⓓ Show the students some real spider webs

3 Listen again to part of the lecture. Then answer the question.
Why does the professor say this: 🎧

- Ⓐ To show how to make an orb web
- Ⓑ To explain the web's composition
- Ⓒ To make a comparison
- Ⓓ To answer a question

Listening Comprehension Complete the following sentences. Use the words in the box.

a. shaped like circles	b. indoor places	c. blades of grass	d. catch insects

1 Spiders use their webs in order to _____ to eat for food.

2 Orb webs are _____ and are found between tree branches.

3 Sheet webs are horizontal webs that are between _____ .

4 Tangled webs are often found in _____ .

Listen to part of a lecture in a paleontology class.

02-13

The Sizes of Dinosaurs

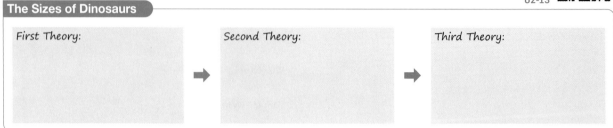

First Theory: ➡ Second Theory: ➡ Third Theory:

1 What is the lecture mainly about?

ⓐ Why some dinosaurs were so big

ⓑ Whether dinosaurs were warm or cold blooded

ⓒ How dinosaurs evolved over time

ⓓ Which dinosaurs were dangerous predators

2 According to the professor, what was the Earth like when dinosaurs lived?
Click on 2 answers.

ⓐ It had a lot of plant life.

ⓑ It was mostly covered with water.

ⓒ It had many other types of animals.

ⓓ It was much warmer than today.

3 Listen again to part of the lecture. Then answer the question.
What can be inferred about the professor when he says this: 🎧

ⓐ He believes that the theory is true.

ⓑ He is conducting research on the theory.

ⓒ He is not convinced the theory is correct.

ⓓ He hopes the theory will be proven false.

🖊 **Listening Comprehension** Complete the following sentences. Use the words in the box.

a. were so big	b. than a house	c. were hollow	d. to defend

1 Dinosaurs could be very small or even bigger _____.

2 Some experts believe dinosaurs _____ because there was a lot of food.

3 Large dinosaurs were able _____ themselves against large predators.

4 The bones of some dinosaurs _____, just like those of birds.

Mastering **Topics** with Conversations **B3**

Listen to part of a conversation between a student and a professor.

02-14

Office Hours

Reason for Contacting Student:	➡	Professor's Response:
	⬉	
Student's Response:		Professor's Solution:
	➡	

1 Why did the professor ask to see the student?

- Ⓐ To show her midterm exam grade to her
- Ⓑ To discuss some work she has not done
- Ⓒ To assign her a new project
- Ⓓ To discuss his most recent lecture

2 According to the professor, what should the students do every week?

- Ⓐ Take a short quiz
- Ⓑ Give a class presentation
- Ⓒ Read the assigned material
- Ⓓ Email some work to him

3 Listen again to part of the conversation. Then answer the question.
What does the professor mean when he says this: 🎧

- Ⓐ The student did not attend the first day of class.
- Ⓑ The student turned in all of her work.
- Ⓒ He forgot to give the student enough time.
- Ⓓ He did not write anything about an assignment.

✎ **Listening Comprehension**   Complete the following sentences. Use the words in the box.

a. the second week	b. asked to see	c. a paper	d. any online assignments

1 The professor _____ the student by email.

2 The student has not done _____ yet.

3 The student did not start class until _____ of the semester.

4 The professor gives the student _____ explaining what to do.

Listen to part of a lecture in an ecology class.

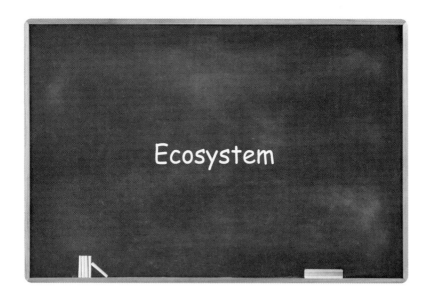

1 What is the professor's attitude toward the student?

- Ⓐ She is complimentary.
- Ⓑ She is impatient.
- Ⓒ She is excited.
- Ⓓ She is critical.

2 Why does the professor mention water and land ecosystems?

- Ⓐ To compare the organisms that live in each of them
- Ⓑ To focus on how large and small both of them can be
- Ⓒ To say that there are more herbivores in land ecosystems than in water ones
- Ⓓ To name some of the types of ecosystems found in each of them

3 According to the professor, which of the following is a microecosystem?

- Ⓐ The Sahara Desert
- Ⓑ A puddle of water
- Ⓒ A jungle
- Ⓓ A coral reef

4 Based on the information in the lecture, indicate which words refer to biotic or abiotic factors. Click in the correct box for each word.

	Biotic Factor	Abiotic Factor
① Monera		
② Climate		
③ Sunlight		
④ Plants		

5 Listen again to part of the lecture. Then answer the question. Why does the professor say this: 🎧

- Ⓐ She wants to begin teaching the class.
- Ⓑ Some students are currently misbehaving.
- Ⓒ The students are not all back from break yet.
- Ⓓ She is ready to hand back their homework.

6 Listen again to part of the lecture. Then answer the question. What does the professor imply when she says this: 🎧

- Ⓐ Ecosystems are too complicated for scientists to study.
- Ⓑ The students need to be familiar with ecosystems.
- Ⓒ Her description of an ecosystem is incomplete.
- Ⓓ Not every ecosystem works in the same way.

Listen to part of a conversation between a student and a museum staff member.

02-16

1   Why does the student visit the museum?

    Ⓐ To get her work assignment from the man

    Ⓑ To see if she can do some volunteer work there

    Ⓒ To look at some of the relics in the museum

    Ⓓ To submit her résumé to the man

2   When does the student want to come to the museum?

    Ⓐ After her classes finish

    Ⓑ Every morning

    Ⓒ In the evenings

    Ⓓ On the weekend

3   What will the student probably do next?

    Ⓐ Start working for the man

    Ⓑ Go back to her dormitory

    Ⓒ Attend her next class

    Ⓓ Have an interview with the man

4   Listen again to part of the conversation. Then answer the question.
What is the purpose of the student's response?

    Ⓐ To provide another suggestion

    Ⓑ To show her disappointment

    Ⓒ To disagree with the man

    Ⓓ To prove she is ready to work

5   Listen again to part of the conversation. Then answer the question.
What can be inferred about the student when she says this: 🎧

    Ⓐ She is willing to work hard.

    Ⓑ She is considering accepting the job.

    Ⓒ She expects payment for her work.

    Ⓓ She thinks she deserves a better assignment.

Star Performer Word Files

- **adaptive** (adj) able to change
  Adaptive animals can survive when there are serious changes in their environments.

- **airborne** (adj) in the air
  Airborne diseases often affect large numbers of people.

- **appendage** (n) a body part, such as an arm or leg, that extends from the main part of the body
  That insect has an extra appendage for sucking blood.

- **ban** (v) to forbid; not to allow or permit something to be used or done
  The government banned the use of some chemicals.

- **benefit** (v) to provide an advantage; to help
  How can we benefit from this new product?

- **breed** (v) to reproduce
  Rabbits can breed very quickly.

- **capability** (n) an ability
  The most advanced computers have many capabilities.

- **carnivorous** (adj) meat-eating
  Sharks and dolphins are both carnivorous animals.

- **control** (v) to run; to manage; to have power over
  This machine can control all of the others in the room.

- **countless** (adj) numerous
  There are countless stars in the galaxy.

- **cover** (v) to describe; to go over
  Could you please cover the material we need to know for the exam?

- **crawl** (v) to move slowly; to move on more than two legs
  The baby is crawling across the floor.

- **decompose** (v) to rot; to break down
  The dead body rapidly began to decompose.

- **drain** (v) to remove the water or some other liquid from something
  You must drain the water before you can work on the pipes.

- **eliminate** (v) to kill; to wipe out
  The farmer wants to eliminate the pests from his fields.

- **enable** (v) to permit; to allow
  This card will enable you to enter every room in the building.

- **enrich** (v) to improve the quality of
  Many inventions have enriched people's daily lives.

- **fearsome** (adj) frightening; very scary
  Dragons are fearsome creatures in most stories.

- **gland** (n) a body part that secretes various substances
  That patient has a problem with his glands.

- **harmful** (adj) dangerous
  Many chemicals are harmful to both humans and animals.

- **herbivore** (n) an animal that only eats vegetation

  A cow is a common **herbivore** found in many places.

- **horizontal** (adj) flat; even; level

  The bricks need to be **horizontal** to make the wall perfect.

- **innate** (adj) natural; inborn

  All animals are born with some **innate** abilities.

- **insecticide** (n) a poison that is used to kill insects

  Some **insecticides** are incredibly powerful and can harm animals other than insects.

- **invisible** (adj) unable to be seen

  Atoms are **invisible** to the human eye.

- **lightweight** (adj) weighing very little

  The bag looks heavy but is actually **lightweight**.

- **microecosystem** (n) a very small ecosystem

  The backyard garden is a **microecosystem**.

- **mucus** (n) a slimy substance found in the nose and the throat

  The body produces extra **mucus** when a person is sick.

- **nectar** (n) a sweet liquid produced by plants

  Butterflies are attracted to the sweet **nectar** of flowers.

- **orb** (n) a sphere; a globe

  The planets look like **orbs** circling the sun.

- **pathogen** (n) an organism such as a bacterium or virus that causes a disease

  The **pathogen** caused the patient to become extremely sick.

- **penetrate** (v) to enter something, often by using force

  The needle must **penetrate** the skin before the medicine is injected.

- **practically** (adv) virtually; almost

  Lisa is **practically** finished with her assignment.

- **soil** (n) ground; earth; dirt

  This dark, rich **soil** is excellent for farming.

- **stagnant** (adj) unmoving

  The water found in swamps is usually **stagnant**.

- **sticky** (adj) having the characteristics of glue

  After working with the glue, the woman's hands were very **sticky**.

- **tangled** (adj) twisted; knotted; snarled

  If you do not comb your hair, it will get **tangled**.

- **thrive** (v) to do well; to reproduce in great numbers

  The colony will **thrive** if everyone works hard.

- **vertically** (adv) upright

  The columns rise **vertically** toward the sky.

- **vibration** (n) a shaking sensation

  An earthquake causes severe **vibrations**.

⬛ Choose the word with the closest meaning to each highlighted word or phrase.

1   Please remove your hats while you are inside.

Ⓐ take in
Ⓑ take out
Ⓒ take away
Ⓓ take off

2   Everyone knows we can depend on Jack to do a good job.

Ⓐ look
Ⓑ consider
Ⓒ rely
Ⓓ expect

3   There are many various reasons why the experiment failed.

Ⓐ different
Ⓑ complicated
Ⓒ unique
Ⓓ interesting

4   Some organisms are so small that people need microscopes to see them.

Ⓐ creatures
Ⓑ germs
Ⓒ molecules
Ⓓ particles

5   Accordingly, there is nothing more they can do to help us.

Ⓐ Although
Ⓑ Despite this
Ⓒ Therefore
Ⓓ Fortunately

6   The defense of the country is every soldier's job.

Ⓐ assault
Ⓑ democracy
Ⓒ trust
Ⓓ protection

⬛ Match each word with the correct definition.

7   claim   •   • Ⓐ something woven by a spider to trap insects in

8   work   •   • Ⓑ the typical weather in a region

9   web   •   • Ⓒ an adornment; an item that makes another thing look better

10 climate   •   • Ⓓ to operate

11 puddle   •   • Ⓔ to declare; to state that something is true

12 decoration   •   • Ⓕ a small pool of water

Part B

Chapter 03 Social Sciences 1 | Conversations

history • archaeology • anthropology • economics • sociology • psychology •
education • geography • political science • linguistics

Mastering **the Question Types**
with Lectures & Conversations

TYPE • 1 Gist-Content   TYPE • 2 Connecting Content   TYPE • 3 Understanding Organization   TYPE • 4 Speaker's Attitude

02-17

Listen to part of a lecture in an education class.

TYPE 1 What is the lecture mainly about?

- Ⓐ The phonics method
- Ⓑ How to use flashcards properly
- Ⓒ Two ways to teach reading
- Ⓓ Why everyone needs to read

TYPE 2 What is the likely outcome of a student who learns to read with the phonics method?

- Ⓐ The student might have a smaller vocabulary than normal.
- Ⓑ The student can teach him or herself many new words.
- Ⓒ The student will enjoy reading new kinds of material.
- Ⓓ The student will have to use flashcards to learn to read.

TYPE 3 How is the lecture organized?

- Ⓐ By having the students provide input in the lecture
- Ⓑ By using the question-and-answer method of lecturing
- Ⓒ By going into detail on individual learning methods
- Ⓓ By reciting information from the students' textbooks

TYPE 4 What is the professor's opinion of the phonics method?

- Ⓐ He thinks it is very effective.
- Ⓑ He believes it is fun to learn.
- Ⓒ He disapproves of it.
- Ⓓ He offers no opinion of it.

✎ Checking Listening Accuracy   Mark the following statements T (true) or F (false).

	T	F	
1	☐	☐	There are four primary ways to teach reading.
2	☐	☐	Students do not learn the alphabet with the phonics method.
3	☐	☐	The phonics method teaches students new words slowly.
4	☐	☐	The look-and-say method may use flashcards.

02-18

Listen to part of a lecture in a history class.

TYPE 5 What is the main topic of the lecture?

    Ⓐ The reasons why Congress wanted a strong central government

    Ⓑ Why Philadelphia was an important early American city

    Ⓒ An early problem between Congress and the American army

    Ⓓ How Washington, D.C. became the capital of the United States

TYPE 6 According to the professor, what city was an early choice to be the U.S. capital?

    Ⓐ New York

    Ⓑ Philadelphia

    Ⓒ Charleston

    Ⓓ Boston

TYPE 7 What will the professor probably do next?

    Ⓐ Continue discussing Washington, D.C.

    Ⓑ Tell the students about the American Revolution

    Ⓒ Explain how Congress passes laws

    Ⓓ Talk about the history of Philadelphia

TYPE 8 Why does the student ask the professor about the choice for the American capital?

    Ⓐ She is unaware of Philadelphia's history.

    Ⓑ She feels that Boston should have been the capital.

    Ⓒ She did not do the reading for the class.

    Ⓓ She has never visited Washington, D.C. before.

✐ Checking Listening Accuracy   **Mark the following statements T (true) or F (false).**

    T   **F**

1 ☐ / ☐ Philadelphia was an early choice for the American capital.

2 ☐ / ☐ The Continental Congress never met in Philadelphia.

3 ☐ / ☐ In 1783, some soldiers interrupted a meeting of Congress.

4 ☐ / ☐ Washington, D.C. is between Virginia and North Carolina.

02-19

Listen to part of a conversation between a student and a gymnasium office employee.

TYPE 9   Why does the student visit the gymnasium office?

- Ⓐ To request to join a team
- Ⓑ To ask which court to use
- Ⓒ To make a reservation
- Ⓓ To borrow some equipment

TYPE 10   According to the man, why is the student unable to use a court?

- Ⓐ The courts are already being used.
- Ⓑ Some cleaning is being done on the courts.
- Ⓒ The gym is getting ready to close.
- Ⓓ She did not make a reservation in time.

TYPE 11   What does the man imply about the squash team?

- Ⓐ The coach is unhappy with its performance.
- Ⓑ It is practicing more than usual this week.
- Ⓒ Its practice time is posted on the bulletin board.
- Ⓓ Several of its members lost their last matches.

TYPE 12   Listen again to part of the conversation. Then answer the question. What is the purpose of the man's response?

- Ⓐ To reject the student's request
- Ⓑ To advise the student not to complain
- Ⓒ To suggest a solution to the student
- Ⓓ To agree with the student

✎ Checking Listening Accuracy   Mark the following statements T (true) or F (false).

	T	F	
1	☐	☐	The student reserved a squash court.
2	☐	☐	The student is a member of the squash team.
3	☐	☐	The man finds an empty court for the student.
4	☐	☐	The student says she will complain to the coach.

Listen to part of a lecture in a psychology class.

02-20

Tolman's Rats

Tolman's Experiment:		Results with No Food for Rats:
		Results with Food for Rats:
		Tolman's Theory:

1   What aspect of Tolman's experiments does the professor mainly discuss?

- Ⓐ The manner in which he conducted experiments
- Ⓑ What animals he used for the experiments
- Ⓒ Where he conducted the experiments
- Ⓓ The place where he conducted the experiments

2   What comparison does the professor make between rats that received food and rats that did not receive food at the end of the maze?

- Ⓐ How quickly they finished the maze
- Ⓑ How interested they were in the maze
- Ⓒ How many mistakes they made in the maze
- Ⓓ How often they got to go through the maze

3   Listen again to part of the lecture. Then answer the question.
What does the professor imply when she says this: 🎧

- Ⓐ She wants the student to expand on the point he makes.
- Ⓑ She thinks the student failed to conduct the experiment.
- Ⓒ She completely agrees with what the student said.
- Ⓓ She is going to show that the student's idea is wrong.

✎ Listening Comprehension   Complete the following sentences. Use the words in the box.

a. any food	b. a cognitive map	c. found the food	d. conducted experiments

1 Edward Tolman _____ with rats in mazes.

2 The rats Tolman put in the mazes always _____ .

3 Later, Tolman did not give the rats _____ at the end.

4 Tolman believed that the rats made _____ , so they learned.

Listen to part of a lecture in a history class.

02-21

The Rosetta Stone

The Rosetta Stone:		Thomas Young:
		Jean-Francois Champollion:

1 In the lecture, the professor describes a number of facts about the Rosetta Stone. Indicate whether each of the following is a fact about the Rosetta Stone.
Click in the correct box for each sentence.

	Fact	Not a Fact
1 It was found in an ancient Egyptian temple.		
2 There was Latin written on it.		
3 Scholars took many years to decipher it.		
4 Thomas Young made the first important discovery about it.		

2 How is the lecture organized?

- Ⓐ By arranging the events chronologically
- Ⓑ By mentioning the roles of important men
- Ⓒ By discussing the translation of the Rosetta Stone
- Ⓓ By following the textbook

3 Listen again to part of the lecture. Then answer the question.
What can be inferred about the professor when she says this: 🎧

- Ⓐ She is able to read and write Demotic.
- Ⓑ She wants to teach the students how to read Demotic.
- Ⓒ She is an expert on ancient languages.
- Ⓓ She thinks the students do not know what Demotic is.

✦Listening Comprehension   Complete the following sentences. Use the words in the box.

a. some French soldiers   b. Jean-Francois Champollion   c. about eighty words   d. three languages

1 _____ found the Rosetta Stone in 1799.

2 The Rosetta Stone contained information in _____ .

3 Thomas Young discovered _____ that were similar in each text.

4 _____ wrote a grammar and a dictionary of hieroglyphics.

Mastering **Topics** with Conversations B3

Listen to part of a conversation between a student and a librarian.

02-22

Service Encounter

Reason for Visiting:

Result:

Student's Response:

Librarian's Response:

1 Why does the student talk to the librarian?

Ⓐ He wants to check out a book from the library.

Ⓑ He cannot find a book he is searching for.

Ⓒ He is looking for the library's e-readers.

Ⓓ He wants to return a book to the library.

2 What can be inferred about the librarian?

Ⓐ She feels bad that she cannot help the student.

Ⓑ She will order more copies of the book the student wants.

Ⓒ She is not interested in helping most students.

Ⓓ She only helps the student because it is her job.

3 What can be inferred about the student?

Ⓐ He will probably buy the book for his e-reader.

Ⓑ He has spoken with the librarian before.

Ⓒ He will turn his homework assignment in late.

Ⓓ He will read the book after it gets returned.

Listening Comprehension Complete the following sentences. Use the words in the box.

a. buy an electronic book	b. are checked out	c. find a book	d. a homework assignment

1 The student is unable to _____ on the library's shelves.

2 Both of the library's copies of the book _____ .

3 The student needs the book for a _____ .

4 The librarian suggests that the student _____ .

02-23

Listen to part of a lecture in a marketing class.

Marketing

Customer Loyalty

1 What aspect of customer loyalty does the professor mainly discuss?

(A) Which stores desire it

(B) How to develop it

(C) Why it earns profits for companies

(D) Its connection with good service

2 According to the professor, how can a store create loyalty with its customers?
Click on 2 answers.

(A) By providing outstanding service

(B) By offering rebates to customers

(C) By giving coupons for free services

(D) By letting customers make exchanges

3 How is the lecture organized?

(A) The professor encourages the students to take part in the lecture.

(B) The professor sets up some case studies for the students to learn.

(C) The professor provides a personal example for the students.

(D) The professor asks questions and then answers them himself.

4 What does the professor imply about customer loyalty?

(A) It is extremely important to places of business.

(B) Most businesses would close without loyal customers.

(C) It is the best way for a store to get new customers.

(D) It has a crucial role in the computer industry.

5 What will the professor probably do next?

(A) Give the class a break

(B) Assign some homework

(C) Finish teaching for the day

(D) Continue his lecture

6 Listen again to part of the lecture. Then answer the question.
What does the professor mean when he says this: 🎧

(A) The student needs to be quiet.

(B) He does not understand the student.

(C) He agrees with the student.

(D) The student has asked a question he cannot answer.

Listen to part of a conversation between a student and a professor.

1   Why does the professor ask to see the student?

 (A) To find out the topic of her upcoming assignment

 (B) To give her a grade on a recent assignment

 (C) To learn why she missed some recent classes

 (D) To tell her to submit her homework by the next day

2   What was the student unable to do in the professor's class?

 (A) Take a test

 (B) Give a presentation

 (C) Write a report

 (D) Do her homework

3   What does the professor want the student to do by the end of the day?

 (A) Turn in a report that is overdue

 (B) Show him a note from her doctor

 (C) Sign up for a time to take an exam

 (D) Complete the rest of her homework

4   Listen again to part of the conversation. Then answer the question. What does the professor imply when he says this: 🎧

 (A) He does not believe the student's excuse.

 (B) He dislikes when students miss his class.

 (C) He expects his students to have perfect attendance.

 (D) He is very upset with the student now.

5   Listen again to part of the conversation. Then answer the question. What does the professor imply when he says this: 🎧

 (A) The student will receive an A on the assignment.

 (B) Most students are worried about his class.

 (C) He is confident in the student's abilities.

 (D) There is nothing difficult for the student to discuss.

Star Performer Word Files

- **accomplish** (v) to do something successfully; to finish

  What do you hope to **accomplish** with that experiment?

- **alphabet** (n) the letters of a language

  Children often learn the **alphabet** at a young age.

- **ancient** (adj) very old

  That story comes from an **ancient** Greek legend.

- **blend** (v) to mix; to combine

  You must **blend** the ingredients to make a mixture.

- **branch** (n) a division

  Mr. Carter works at the **branch** located downtown.

- **capital** (n) the city in which the national government of a country is located

  The **capital** of Italy is Rome.

- **combination** (n) a mixture; a grouping of two or more things

  A **combination** of factors resulted in her getting hired.

- **conduct** (v) to do; to carry out; to attempt

  It is necessary to **conduct** the experiment in total darkness.

- **decipher** (v) to decode; to figure out

  They are trying to **decipher** what the coded message means.

- **declare** (v) to state; to say

  The doctor **declared** that the patient was completely healed.

- **disrupt** (v) to upset; to disturb; to interfere with

  The thunderstorm **disrupted** the picnic they had planned.

- **entirely** (adv) totally; completely

  Your ideas are **entirely** incorrect and need to be rethought.

- **federal** (adj) national

  Some believe that the **federal** government has too much power.

- **focal point** (n) a center

  We should go to the **focal point** of the incident.

- **formative** (adj) influential; shaping; decisive

  Mary's **formative** years were spent in Asia.

- **fort** (n) a military base

  The soldiers were supposed to protect the **fort** from enemy attacks.

- **level** (n) a stage; a rank

  There are two more **levels** for him to complete.

- **loyalty** (n) devotion or faithfulness to a person

  Loyalty to one's country is very important.

- **maze** (n) a labyrinth; a jumbled network of paths

  It took them three hours to get through the **maze** and to find the exit.

- **memorization** (n) the act of remembering something

  For some, **memorization** is easy, yet it is difficult for others.

- **method** (n) a way; a manner

  There are several **methods** you can use to solve the problem.

- **obsolete** (adj) outdated; no longer useful

  Vacuum tubes are **obsolete**, so they are no longer used in computers.

- **performance** (n) an ability; an act

  Tim's job **performance** was outstanding, so he got promoted.

- **phonics** (n) a reading method that involves learning how to pronounce various sounds

  The teachers prefer to teach reading by using **phonics**.

- **profit** (n) earnings

  How much **profit** did the company earn last year?

- **promptly** (adv) immediately

  All employees are expected to reply to email **promptly**.

- **psychology** (n) the study of the mind

  Wendy decided to take a class in **psychology** this semester.

- **rebate** (n) a money-back offer

  The store is offering a **rebate** to customers who buy that product.

- **recognize** (v) to know

  Nobody **recognized** Peter after he shaved his beard.

- **recommendation** (n) advice; an offer; a proposal

  You need a **recommendation** before you can get hired by that law firm.

- **reward** (v) to give as a prize

  How are they going to **reward** Joe for winning the big contract?

- **riot** (n) a public disorder that often becomes violent

  The police came to stop the **riot** and arrest the demonstrators.

- **roughly** (adv) about; approximately; around

  It takes **roughly** ten minutes to get to the park from here.

- **scholar** (n) an academic; a researcher

  She decided to become a **scholar** and to work at the university.

- **text** (n) a written work; a book

  This is a rare old **text**, so be careful with it.

- **translation** (n) the act of changing something from one language to another

  The **translation** of the passage had many mistakes in it.

- **treat** (v) to care for; to take care of

  Always **treat** your children kindly.

- **upgrade** (v) to improve the quality of

  You had better **upgrade** your computer since it is getting old.

- **urge** (n) a desire

  I had a sudden **urge** to get something to eat.

- **warranty** (n) a guarantee, often for something that has been purchased

  The shop offers a two-year **warranty** on every product it sells.

Vocabulary Review

Choose the word with the closest meaning to each highlighted word or phrase.

1 The scientist tried to conduct the test in a short amount of time.

   Ⓐ research
   Ⓑ result
   Ⓒ practice
   Ⓓ experiment

2 There are several customers in the store right now.

   Ⓐ shoppers
   Ⓑ employees
   Ⓒ clerks
   Ⓓ managers

3 We think that your proposal is very logical.

   Ⓐ reasonable
   Ⓑ essential
   Ⓒ hasty
   Ⓓ unfair

4 They were originally scheduled to leave at six in the morning.

   Ⓐ partially
   Ⓑ decidedly
   Ⓒ happily
   Ⓓ initially

5 The students had to determine the main idea of the story they were reading.

   Ⓐ first
   Ⓑ hidden
   Ⓒ primary
   Ⓓ thematic

6 You basically need to bring enough supplies for three days.

   Ⓐ apparently
   Ⓑ essentially
   Ⓒ considerably
   Ⓓ possibly

Match each word with the correct definition.

7 manager   •   • Ⓐ a desire to eat

8 century   •   • Ⓑ the building of something

9 construction   •   • Ⓒ a director

10 consider   •   • Ⓓ an ancient king of Egypt

11 pharaoh   •   • Ⓔ to think about

12 hunger   •   • Ⓕ a period of 100 years

Part B

Chapter 04 **Social Sciences 2 | Conversations**

history • archaeology • anthropology • economics • sociology • psychology •
education • geography • political science • linguistics

02-25

Listen to part of a lecture in an archaeology class.

TYPE 1 What is the lecture mainly about?

    Ⓐ Various aspects of Mayan civilization

    Ⓑ When Mayan culture began to develop

    Ⓒ The methods the Mayans used to write with

    Ⓓ The role of the Spanish in Mayan culture

TYPE 2 What can be inferred about Mayan temples and palaces?

    Ⓐ They were decorated with art and writing.

    Ⓑ It took years for the Mayans to construct them.

    Ⓒ Pots and figures have been found there.

    Ⓓ Mayans visited them to learn to write.

TYPE 3 Why does the professor mention the Spanish conquerors?

    Ⓐ To announce that they defeated the Mayans in battle

    Ⓑ To talk about their role in developing Mayan culture

    Ⓒ To explain why there are few written Mayan records

    Ⓓ To say that they stole many Mayan figures and pottery

TYPE 4 Listen again to part of the lecture. Then answer the question.
What does the professor mean when she says this: 🎧

    Ⓐ Mayan works of metals are found in museums.

    Ⓑ Archaeologists highly value Mayan metal works.

    Ⓒ She will show her students some examples of Mayan art.

    Ⓓ Most Mayan metal objects have not survived.

✎**Checking Listening Accuracy** Mark the following statements T (true) or F (false).

      T   F

1 ☐ / ☐ The Mayans had city-states that were surrounded by farms.

2 ☐ / ☐ The Mayans often used paper to write on.

3 ☐ / ☐ Many Mayan books have survived to the present day.

4 ☐ / ☐ The Spanish destroyed many of the Mayans' written records.

02-26

Listen to part of a lecture in a history of urbanization class.

TYPE 5 What aspect of zoning laws does the professor mainly discuss?

Ⓐ The purposes that they serve

Ⓑ The major zones found in cities

Ⓒ The most popular types of zones

Ⓓ The origins of zoning laws

TYPE 6 According to the professor, who is responsible for passing zoning laws?

Ⓐ Local governments

Ⓑ Mayors of towns

Ⓒ State governments

Ⓓ The federal government

TYPE 7 What does the professor imply about the location of a stadium?

Ⓐ It would be in a commercial zone.

Ⓑ It would be in a recreational zone.

Ⓒ It would be in a residential zone.

Ⓓ It would be in an agricultural zone.

TYPE 8 Listen again to part of the lecture. Then answer the question.
Why does the professor say this: 🎧

Ⓐ To indicate that her lecture is almost complete

Ⓑ To encourage the students to give her an answer

Ⓒ To insist that her opinion is the correct one

Ⓓ To imply she knows the answers to her questions

🎵 **Checking Listening Accuracy** **Mark the following statements T (true) or F (false).**

T   F

1 ☐ / ☐ Zoning laws are usually passed by city and state governments.

2 ☐ / ☐ Residential zones are for houses and apartment buildings.

3 ☐ / ☐ Industrial zones are for factories and farms.

4 ☐ / ☐ Zoning laws keep buildings out of places where they should not be.

02-27

Listen to part of a conversation between a student and a laboratory assistant.

TYPE 9 Why does the student visit the laboratory assistant?

- Ⓐ To give her his laboratory report
- Ⓑ To ask for a new assignment
- Ⓒ To apply for a job at the laboratory
- Ⓓ To get directions to the chemistry laboratory

TYPE 10 What is the student majoring in?
Click on 2 answers.

- Ⓐ Biology
- Ⓑ Physics
- Ⓒ Chemistry
- Ⓓ Engineering

TYPE 11 What can be inferred about the laboratory assistant?

- Ⓐ She is a graduate student at the university.
- Ⓑ She is going to teach a biology class soon.
- Ⓒ She is uninterested in hiring the student.
- Ⓓ She has a lot of work in the laboratory.

TYPE 12 Listen again to part of the conversation. Then answer the question.
What does the laboratory assistant mean when she says this: 🎧

- Ⓐ She has to prepare for an upcoming lab soon.
- Ⓑ The student is speaking too quickly.
- Ⓒ The student should stop working so fast.
- Ⓓ She is not ready to hire the student.

✎**Checking Listening Accuracy**   Mark the following statements T (true) or F (false).

	T	F	
1	☐	☐	The student visits a biology laboratory.
2	☐	☐	There will be a lab class in the next half hour.
3	☐	☐	The student is working on a double major.
4	☐	☐	The laboratory assistant does not need any help.

Mastering **Topics** with Lectures

Listen to part of a lecture in an economics class.

02-28

Marketing

Short-Term Marketing	→	Long-Term Marketing:
		Social Media:

1 According to the professor, why do businesses send people to trade shows?

    (A) To learn various skills

    (B) To purchase new products

    (C) To find more clients

    (D) To recruit potential employees

2 What does the professor imply about public relations firms?

    (A) Companies may use them for a long time.

    (B) They cost too much for small businesses.

    (C) They are useful only in some industries.

    (D) Some of them help with product promotions.

3 Based on the information in the lecture, indicate which statements refer to short-term marketing and long-term marketing.
Click in the correct box for each sentence.

	Short-Term Marketing	Long-Term Marketing
1 May involve special sales at stores		
2 Requires extensive use of social media		
3 Involves product placement optimization		
4 Can include the promotions of products		

Listening Comprehension   Complete the following sentences. Use the words in the box.

a. up to one year	b. social media	c. revenues and profits	d. in the future

1 Marketing lets companies increase their _____ .

2 Short-term marketing may last for _____ .

3 Most businesses do not plan for events far _____ .

4 _____ may be used for short-term and long-term marketing.

Mastering **Topics** with Lectures B2

Listen to part of a lecture in a marketing class.

Internet Advertising

02-29

TV and Print Media Ads:	Internet Ads:

1 What is the lecture mainly about?

ⓐ The uses of television commercials

ⓑ Print media such as newspapers and magazines

ⓒ The costs involved with advertisements

ⓓ The benefits of Internet advertising

2 How does the professor organize the information about the advantages of Internet advertising that he presents to the class?

ⓐ By focusing on its advantages and disadvantages

ⓑ By providing a list of major Internet advertisers

ⓒ By comparing it with other forms of advertising

ⓓ By showing how advertisers utilize individual websites

3 Based on the information in the lecture, indicate which statements refer to Internet advertisements and television commercials.
Click in the correct box for each sentence.

	Internet Advertisements	Television Commercials
1 They can cost millions of dollars.		
2 They can be targeted to a specific audience.		
3 They were once worth the money that advertisers spent.		
4 They are usually cheap to make.		

✎**Listening Comprehension** Complete the following sentences. Use the words in the box.

a. getting their news	b. marketing segment	c. specific groups	d. make and air

1 Television will soon no longer be the largest _____ .

2 More people are _____ from the Internet nowadays.

3 TV commercials can cost millions of dollars to _____ .

4 It is possible to advertise to _____ of people on the Internet.

Mastering **Topics** with Conversations B3

Listen to part of a conversation between a student and a professor.

02-30

Office Hours

Reason for Visiting:	→	Professor's Response:
Student's Response:	↖ →	Professor's Comment:

1 Why does the student visit the professor?

- Ⓐ To ask for some research material
- Ⓑ To discuss a play by Shakespeare with him
- Ⓒ To tell him about an assignment she is doing
- Ⓓ To submit the essay that she finished

2 What is the professor's opinion of the student's paper topic?

- Ⓐ It is unacceptable to him.
- Ⓑ It is a unique idea.
- Ⓒ It needs to be more developed.
- Ⓓ It would be better as a long paper.

3 Listen again to part of the conversation. Then answer the question. What does the student imply when she says this: 🎧

- Ⓐ She is an English major specializing in Shakespeare.
- Ⓑ The professor will be her teacher in a future class.
- Ⓒ She will ask the professor to become her advisor.
- Ⓓ She has not taken enough classes on English literature.

Listening Comprehension Complete the following sentences. Use the words in the box.

a. a short essay	b. favorite plays	c. develop her idea	d. the historical context

1 *A Midsummer Night's Dream* is one of the student's _____ .

2 The student wants to write about _____ of the play.

3 The professor says the student's topic is too detailed for _____ .

4 The student decides to _____ into a longer paper later.

02-31

Listen to part of a lecture in a history class.

History

1   What is the main topic of the lecture?

    Ⓐ The importance of food in ancient societies

    Ⓑ Methods of food preservation in the past

    Ⓒ The foods that people in ancient cultures ate

    Ⓓ The role of food in ancient armies

2   Why does the professor explain some options for eating that modern-day people have?

    Ⓐ To note why few people today go hungry

    Ⓑ To ask the students for their opinions on food

    Ⓒ To prove that modern farming methods are effective

    Ⓓ To show how fortunate people are today

3   According to the professor, what was an advantage of having grain as a major food source?

    Ⓐ It had a very short growing season.

    Ⓑ It could be stored for a long time.

    Ⓒ It was easy to transform into bread.

    Ⓓ It cost less than fruits and vegetables.

4   Why does the professor discuss granaries?

    Ⓐ To name the civilizations that utilized them

    Ⓑ To answer a question asked by a student

    Ⓒ To mention why they were so well protected

    Ⓓ To explain why some societies gave away free grain

5   What will the professor probably do next?

    Ⓐ Show a short movie to the class

    Ⓑ Ask the class to look at their textbooks

    Ⓒ Continue to lecture on the topic

    Ⓓ Have some students give their presentations

6   Listen again to part of the lecture. Then answer the question.
What does the professor imply when she says this: 🎧

    Ⓐ There were often riots when food was not free.

    Ⓑ Problems concerning food supplies were common.

    Ⓒ Farmers were the least likely people to cause problems.

    Ⓓ Some populations revolted when there was no food.

02-32

Listen to part of a conversation between a student and a housing office employee.

1   Why does the student visit the housing office?

    Ⓐ To ask for directions to another office

    Ⓑ To find out about some money he owes

    Ⓒ To complain about a fine that he received

    Ⓓ To see if he can get a new roommate

2   Why does the student need some copies of his transcript?

    Ⓐ To send to the graduate schools he is applying to

    Ⓑ To get some copies to give to his family members

    Ⓒ To make sure that his grades are all accurate

    Ⓓ To send to places where he is applying for jobs

3   What can be inferred about the student?

    Ⓐ He is displeased with his roommate.

    Ⓑ He is willing to pay the money he owes.

    Ⓒ He thinks his grades should be higher.

    Ⓓ He is angry that he cannot get his transcript.

4   What does the student imply about his roommate?

    Ⓐ His roommate is careless with other people's property.

    Ⓑ His roommate should pay for all of the damage.

    Ⓒ His roommate does not have very much money.

    Ⓓ His roommate will visit the housing office later.

5   Listen again to part of the conversation. Then answer the question.
    What is the purpose of the student's response?

    Ⓐ To express his surprise

    Ⓑ To agree with the woman

    Ⓒ To acknowledge a problem

    Ⓓ To deny he was at fault

Star Performer Word Files

- **accidental** (adj) by accident; not on purpose; unintentional

  Brad's mistake was **accidental**, so no one got upset about it.

- **advanced** (adj) developed; sophisticated; higher

  There are many **advanced** societies all around the world.

- **agricultural** (adj) related to farming

  Agricultural methods have improved over thousands of years.

- **aim** (v) to intend or direct at someone or something

  The special offer is **aimed** at teens and young adults.

- **ashore** (adv) onto land; to the shore

  The sailors swam **ashore** after their ship sank.

- **bark** (n) the hard outer layer of a tree

  The **bark** of some trees can be extremely thick.

- **civilization** (n) society

  The first **civilizations** arose in the Middle East thousands of years ago.

- **clay** (n) a type of soil or earth

  The **clay** in that region is good for making pots.

- **collapse** (n) a downfall

  The **collapse** of the bridge surprised everyone.

- **confused** (adj) puzzled; not understanding something

  I am sorry, but I am **confused** by your statement.

- **conqueror** (n) a person who defeats another

  Conquerors in ancient times often led powerful armies.

- **discount** (n) an amount reduced from a regular price

  She received a **discount** of thirty percent when she bought the book.

- **district** (n) a region; an area; a neighborhood

  Sue lives in the downtown **district** of her city.

- **dominate** (v) to control; to rule over

  A dictator **dominates** the entire country that he rules.

- **exceptional** (adj) outstanding; excellent

  Some **exceptional** students may receive scholarships.

- **extensive** (adj) lengthy; lasting a long time

  The **extensive** journey took more than three years to complete.

- **factory** (n) a building in which products are manufactured

  More than 200 people work at that computer-manufacturing **factory**.

- **fortunate** (adj) lucky

  We are **fortunate** that it did not snow too heavily today.

- **granary** (n) a building in which people store grain

  The guards are protecting the **granary** from thieves who want to steal grain.

- **harvest** (v) to gather crops from the field

  Many farmers **harvest** their crops in September or October.

- **intentional** (adj) on purpose

  The omission of information was **intentional**.

- **moisture** (n) dampness; water

  The **moisture** on plants in the morning is called dew.

- **optimize** (v) to make as good as possible

  It will take more time for the expert to **optimize** the program.

- **option** (n) a choice

  We are out of **options**, so we have to do what he says.

- **originate** (v) to come from

  Coffee beans are believed to have **originated** in Africa.

- **overtake** (v) to pass; to go beyond; to take the lead

  The company will **overtake** its competitors and become the leader in the industry.

- **process** (n) a method or way of doing something

  Please explain the entire **process** one more time.

- **professional** (adj) relating to a certain industry or occupation

  She attends several **professional** events throughout the year.

- **profit** (n) the money left over after all expenses are paid

  We hope to increase our **profits** by more than ten percent this year.

- **promotion** (n) a special offer, often given by a business

  The store is having a **promotion** for new shoppers this weekend.

- **reasonable** (adj) making sense; logical

  Please try to find a **reasonable** solution to the problem.

- **residential** (adj) related to a group of residences or homes

  There are no factories at all in this **residential** area.

- **revenue** (n) income; money that a person or business takes in

  Revenues for the past three months were down a bit.

- **ruins** (n) the remains of fallen or destroyed buildings

  Many tourists have visited the **ruins** of the ancient temple.

- **segment** (n) a section; a part

  The miniseries will be aired in ten different **segments**.

- **spoil** (v) to go bad; to rot

  Food will **spoil** if it is not refrigerated.

- **surround** (v) to encircle; to be on all sides of someone or something

  The police **surrounded** the building that the bank robbers were in.

- **undernourished** (adj) not having enough food or nutrients; underfed

  Many children around the world are **undernourished**.

- **warehouse** (n) a building in which goods are stored

  The products were taken off the ship and brought to the **warehouse**.

- **zone** (n) a region; an area; a district

  The industrial **zone** of the city is located in that direction.

Vocabulary **Review**

Choose the word with the closest meaning to each highlighted word or phrase.

1   The ideas proposed by Jane were outstanding, so they were quickly utilized.

   (A) excellent
   (B) creative
   (C) efficient
   (D) praiseworthy

2   The government passed some laws concerning manufacturing.

   (A) ideas
   (B) regulations
   (C) representatives
   (D) theories

3   The recipe requires two cups of sugar to be added.

   (A) makes
   (B) requests
   (C) writes
   (D) needs

4   How long will it take to erect that tower?

   (A) build
   (B) design
   (C) plan
   (D) support

5   It is possible to preserve old books by taking good care of them.

   (A) print
   (B) edit
   (C) save
   (D) write

6   This food contains many important vitamins and minerals.

   (A) provides
   (B) creates
   (C) requires
   (D) has

Match each word with the correct definition.

7   population   •

8   pottery   •

9   engage in   •

10   retain   •

11   jungle   •

12   starve   •

•   (A) to be very hungry; not to be able to eat any food

•   (B) the number of people living in a certain place

•   (C) to do; to become involved in

•   (D) a hot, wet region with thick vegetation

•   (E) ceramics

•   (F) to keep; to avoid losing

Part B

Chapter 05 **Physical Sciences 1 | Conversations**

astronomy • physics • chemistry • geology • environmental science • meteorology •
mineralogy • astrophysics • geophysics • physical chemistry

02-33

Listen to part of a lecture in a meteorology class.

TYPE 1 What is the lecture mainly about?

    Ⓐ The northern lights

    Ⓑ Auroras

    Ⓒ The Earth's magnetic field

    Ⓓ The Northern and Southern hemispheres

TYPE 2 Based on the information in the lecture, do the following statements refer to the causes or effects of auroras?
Click in the correct box for each sentence.

	Cause	Effect
① Green lights appear in the sky.		
② Nitrogen atoms in the atmosphere get excited.		
③ Solar winds reach the Earth's magnetic field.		
④ The electrons in oxygen atoms give off energy.		

TYPE 3 Why does the professor mention the equinox?

    Ⓐ To explain when the equinox takes place

    Ⓑ To answer a question from a student

    Ⓒ To say when auroras most often occur

    Ⓓ To describe the Earth's rotation

TYPE 4 What is the student's opinion of auroras?

    Ⓐ He is hopeful of seeing them again.

    Ⓑ He thinks they are nice to look at.

    Ⓒ He is confused about their origins.

    Ⓓ He is bothered by them.

✎ Checking Listening Accuracy Mark the following statements T (true) or F (false).

    T   F

1 ☐ / ☐ The aurora australis are seen in the Northern Hemisphere.

2 ☐ / ☐ The equinox takes place in March and November.

3 ☐ / ☐ Auroras are the result of solar winds hitting the ozone layer.

4 ☐ / ☐ Oxygen and nitrogen atoms are responsible for auroras.

02-34

Listen to part of a lecture in a geology class.

TYPE 5 What aspect of the Mohs Scale of Hardness does the professor mainly discuss?

- Ⓐ Who created it
- Ⓑ How it rates minerals
- Ⓒ When it was made
- Ⓓ Which mineral is the hardest

TYPE 6 What is the softest substance on the Mohs Scale of Hardness?

- Ⓐ Gypsum
- Ⓑ Diamond
- Ⓒ Talc
- Ⓓ Topaz

TYPE 7 What can be inferred about diamonds?

- Ⓐ They can be scratched by quartz.
- Ⓑ They were not rated by Mohs.
- Ⓒ They can scratch anything.
- Ⓓ They are close to glass in hardness.

TYPE 8 Why does the professor tell the students to look in their textbooks?

- Ⓐ So that they can conduct an experiment on hardness
- Ⓑ So that they can read more about Friedrich Mohs
- Ⓒ So that they can learn about the hardness of diamonds
- Ⓓ So that they can see the minerals listed on the Mohs scale

✐ Checking Listening Accuracy   Mark the following statements T (true) or F (false).

	T	F	
1	☐	☐	Hardness refers to a material's ability to scratch other objects.
2	☐	☐	Friedrich Mohs was the first person to realize how hard diamonds are.
3	☐	☐	Diamonds are the hardest material that men know about.
4	☐	☐	Steel has a hardness that is higher than iron.

02-35

Listen to part of a conversation between a student and a professor.

TYPE 9   Why does the student visit the professor?

    Ⓐ To ask to borrow one of the professor's books

    Ⓑ To get some information on his research paper

    Ⓒ To find out what resources he needs to use for a paper

    Ⓓ To show the professor a book he wants to use

TYPE 10   What does the professor tell the student to do?

    Ⓐ Rewrite his paper

    Ⓑ Find some more sources

    Ⓒ Conduct another experiment

    Ⓓ Read an article in the book

TYPE 11   What will the student probably do next?

    Ⓐ Remain in the professor's office

    Ⓑ Borrow the professor's book

    Ⓒ Attend a class

    Ⓓ Visit the library

TYPE 12   Listen again to part of the conversation. Then answer the question. What is the purpose of the student's response?

    Ⓐ To ask the professor to repeat himself

    Ⓑ To express his confusion

    Ⓒ To agree with the professor

    Ⓓ To dispute the professor's comment

✐ Checking Listening Accuracy   Mark the following statements T (true) or F (false).

	T	F	
1	☐ / ☐		The professor gives the student a book to look at.
2	☐ / ☐		The student originally wants to use one book for his research paper.
3	☐ / ☐		The professor tells the student to use several books.
4	☐ / ☐		The student refuses to accept the professor's advice.

Mastering **Topics** with Lectures

Listen to part of a lecture in a chemistry class.

02-36

Mixtures

Characteristics:	Heterogeneous Mixtures:
	Homogenous Mixtures:
	Separating Salt from Water:

1 What is the main topic of the lecture?

Ⓐ The two types of mixtures

Ⓑ The differences between compounds and mixtures

Ⓒ How to separate the parts of a mixture

Ⓓ Different types of homogenous mixtures

2 Based on the information in the lecture, indicate which statements refer to heterogeneous mixtures or homogenous mixtures.
Click in the correct box for each sentence.

	Heterogeneous Mixture	Homogenous Mixture
① Its parts may often be separated by hand.		
② An example of it is salt dissolved in water.		
③ Its parts often appear to be the same color.		
④ It is often easy to see its individual parts.		

3 Listen again to part of the lecture. Then answer the question.
What does the professor imply when he says this: 🎧

Ⓐ The lecture he is teaching is difficult to understand.

Ⓑ He expects the students to answer his question.

Ⓒ The class has already studied chemical compounds.

Ⓓ The information he is discussing will be on a test.

Listening Comprehension Complete the following sentences. Use the words in the box.

a. easy to see	b. a homogenous mixture	c. chemically combine	d. more difficult

1 Items in a mixture do not _____ with each other.

2 The parts of a heterogeneous mixture are _____ .

3 It is _____ to separate the parts of a homogenous mixture.

4 One example of _____ is the air in the atmosphere.

Listen to part of a lecture in an environmental science class.

02-37

Global Cooling

The Little Ice Age:		Why There Are Ice Ages:

1 What is the professor's opinion of global cooling?

- (A) She doubts that it will ever happen.
- (B) She thinks it would benefit the planet.
- (C) She feels it will occur in a few centuries.
- (D) She believes it could happen soon.

2 In the lecture, the professor describes a number of facts about the Little Ice Age. Indicate whether each of the following is a fact about the Little Ice Age.
Click in the correct box for each sentence.

	Fact	Not a Fact
1 There was less rain in summer during it.		
2 It ended around 1800.		
3 Temperatures in the Northern Hemisphere remained the same.		
4 There was a lack of food during it.		

3 Why does the professor mention sunspots?

- (A) To state that the sun produces thousands of them
- (B) To explain how they can affect temperatures on the Earth
- (C) To say that they are large storms on the sun's surface
- (D) To discuss their effect on the orbit of the Earth

Listening Comprehension Complete the following sentences. Use the words in the box.

a. a lack of sunspots	b. the Little Ice Age	c. the Earth's orbit	d. global cooling

1 _____ has taken place on the Earth in the past.

2 _____ lasted from around 1300 to 1800.

3 Some scientists think changes in _____ make the temperature drop.

4 _____ might affect temperatures on the Earth.

Mastering **Topics** with Conversations

Listen to part of a conversation between a student and the dean of students.

02-38

Service Encounter

Reason for Visiting:

Dean's Questions:

Student's Response:

Dean's Decision:

1 What are the speakers mainly discussing?

- Ⓐ An idea for financing the student has
- Ⓑ An award which the student won
- Ⓒ A contest the student wants to begin
- Ⓓ A project the student would like to start

2 What does the student want to focus on?

- Ⓐ Local current events
- Ⓑ Music, art, and culture
- Ⓒ Sporting events
- Ⓓ News from around the world

3 What can be inferred about the student?

- Ⓐ He will pay for the project himself.
- Ⓑ He will meet the dean next week.
- Ⓒ He will attend class after the meeting ends.
- Ⓓ He met the dean before in the past.

✎ **Listening Comprehension**   Complete the following sentences. Use the words in the box.

| a. publishing a magazine | b. a detailed budget | c. nine students | d. a new magazine |

1 The student visits the dean to discuss _____ .

2 _____ are willing to write for the student.

3 The dean states that _____ is not cheap.

4 The dean tells the student to come up with _____ .

02-39

Listen to part of a lecture in an astronomy class.

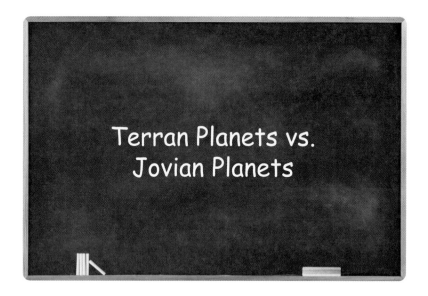

Terran Planets vs.
Jovian Planets

1 What is the main topic of the lecture?

    (A) The solar system

    (B) The major planets

    (C) The dwarf planets

    (D) The Terran planets

2 How is the lecture organized?

    (A) By discussing the relationships of the planets to the sun

    (B) By describing the planets in order according to their sizes

    (C) By focusing first on the Terran planets and then on the Jovians

    (D) By comparing and contrasting the Terran and Jovian planets

3 What comparison does the professor make between Mercury and Neptune?

    (A) He compares the lengths of their orbits.

    (B) He compares the number of moons they have.

    (C) He compares their individual sizes.

    (D) He compares the makeup of their cores.

4 According to the professor, how did the solar system begin?

    (A) As a double star system

    (B) As a system with ten planets

    (C) As a spinning disk

    (D) As a system with only gas giants

5 Listen again to part of the lecture. Then answer the question.
Why does the professor say this: 🎧

    (A) To answer a student's question

    (B) To focus on Earth's small size

    (C) To complete his discussion of Jupiter

    (D) To make a comparison

6 Listen again to part of the lecture. Then answer the question.
What does the professor imply when he says this: 🎧

    (A) He is not interested in how the gas giants formed.

    (B) He will talk about that subject later.

    (C) He wants to finish talking about the planets.

    (D) There is not much time left in class.

02-40

Listen to part of a conversation between a student and a professor.

1 Why did the professor ask to see the student?

    (A) To discuss the student's paper

    (B) To give the student a grade

    (C) To assign the student some work

    (D) To tell the student about an article

2 Why did the student write the essay?

    (A) To get some extra credit

    (B) To complete a class assignment

    (C) To submit it to a journal

    (D) To apply for an internship

3 What is the professor's opinion of the student's writing ability?

    (A) It needs to be improved.

    (B) It is outstanding.

    (C) It is the best he has ever seen.

    (D) It is about average.

4 What kind of paper does the professor want the student to write?

    (A) A newspaper article

    (B) A critical writing essay

    (C) An interview

    (D) An expository paper

5 What will the student probably do next?

    (A) Ask the professor for help

    (B) Register for a class

    (C) Visit the library

    (D) Rewrite her paper

Star Performer Word Files

- **appear** (v) to look like; to seem

  This **appears** to be a difficult topic.

- **atmosphere** (n) the air

  Most of the Earth's **atmosphere** is nitrogen and oxygen.

- **bond** (v) to join; to unite; to combine

  Some elements **bond** more easily than others.

- **collide** (v) to run into

  The car **collided** with another when it ran the red light.

- **combine** (v) to join; to unite

  The scientist **combined** several liquids to make a mixture.

- **component** (n) a part; something that makes up a larger thing

  One of the main **components** of the computer is broken.

- **composition** (n) the makeup of something; all of the parts that something is made of

  What is the **composition** of that chemical compound?

- **core** (n) a center

  The **core** of the Earth is made mostly of nickel and iron.

- **crazy** (adj) strange; unusual

  Some ideas seem **crazy** but actually work quite well.

- **crop** (n) a plant that people grow in order to eat

  Farmers plant their **crops** in spring and harvest them in fall.

- **curious** (adj) interested; nosy; inquisitive

  The police are **curious** about how the criminals managed to escape.

- **dense** (adj) thick

  The material is too **dense** to see through.

- **differ** (v) to vary; to be different from

  Describe three ways in which they **differ** from one another.

- **distinguish** (v) to tell the difference between two or more things

  It is difficult to **distinguish** some species from others.

- **drop** (v) to decrease rapidly

  The temperature started to **drop** as the snowstorm approached.

- **dwarf** (n) someone or something that is very small

  That animal is a **dwarf**, so it is smaller than other animals of its kind.

- **emit** (v) to send out

  That machine is **emitting** a strange sound.

- **evaporate** (v) to vanish; to disappear

  Water will **evaporate** when the sun's rays shine on it.

- **excite** (v) to stimulate; to agitate; to cause to move

  The atoms are getting **excited**, so they are heating up.

- **expect** (v) to anticipate; to believe

  When do you **expect** the results of the survey to be complete?

- **extremely** (adv) very; highly

  The chances of an earthquake happening here are **extremely** low.

- **famine** (n) a period in which there is little or no food available

  During times of **famine**, people may often starve to death.

- **freeze** (v) to change from a liquid to a solid form

  Water **freezes** at zero degrees Celsius.

- **giant** (n) someone or something that is very large

  The man was a **giant** and stood more than 210 centimeters tall.

- **heterogeneous** (adj) different; varied; mixed

  Can you describe the characteristics of these **heterogeneous** mixtures?

- **homogenous** (adj) alike; similar

  That is a **homogenous** substance she is examining.

- **latitude** (n) the distance north or south of the equator someone or something is

  They must determine their **latitude** to find their location.

- **mar** (v) to damage

  If you **mar** the painting, you will damage it.

- **mineralogist** (n) a person who studies minerals

  She is studying to become a **mineralogist** in the future.

- **orbit** (n) the path an object takes around another, such as Earth around the sun

  The **orbit** of Earth around the sun takes 365 days to complete.

- **overview** (n) a summary; a general study

  The manager requested an **overview** of the ongoing project.

- **resist** (v) to oppose

  The body's immune system tries to **resist** harmful viruses.

- **satellite** (n) a moon

  Mars has two **satellites** orbiting it while Venus has none.

- **scratch** (v) to scrape; to damage

  Cats like to **scratch** furniture such as sofas.

- **separate** (v) to divide

  The scientists are using a centrifuge to **separate** the parts of the mixture.

- **solar** (adj) related to the sun

  Solar power is still not efficient.

- **substance** (n) material; matter

  This is a mysterious **substance** that scientists are still examining.

- **sunspot** (n) a dark spot that sometimes appears on the sun

  In recent years, there have been few **sunspots** on the sun's surface.

- **theory** (n) an idea; a hypothesis

  A **theory** must be tested many times to be proven correct.

- **tilted** (adj) slanted; skewed

  That painting hanging on the wall is slightly **tilted**.

Vocabulary Review

Choose the word with the closest meaning to each highlighted word or phrase.

1 There is a lot of advanced machinery in that factory.
   (A) designs
   (B) computers
   (C) automobiles
   (D) equipment

2 The employees expect to complete the project in a few hours.
   (A) finish
   (B) rewrite
   (C) correct
   (D) begin

3 They are trying to determine the major cause of the failure of the experiment.
   (A) initial
   (B) main
   (C) possible
   (D) damaging

4 The explosion damaged several buildings in the neighborhood.
   (A) constructed
   (B) concerned
   (C) exploded
   (D) harmed

5 You must prevent everyone from entering that room.
   (A) request
   (B) enable
   (C) stop
   (D) invite

6 Eric decided to remain at the office to complete the project.
   (A) stay
   (B) work
   (C) practice
   (D) research

Match each word with the correct definition.

7 measure •
8 age •
9 uniform •
10 filter •
11 rate •
12 glacier •

• (A) to calculate the size or weight of something
• (B) a device that can remove impurities from a liquid
• (C) a huge flowing sheet of ice
• (D) to rank
• (E) the same; identical; alike
• (F) an era; a period of time

Part B

Chapter 06   Physical Sciences 2 | Conversations

astronomy • physics • chemistry • geology • environmental science • meteorology •
mineralogy • astrophysics • geophysics • physical chemistry

02-41

Listen to part of a lecture in a chemistry class.

TYPE 1 What is the lecture mainly about?

ⓐ The most important chemistry terms

ⓑ Organic and inorganic compounds

ⓒ Why there are many carbon compounds

ⓓ The characteristics of carbon compounds

TYPE 2 Based on the information in the lecture, indicate which statements refer to organic or inorganic compounds.
Click in the correct box for each statement.

	Organic Compounds	Inorganic Compounds
1 Include all living organisms		
2 Boil at lower temperatures		
3 Can easily bond with other elements		
4 Are the less common type of compound		

TYPE 3 How does the professor organize the information about organic compounds that she presents to the class?

ⓐ By listing their characteristics

ⓑ By giving examples of carbon compounds

ⓒ By focusing on how they are created

ⓓ By describing their role in organic chemistry

TYPE 4 Listen again to part of the lecture. Then answer the question.
What can be inferred about the professor when she says this: 🎧

ⓐ She believes that the students should already know these terms.

ⓑ She wants the students to do well in her class.

ⓒ She dislikes when students do not listen in her class.

ⓓ She feels she is giving the students important information.

✐ Checking Listening Accuracy   Mark the following statements T (true) or F (false).

    T   **F**

1 ☐ / ☐   A compound is made when two or more elements unite.

2 ☐ / ☐   There are three main branches of chemistry.

3 ☐ / ☐   All living organisms contain carbon.

4 ☐ / ☐   There are more carbon compounds than non-carbon compounds.

02-42

Listen to part of a lecture in an environmental science class.

TYPE 5   Why does the professor explain the Dust Bowl?

    Ⓐ To mention that it caused a mass migration

    Ⓑ To name all of the states that it affected

    Ⓒ To point out its connection with erosion

    Ⓓ To state how many people it harmed

TYPE 6   According to the professor, how can wind erosion harm farmers?

    Ⓐ By sending dust into the air

    Ⓑ By blowing away fertile soil

    Ⓒ By keeping crops from getting water

    Ⓓ By causing crops to fall down

TYPE 7   What can be inferred about the Dust Bowl?

    Ⓐ It lasted for more than one decade.

    Ⓑ It caused many Americans to starve.

    Ⓒ It killed a large number of people.

    Ⓓ It was not a unique event in history.

TYPE 8   Listen again to part of the lecture. Then answer the question.
What does the professor imply when he says this: 🎧

    Ⓐ Governments should make farmers use sustainable farming.

    Ⓑ It is possible to prevent erosion from happening.

    Ⓒ Erosion does not always cause problems for farmers.

    Ⓓ Farmers can profit from sustainable farming.

✒ **Checking Listening Accuracy**   Mark the following statements T (true) or F (false).

    T   F

1 ☐ / ☐ The Grand Canyon took a long time to form.

2 ☐ / ☐ Erosion can occur in a short period of time.

3 ☐ / ☐ The Dust Bowl happened in the Great Plains.

4 ☐ / ☐ Mass migrations can sometimes cause erosion.

02-43

Listen to part of a conversation between a student and a housing office employee.

TYPE 9   Why does the student visit the housing office?

Ⓐ   To have the man fix a broken machine

Ⓑ   To demand that the school make some changes

Ⓒ   To complain about the washing machines

Ⓓ   To ask for a refund on the money she spent

TYPE 10   What does the student say about the washing machines?
Click on 2 answers.

Ⓐ   The price of using them has gone up.

Ⓑ   They seem to break down frequently.

Ⓒ   They do not clean clothes very well.

Ⓓ   They are not big enough for her.

TYPE 11   What can be inferred about the student?

Ⓐ   She blames the man for her problems.

Ⓑ   She is unhappy about the current situation.

Ⓒ   She is going to move out of her dormitory.

Ⓓ   She dislikes having to wash her own clothes.

TYPE 12   Listen again to part of the conversation. Then answer the question.
What can be inferred from the man's response to the student?

Ⓐ   He is not interested in the student's opinion.

Ⓑ   He has heard other similar complaints.

Ⓒ   He wants the student to continue talking.

Ⓓ   He lacks the time to speak with the student.

✎ Checking Listening Accuracy   Mark the following statements T (true) or F (false).

	T	F	
1	☐	☐	The student is talking about a problem in her dormitory.
2	☐	☐	The student says that the washing machines are too small.
3	☐	☐	It costs one dollar to wash clothes now.
4	☐	☐	The man will speak to his boss about the washing machines.

Listen to part of a lecture in a geology class.

02-44

Antarctica

Plate Tectonics:

→

Effects on Antarctica:

1   Based on the information in the lecture, indicate which sentences refer to the causes or effects of the movement of Antarctica.
Click in the correct box for each sentence.

	Cause	Effect
1 Antarctica is currently at the bottom of the Earth.		
2 The Earth's crust is made of many plates.		
3 The Earth's mantle creates convection waves.		
4 India became separated from Antarctica.		

2   According to the professor, what did the ice do to Antarctica?

   Ⓐ It made the dinosaurs living on it all die.

   Ⓑ It made the continent move slowly.

   Ⓒ It killed many plants and animals.

   Ⓓ It increased the elevation of the continent.

3   What does the professor imply about Antarctica?

   Ⓐ It will move beside Africa in the future.

   Ⓑ It is almost as large as South America.

   Ⓒ It contains fossils of tropical creatures.

   Ⓓ It has several types of plants growing on it.

Listening Comprehension Complete the following sentences. Use the words in the box.

a. combined to form	b. plate tectonics	c. twenty-five million years	d. dinosaur fossils

1 Scientists in Antarctica recently found some _____ there.

2 _____ describes the movement of the plates on the crust.

3 Several landmasses once _____ a supercontinent.

4 Antarctica has been in its current location for _____ .

Listen to part of a lecture in a physics class.

02-45

Sir Isaac Newton

Sir Isaac Newton:	Newton's Experiments with Light:	The Newtonian Telescope:

1 What aspect of Sir Isaac Newton's life does the professor mainly discuss?

(A) His research on light

(B) His making of a telescope

(C) His experiments with prisms

(D) His work with particles

2 Why does the professor mention the reflecting telescope?

(A) To show how it is better than other telescopes

(B) To prove that it gathers light well

(C) To describe how it works

(D) To note that Newton invented it

3 Listen again to part of the lecture. Then answer the question.
Why does the professor say this: 🎧

(A) To check on the date

(B) To answer a question

(C) To correct himself

(D) To make a decision

Listening Comprehension Complete the following sentences. Use the words in the box.

a. the laws of motion	b. the reflecting telescope	c. to bend light	d. the light spectrum

1 Sir Isaac Newton did work on gravity and _____ .

2 A prism is able _____ that passes through it.

3 There are a total of seven colors in _____ .

4 _____ is sometimes called the Newtonian telescope.

Mastering **Topics** with Conversations B3

Listen to part of a conversation between a student and a professor.

02-46

Office Hours

Student's Request:

Student's Response:

Professor's Response:

Professor's Comment:

1 What are the speakers mainly discussing?

Ⓐ How the student can get into graduate school

Ⓑ The professor's upcoming philosophy class

Ⓒ The student's desire to be a teaching assistant

Ⓓ The rough draft that the student wrote

2 What can be inferred about the student?

Ⓐ His major is Philosophy.

Ⓑ He gets good grades.

Ⓒ He is upset with the professor.

Ⓓ He plans to graduate next year.

3 What does the professor imply about the student?

Ⓐ He needs to improve his writing skills.

Ⓑ He should take more of her classes.

Ⓒ He is currently an undergraduate.

Ⓓ He needs experience to become a teaching assistant.

✐ Listening Comprehension   Complete the following sentences. Use the words in the box.

a. a teaching assistant	b. graduate students	c. rough draft	d. thanks the professor

1 The professor believes the student's _____ looks good.

2 The student wants to become _____ in a philosophy class.

3 The professor says that most teaching assistants are _____ .

4 The student _____ for explaining the situation to him.

02-47

Listen to part of a lecture in an environmental science class.

Environmental Science

1   What is the main topic of the lecture?

    Ⓐ Where many rivers usually dry up

    Ⓑ How humans can affect rivers

    Ⓒ What can cause rivers to dry up

    Ⓓ Some drastic changes to the Earth

2   According to the professor, where have some rivers dried up in the past?

    Ⓐ The Amazon Rainforest

    Ⓑ North Africa

    Ⓒ Europe

    Ⓓ North America

3   How is the lecture organized?

    Ⓐ The professor talks about the process by which a river dried up in the past.

    Ⓑ The professor shows the students pictures of how rivers have disappeared.

    Ⓒ The professor describes some places where rivers have vanished.

    Ⓓ The professor lists some reasons for rivers drying up and then discusses them.

4   What does the professor imply about the effects of humans on rivers?

    Ⓐ Dams are the only manmade way to make rivers disappear.

    Ⓑ Some humans want certain rivers to dry up.

    Ⓒ Many people are trying to protect rivers.

    Ⓓ Humans can make rivers dry up quickly.

5   Based on the information in the lecture, indicate which sentences refer to each reason why rivers dry up.
Click in the correct box for each sentence.

	Climate Change	Landscape	Humans
1 A volcano may erupt and block a river.			
2 Silt may block a river's flow.			
3 Rain may fall less often in a region.			
4 A dam may block the flow of a river.			

6   Listen again to part of the lecture. Then answer the question.
What does the professor mean when she says this: 🎧

    Ⓐ There is not enough time to discuss that topic.

    Ⓑ She doubts the Nile or the Amazon will dry up.

    Ⓒ The student is most likely correct.

    Ⓓ The Nile and the Amazon are young rivers.

02-48

Listen to part of a conversation between a student and a parking office employee.

1 Why does the student visit the parking office?

    (A) To request a parking sticker

    (B) To find out which parking lots are open

    (C) To protest some tickets he received

    (D) To pay a fine for illegal parking

2 Why did the student park in a different parking lot than normal?

    (A) A security guard told him to park there.

    (B) There was no room in his regular lot.

    (C) He did not have time to park elsewhere.

    (D) The parking lot was near his dormitory.

3 Why does the employee tell the student about the other complaints?

    (A) To encourage the student to pay his fines

    (B) To explain why he believes the student

    (C) To show that he is annoyed by all of the complaints

    (D) To request that the student stop complaining

4 What is the employee's attitude toward the student?

    (A) He is uninterested in the student's problem.

    (B) He is impatient with the student.

    (C) He does not believe the student.

    (D) He is polite to the student.

5 Why does the student mention Daryl Smith?

    (A) To state that Daryl Smith is his student advisor

    (B) To name someone who can prove his story is true

    (C) To complain about how Daryl Smith treated him

    (D) To compliment him for the work that he did

Star Performer Word Files

- **alter** (v) to change

  The floods caused by the hurricane **altered** the shape of the land.

- **barren** (adj) sterile; unfertile; unproductive

  After the drought ended, much of the land remained **barren**.

- **blockage** (n) an obstruction; something that blocks another thing

  The **blockage** of the filters caused the machine to break down.

- **boil** (v) to change from a liquid to a gaseous state

  It usually takes water a few minutes to begin to **boil**.

- **complex** (adj) complicated

  Complex problems can be solved easily thanks to computers.

- **convection** (n) the transfer of heat through circulation

  Many people have **convection** ovens in their kitchens.

- **disrupt** (v) to disturb; to interfere with

  The protesters **disrupted** the meeting with some shareholders.

- **distort** (v) to alter; to deform; to change in a negative manner

  The reporter **distorted** the news and gave an untruthful account in his article.

- **drastic** (adj) serious; severe

  The equipment is in need of **drastic** repairs.

- **drought** (n) a long period of time when little or no rain or snow falls

  Because of the **drought**, the water level of the lake is low.

- **dusty** (adj) dirty; covered with dust or dirt

  No one cleaned the room for a long time, so the floor is **dusty**.

- **expert** (n) a person who knows a lot about a particular subject

  Jason is an **expert** in the field of electronics.

- **extinct** (adj) no longer alive as a species

  The dinosaurs went **extinct** millions of years ago.

- **fossil** (n) the preserved remains of a dead organism

  Fossils teach researchers many things about the past.

- **gather** (v) to collect

  They must **gather** supplies before going on their trip.

- **gravity** (n) the force that causes all objects to attract one another

  The **gravity** on the moon is 1/6 of the gravity on the Earth.

- **inorganic** (adj) not alive; lifeless; inert

  A rock is an example of an **inorganic** substance.

- **interact** (v) to work together; to communicate with

  The parents enjoy watching the students and the teachers **interact** with one another.

- **interrupt** (v) to disrupt; to break into

  Please do not **interrupt** the speaker during her talk.

- **mantle** (n) the second layer of the Earth

  Part of the **mantle** is solid while the rest is formed of melted rock.

- **melt** (v) to change from a solid to a liquid state

  The ice will **melt** if the temperature goes above freezing.

- **migration** (n) the movement of people or animals from one place to another

  During the fall **migration**, birds fly south for winter.

- **obvious** (adj) clear; apparent

  It is **obvious** how we can solve this problem.

- **occurrence** (n) an event; a happening

  There was a strange **occurrence** last night.

- **optics** (n) the study of light

  Dave is currently studying **optics** at school.

- **organic** (adj) living; alive; natural

  Organic food has become popular in many places nowadays.

- **overuse** (n) excessive use; the act of using something too much

  The **overuse** of farmland can cause it to become less productive.

- **particle** (n) a tiny part of something bigger

  Sand is comprised of extremely tiny **particles**.

- **polar** (adj) related to one of the poles

  Polar explorers need to bring sufficient supplies with them.

- **reaction** (n) a response; an effect

  The politicians were surprised by the people's **reaction** to the new law.

- **refract** (v) to bend

  Light gets **refracted** when it hits water.

- **significant** (adj) important; crucial

  A **significant** number of volunteers signed up to help.

- **silt** (n) soil that is carried in moving water such as a river or stream

  The Amazon River carries a great amount of **silt** to the ocean.

- **supercontinent** (n) an enormous landmass formed by two or more continents

  One **supercontinent** from the past is called Pangaea.

- **thankfully** (adv) luckily; fortunately; happily

  Thankfully, no one was hurt when the two cars hit each other.

- **topmost** (adj) uppermost

  The **topmost** layer of soil was blown away by the wind.

- **topsoil** (n) fertile land on the surface of the ground

  The **topsoil** in this area is full of rich black earth.

- **unearth** (v) to dig up

  The archaeologists are trying to **unearth** the ruins of the ancient city.

- **vanish** (v) to disappear

  The creature appeared to **vanish** because it was so dark.

- **wasteland** (n) a desert; a wilderness

  No one is able to live in that **wasteland** for any length of time.

⊙ Vocabulary **Review**

❗ Choose the word with the closest meaning to each highlighted word or phrase.

1   A gigantic wave caused the ship to sink in
    the ocean.

   Ⓐ huge
   Ⓑ deadly
   Ⓒ unexpected
   Ⓓ swift

2   The attempt to rescue the miners ended up
    as a complete disaster.

   Ⓐ success
   Ⓑ destruction
   Ⓒ catastrophe
   Ⓓ event

3   Try to avoid making any mistakes in your
    report.

   Ⓐ errors
   Ⓑ graphs
   Ⓒ responses
   Ⓓ statements

4   You must learn to adapt and get used to
    your surroundings.

   Ⓐ respond
   Ⓑ propose
   Ⓒ search for
   Ⓓ change

5   The results from the experiment indicate that
    the theory is correct.

   Ⓐ promise
   Ⓑ show
   Ⓒ guess
   Ⓓ assume

6   There is some strange liquid oozing from the
    floor.

   Ⓐ dropping
   Ⓑ gushing
   Ⓒ seeping
   Ⓓ climbing

❗ Match each word with the correct definition.

7   definition   •   • Ⓐ a dry, often hot, place

8   desert   •   • Ⓑ to run, as in a river or a stream

9   erupt   •   • Ⓒ the meaning of a word

10   flow   •   • Ⓓ a group; a class

11   unite   •   • Ⓔ to combine; to join together

12   category   •   • Ⓕ to explode, like a volcano

126

Part B

Chapter 07 **Arts 1** | **Conversations**

city planning • art history • literature • music • industrial design • visual arts • crafts • architecture • film • photography

Listen to part of a lecture in a music class.

02-49

TYPE 1 What aspect of Bela Bartok does the professor mainly discuss?

　Ⓐ His early life

　Ⓑ His work with folk music

　Ⓒ His piano compositions

　Ⓓ His mother's influence on him

TYPE 2 What can be inferred about music from Romania and Slovakia?

　Ⓐ It was livelier than Hungarian music.

　Ⓑ It involved music that was nationalistic.

　Ⓒ It stressed piano music.

　Ⓓ It was influenced by gypsies.

TYPE 3 Why does the professor mention Bela Bartok's mother?

　Ⓐ To name a person who affected his music

　Ⓑ To state that she used to be a gypsy

　Ⓒ To claim that she had come from Hungary

　Ⓓ To say that she taught him to compose music

TYPE 4 What is the student's opinion of the music she heard?

　Ⓐ She thinks it was original.

　Ⓑ She enjoyed hearing it.

　Ⓒ She wants to hear it again.

　Ⓓ She is unimpressed by it.

✎ Checking Listening Accuracy   Mark the following statements T (true) or F (false).

	T	F	
1	☐	☐	Bela Bartok lived during the twentieth century.
2	☐	☐	Bela Bartok's mother had a great influence on him.
3	☐	☐	Much Hungarian folk music came from gypsies.
4	☐	☐	Bela Bartok created many original Hungarian folk songs.

02-50

Listen to part of a lecture in an art history class.

TYPE 5   What is the main topic of the lecture?

    Ⓐ   How to make a mural

    Ⓑ   Where murals are found

    Ⓒ   The most famous murals

    Ⓓ   Some facts about murals

TYPE 6   What is a mural?

    Ⓐ   A painting found on the outside of a building

    Ⓑ   A painting made on a wall, floor, or ceiling

    Ⓒ   A painting that is done on a piece of canvas

    Ⓓ   A painting that gives a special kind of message

TYPE 7   What will the professor probably do next?

    Ⓐ   Ask the students for their thoughts on murals

    Ⓑ   Show some slides to the students

    Ⓒ   Continue discussing the history of murals

    Ⓓ   Start a class discussion

TYPE 8   Listen again to part of the lecture. Then answer the question.
What does the professor imply when she says this: 🎧

    Ⓐ   Murals are some of the oldest types of art.

    Ⓑ   Prehistoric murals were very simplistic.

    Ⓒ   She thinks that early murals are primitive.

    Ⓓ   The first murals are in poor condition.

Checking Listening Accuracy   Mark the following statements T (true) or F (false).

	T	F	
1	☐	☐	A mural is smaller than most other types of paintings.
2	☐	☐	Prehistoric men made some murals inside caves.
3	☐	☐	Some Greek murals have been found in Pompeii.
4	☐	☐	Renaissance masters made some creative murals.

02-51

Listen to part of a conversation between a student and a professor.

TYPE 9   What are the speakers mainly discussing?

  (A) A paper the student needs to write

  (B) The student's application for a job

  (C) An assignment the student turned in

  (D) The student's recent lateness for class

TYPE 10   What did the student do recently?

  (A) She found a job on campus.

  (B) She became a teaching assistant.

  (C) She gave a presentation in class.

  (D) She began working as an intern.

TYPE 11   What can be inferred about the student?

  (A) She is going to graduate this semester.

  (B) She caused a problem in a recent class.

  (C) She lives in the downtown area.

  (D) She hopes to attend graduate school.

TYPE 12   Listen again to part of the conversation. Then answer the question.
Why does the professor say this: 🎧

  (A) To thank the student for giving him a paper

  (B) To tell the student she needs to attend every class

  (C) To require the student to try harder in class

  (D) To show he understands the student's problem

⏴ Checking Listening Accuracy   Mark the following statements T (true) or F (false).

        T   F

1   ☐ / ☐   The student has been late for four classes.

2   ☐ / ☐   The student has an internship at a consulting firm.

3   ☐ / ☐   The student was late because she missed the bus.

4   ☐ / ☐   The professor tells the student to come into the room quietly.

Listen to part of a lecture in an art history class.

02-52

The Dada Art Movement	
Characteristics:	Marcel Duchamp:
	Reactions to Dadaism:

1 Why does the professor explain what non-art is?

- Ⓐ To respond to a student's question
- Ⓑ To compare it with anti-art
- Ⓒ To describe a popular new art form
- Ⓓ To describe the works of Marcel Duchamp

2 According to the professor, why was the Dada Art Movement founded?

- Ⓐ Some artists in Switzerland were bored with regular art.
- Ⓑ There was a need for a new genre of art.
- Ⓒ It was a response to the violence of World War I.
- Ⓓ Some artists were trying to combine art and literature.

3 What is the student's opinion of Dadaist art?

- Ⓐ She appreciates its originality.
- Ⓑ She believes it is not real art.
- Ⓒ She thinks some of it is acceptable.
- Ⓓ She gives no opinion about it.

✎ Listening Comprehension Complete the following sentences. Use the words in the box.

a. Marcel Duchamp	b. World War I	c. pieces of non-art	d. strongly disliked

1 The Dada Art Movement started during _____ .

2 The artists in the Dada Art Movement created _____ .

3 _____ was one of the Dadaist artists.

4 Much of the public _____ the works of the Dadaists.

Mastering **Topics** with Lectures

Listen to part of a lecture in an art history class.

02-53

Frederic Remington

| Frederic Remington | ➡ | Remington's Artwork: |

1 What aspect of Frederic Remington does the professor mainly discuss?

   Ⓐ The time he spent in the West

   Ⓑ His most famous sculptures

   Ⓒ The work he did for magazines

   Ⓓ The characteristics of his art

2 How does the professor organize the information about Remington's artwork that he presents to the class?

   Ⓐ He names some works of art and then discusses them.

   Ⓑ He compares Remington's paintings with works by other artists.

   Ⓒ He describes Remington's artwork while showing slides of it.

   Ⓓ He stresses the works that Remington made of the landscape.

3 Listen again to part of the lecture. Then answer the question.
Why does the professor say this: 🎧

   Ⓐ To describe the colors in a painting

   Ⓑ To give his opinion of Remington's work

   Ⓒ To point out something in a painting

   Ⓓ To discuss his favorite work by Remington

Listening Comprehension Complete the following sentences. Use the words in the box.

| a. most famous work | b. the American West | c. people and animals | d. popular magazines |

1 Much of Frederic Remington's works were printed in _____ .

2 People believed that Frederic Remington was an expert on _____ .

3 _____ are common subjects in Frederic Remington's paintings.

4 Frederic Remington's _____ is a sculpture.

Listen to part of a conversation between a student and a financial aid office employee.

02-54

Service Encounter

Reason for Visiting:		Employee's Question:
Student's Response:		Employee's Comment:

1 Why does the student explain her family situation?

- Ⓐ To complain about her parents losing their jobs
- Ⓑ To mention the reason that she is quitting school
- Ⓒ To tell the man why she needs financial aid
- Ⓓ To indicate why she wants some more student loans

2 How much of her tuition is the student currently paying?

- Ⓐ None of it
- Ⓑ Half of it
- Ⓒ Most of it
- Ⓓ All of it

3 What does the man imply about the student?

- Ⓐ She will probably receive some financial aid.
- Ⓑ The student will likely have to quit school.
- Ⓒ Her grades are too low for her to get a scholarship.
- Ⓓ The student should get a part-time job to earn money.

✎ Listening Comprehension **Complete the following sentences. Use the words in the box.**

a. twin brothers	b. her tuition	c. help the student	d. economic status

1 The student says that she needs some help with _____ .

2 The employee wants to know about the student's current _____ .

3 The student's _____ are going to start college next semester.

4 The employee says that the school will probably be able to _____ .

02-55

Listen to part of a lecture in a film class.

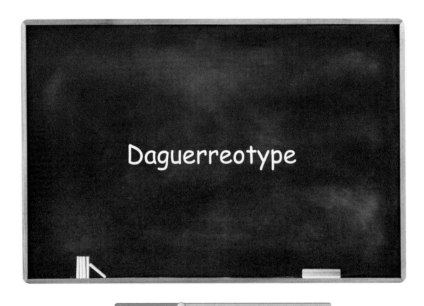

Daguerreotype

1   Why does the professor explain how the daguerreotype worked?

    (A) To make sure the students know the exact steps involved

    (B) To stress the different chemicals that were used

    (C) To show the students how complicated it was

    (D) To give the students a demonstration of how to use it

2   According to the professor, how was the daguerreotype limited?
Click on 2 answers.

    (A) The chemicals it used were very expensive.

    (B) An image it made could not be reproduced.

    (C) It was hard to photograph objects in the light.

    (D) The pictures it created were easily damaged.

3   What is the likely outcome of taking a picture with a daguerreotype with an exposure time of five minutes?

    (A) The image will be unclear.

    (B) The picture will be overexposed.

    (C) The image will look perfect.

    (D) The picture will be too dark.

4   Why does the professor mention that new photographic processes were invented after the daguerreotype?

    (A) To state the improvements that they made

    (B) To introduce the next part of her lecture

    (C) To explain how they created modern cameras

    (D) To respond to a question a student asks

5   What is the professor's opinion of the daguerreotype?

    (A) It was fairly primitive technology.

    (B) It has an important global legacy.

    (C) It revolutionized how people lived.

    (D) It was too expensive to be influential.

6   Listen again to part of the lecture. Then answer the question.
What does the professor imply when she says this: 🎧

    (A) The students can look up the correct spelling.

    (B) She wants to discuss the daguerreotype.

    (C) She has just spelled a difficult word.

    (D) She enjoys trying to make jokes in class.

02-56

Listen to part of a conversation between a student and a professor.

1 What are the speakers mainly discussing?

(A) The student's current part-time job

(B) An offer the professor makes to the student

(C) A special project the student is working on

(D) A class the professor is offering in the summer

2 What is the student going to do in the summer?

(A) Go back to his parents' home

(B) Apply for a grant with the professor

(C) Work on his senior thesis

(D) Take a summer school class

3 What does the professor want the student to do?

(A) Transcribe some interviews

(B) Get a job in the library

(C) Help the professor get a grant

(D) Conduct some research for the professor

4 Listen again to part of the conversation. Then answer the question.
What does the professor imply when he says this: 🎧

(A) The student needs a drink of water.

(B) The student should try to calm down.

(C) The student ran to get to his office.

(D) The student is always in a hurry.

5 Listen again to part of the conversation. Then answer the question.
What is the purpose of the professor's response?

(A) To make fun of the student

(B) To criticize the student

(C) To compliment the student

(D) To agree with the student

★ Star Performer Word Files

- **abstract** (adj) not realistic; nonfigurative

  Some **abstract** artists have sold their works for millions of dollars.

- **absurd** (adj) silly; inane; ridiculous

  That suggestion was **absurd**, so everyone ignored it.

- **canvas** (n) a type of cloth on which an artist paints a picture

  Julie is painting a picture on a large **canvas**.

- **chemist** (n) a person who studies chemistry

  Two **chemists** are still working in the laboratory.

- **complicated** (adj) complex; detailed; involved

  The solution was **complicated**, but it worked perfectly.

- **composer** (n) a person who writes music

  Mozart and Handel are two famous **composers** from the past.

- **depict** (v) to show; to portray

  Brian was **depicted** as a criminal when he was actually a good man.

- **exaggeration** (n) an overstatement; hyperbole

  It is an **exaggeration** to say that millions of people attended the rally.

- **expand** (v) to become larger; to increase in size

  Some stars **expand** to enormous sizes before they die.

- **exposure** (n) the act of letting light shine on something

  What is the necessary **exposure** time for that camera?

- **fascination** (n) appeal; attraction

  Lee's **fascination** with machines made him become an engineer.

- **focus** (v) to concentrate on; to look at something closely

  You need to **focus** more closely on the work that we are doing.

- **folk** (adj) relating to common people

  There are many unique **folk** tales in cultures around the world.

- **fume** (n) smoke

  The **fumes** were so thick that they had to wear masks.

- **gypsy** (n) a nomad who often comes from Southeastern Europe

  Many people distrust **gypsies** and therefore treat them poorly.

- **humorous** (adj) funny; comical

  Karen's speech was so **humorous** that people were constantly laughing.

- **influence** (v) to have an effect on

  Ron **influenced** his children to become doctors.

- **intellectual** (n) a scholar; a thinker; a smart person

  Many **intellectuals** prefer to work at universities.

- **interest** (n) something that a person likes or enjoys

  One of Joe's main **interests** is learning foreign languages.

- **landscape** (n) the appearance of the land

  The **landscape** here is some of the most beautiful in the country.

- **latent** (adj) hidden; idle; sleeping

  There are some **latent** defects in that computer software.

- **limitation** (n) a restriction; a restraint

  Smart people should be aware of their **limitations**.

- **master** (n) a person who excels at something; an expert

  He is a **master** at designing complex systems.

- **nationalistic** (adj) patriotic

  Their **nationalistic** feelings led them to serve their country in the military.

- **neutral** (adj) impartial; having chosen no sides

  A judge should be **neutral** when two people have a dispute.

- **obviously** (adv) apparently; clearly

  She is **obviously** upset about her current situation.

- **outrageous** (adj) extreme; shocking

  It was **outrageous** for Sam to ask for a big bonus.

- **perfect** (v) to make ideal; to complete in the best possible way

  Before we can sell this product, we must **perfect** it.

- **prehistoric** (adj) relating to the time before recorded history; primitive

  During **prehistoric** times, man was uncivilized.

- **process** (n) a way of doing something; a method

  Follow the correct **process**, or you will make many mistakes.

- **publish** (v) to print, as in a book, newspaper, or magazine

  The company will **publish** his book in about two months.

- **pun** (n) a play on words

  Many people do not think **puns** are funny.

- **regard** (v) to consider; to believe

  We **regarded** him with respect when he won the race.

- **repulsed** (adj) disgusted

  I am **repulsed** by your suggestion.

- **scribble** (v) to write quickly

  Peter **scribbled** down the words as fast as he could.

- **sculpture** (n) a statue

  This **sculpture** was created by Michelangelo.

- **tribute** (n) praise of another; an acknowledgement of another

  His book was written as a **tribute** to his old professor.

- **violent** (adj) rough; severe

  The thugs were engaging in **violent** behavior.

- **visible** (adj) able to be seen; clear; apparent

  The ocean should become **visible** in just a few moments.

- **volcano** (n) a mountain from which lava may come

  When a **volcano** erupts, it can cause a huge amount of damage.

Vocabulary **Review**

Choose the word with the closest meaning to each highlighted word or phrase.

1   Please erase those obscene remarks from your notebook.
   (A) false
   (B) silly
   (C) rude
   (D) traditional

2   Despite being in a tremendous amount of pain, Tim drove himself to the hospital.
   (A) minor
   (B) apparent
   (C) somewhat
   (D) great

3   The child disappeared and was never seen again.
   (A) ran away
   (B) vanished
   (C) escaped
   (D) died

4   Have you ever tried to compose any music?
   (A) write
   (B) play
   (C) listen to
   (D) perform

5   You mistakenly confused me for someone else.
   (A) frequently
   (B) surprisingly
   (C) erroneously
   (D) possibly

6   Most animals are wild and cannot be domesticated.
   (A) untamed
   (B) ferocious
   (C) solitary
   (D) playful

Match each word with the correct definition.

7   decade   •   • (A) a period of ten years

8   permanently   •   • (B) after some time

9   fake   •   • (C) forever; eternally

10   eventually   •   • (D) to draw; to paint

11   illustrate   •   • (E) very angry or upset

12   furious   •   • (F) false; not real

Part B

Chapter 08 **Arts 2 | Conversations**

city planning • art history • literature • music • industrial design • visual arts • crafts • architecture • film • photography

02-57

Listen to part of a lecture in a literature class.

TYPE 1   What aspect of Christopher Marlowe does the professor mainly discuss?
Click on 2 answers.

- (A) His life
- (B) His work
- (C) His fame
- (D) His education

TYPE 2   According to the professor, what was tragic about Christopher Marlowe's life?

- (A) His poor education
- (B) The way that he died
- (C) His life of poverty
- (D) The death of his family

TYPE 3   Why does the professor mention *Tamburlaine the Great*?

- (A) To describe the story in it
- (B) To quote a famous line from it
- (C) To compare it with *The Massacre at Paris*
- (D) To state when it was written

TYPE 4   What is the professor's opinion of Christopher Marlowe?

- (A) He says that Marlowe did not write enough.
- (B) He thinks Marlowe was a great writer.
- (C) He believes Marlowe needed some improvements.
- (D) He enjoys the comedies that Marlowe wrote.

Checking Listening Accuracy   Mark the following statements T (true) or F (false).

	T	F	
1	☐	☐	The professor says that *Dr. Faustus* was a masterpiece.
2	☐	☐	Christopher Marlowe died in his forties.
3	☐	☐	Christopher Marlowe never went to college.
4	☐	☐	The professor will read some scenes from Christopher Marlowe's work next.

02-58

Listen to part of a lecture in an art history class.

TYPE 5   What aspect of Cubism does the professor mainly discuss?

- Ⓐ What its origin and features are
- Ⓑ Who created it
- Ⓒ Where its name comes from
- Ⓓ What influenced it

TYPE 6   According to the professor, who created the term Cubism?

- Ⓐ Pablo Picasso
- Ⓑ A French art critic
- Ⓒ An African artist
- Ⓓ Paul Cezanne

TYPE 7   What can be inferred about Cubism?

- Ⓐ The only painters who used it were Picasso and Braque.
- Ⓑ Paintings in the Cubist style are very valuable.
- Ⓒ It was the most popular modern art movement.
- Ⓓ Not all Cubist artwork looks the same.

TYPE 8   Listen again to part of the lecture. Then answer the question. What does the professor imply when he says this: 🎧

- Ⓐ The students had homework on realistic art.
- Ⓑ He is interested in teaching abstract art.
- Ⓒ The class has already discussed abstract art.
- Ⓓ He is going to give the students a test soon.

Checking Listening Accuracy   Mark the following statements T (true) or F (false).

	T	F	
1	☐	☐	Cubism was created in the nineteenth century.
2	☐	☐	Pablo Picasso was one of the creators of Cubism.
3	☐	☐	Cubist art uses geometric shapes.
4	☐	☐	There were three major styles of Cubism.

Listen to part of a conversation between a student and a bookstore employee.

TYPE 9   What are the speakers mainly talking about?

02-59

     Ⓐ   The number of students in a class

     Ⓑ   The price of the student's textbook

     Ⓒ   A class that the student is enrolled in

     Ⓓ   A book the student is looking for

TYPE 10   Why did the bookstore order only twenty copies of the book?

     Ⓐ   Many students buy their books elsewhere.

     Ⓑ   There are twenty-five students in the class.

     Ⓒ   The publisher did not print enough copies.

     Ⓓ   Someone at the bookstore made a mistake.

TYPE 11   What will the student probably do next?

     Ⓐ   Pay for his purchase

     Ⓑ   Find another textbook

     Ⓒ   Visit the library

     Ⓓ   Order the book online

TYPE 12   Listen again to part of the conversation. Then answer the question. What does the employee imply when she says this: 🎧

     Ⓐ   She does not usually buy expensive books.

     Ⓑ   The bookstore frequently has expensive books.

     Ⓒ   The textbook the student wants costs a lot.

     Ⓓ   Only cheap books are sold at the bookstore.

✎ **Checking Listening Accuracy**   **Mark the following statements T (true) or F (false).**

     T   F

1   ☐ / ☐   The student cannot find a book he is looking for.

2   ☐ / ☐   The book the student wants was never ordered.

3   ☐ / ☐   Many students order their books online these days.

4   ☐ / ☐   The woman suggests ordering the book from the bookstore.

Listen to part of a lecture in an arts and crafts class.

02-60

Quilts

The Three Parts of Quilts:	How People Make Quilts:
	What Quilts May Show:

1 What is the batting?

ⓐ The top layer of the quilt

ⓑ The decorative part of the quilt

ⓒ The bottom layer of the quilt

ⓓ The soft, thick part of the quilt

2 Why does the professor mention quilting bees?

ⓐ To say where quilts were first invented

ⓑ To discuss a social event centered on quilts

ⓒ To describe a traditional American custom

ⓓ To explain why some quilts have many patterns

3 What will the professor probably do next?

ⓐ Begin a class discussion

ⓑ Show some pictures of quilts

ⓒ Finish giving her lecture

ⓓ Demonstrate the quilt-making process

Listening Comprehension Complete the following sentences. Use the words in the box.

a. separate layers	b. display quilts	c. their family history	d. the border

1 Some people _____ instead of using them as bedding.

2 All quilts are made of three _____.

3 Once _____ is added to the quilt, it is complete.

4 Some people make quilts that show _____.

Listen to part of a lecture in a film class.

02-61

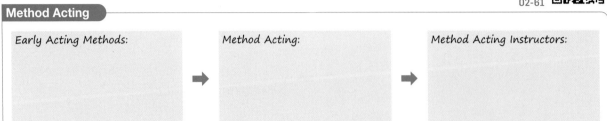

Method Acting

| Early Acting Methods: | Method Acting: | Method Acting Instructors: |

1 Why does the professor explain method acting?

Ⓐ To contrast it with the acting style that came before it

Ⓑ To talk about a movie that they just watched in class

Ⓒ To answer a question that a student asks her

Ⓓ To instruct the students on the proper way to act

2 What is the professor's opinion of *On the Waterfront*?

Ⓐ It should have received many awards.

Ⓑ It was the best movie of its generation.

Ⓒ It was an outstanding movie.

Ⓓ It is a movie of little importance.

3 Based on the information in the lecture, indicate which sentences refer to method acting or the acting style before method acting.
Click in the correct box for each sentence.

	Method Acting	The Acting Style before Method Acting
1 Actors used exaggerated gestures.		
2 Actors made very loud exclamations.		
3 Actors used their own experiences.		
4 Actors tried to understand the characters they were playing.		

Listening Comprehension Complete the following sentences. Use the words in the box.

| a. the 1940s and 1950s | b. was the founder | c. Elia Kazan | d. method actors |

1 Konstantin Stanislavski _____ of the school of method acting.

2 _____ try to become the characters that they are playing.

3 _____ directed *On the Waterfront*, which used method acting.

4 Method acting became more popular in _____ .

Mastering **Topics** with Conversations B3

Listen to part of a conversation between a student and a professor.

02-62

Office Hours

Reason for Visiting: ➡   Professor's Response:

Student's Question: ↙ ➡   Professor's Response:

1   Why does the student visit the professor?

Ⓐ To ask to drop a class of his that she is taking

Ⓑ To talk to him about a seminar he is teaching

Ⓒ To discuss the history of economics with him

Ⓓ To find out how many students are in his class

2   What does the professor say about his class?

Ⓐ It is going to be held in the morning.

Ⓑ The students must all give presentations.

Ⓒ There are only fifteen students in it.

Ⓓ He lets the students conduct some classes.

3   Listen again to part of the conversation. Then answer the question.
What does the student imply when she says this: 🎧

Ⓐ She is upset she cannot get into the class.

Ⓑ She thinks the professor is being unfair to her.

Ⓒ She will put her name on the waiting list.

Ⓓ She is going to enroll in another class.

Listening Comprehension   Complete the following sentences. Use the words in the box.

a. will look for	b. a seminar	c. the waiting list	d. the History Department

1 The student says that she belongs to _____.

2 The student wants to sign up for _____ that the professor will teach.

3 The professor offers to let the student sign up on _____.

4 The student mentions that she _____ another seminar.

02-63

Listen to part of a lecture in an art history class.

1   What is the passage mainly about?

    (A) The Cubist Art Movement

    (B) The life and work of Paul Cezanne

    (C) The effects of short brushstrokes

    (D) Art in the late nineteenth century

2   According to the professor, what kind of painter was Cezanne?

    (A) A Realist

    (B) An Impressionist

    (C) A Pop Artist

    (D) A Modernist

3   Why does the professor explain Cezanne's personality?

    (A) To mention why he was almost never happy

    (B) To talk about his relationship with his father

    (C) To tell the students why Cezanne moved to Paris

    (D) To note some characteristics of his paintings

4   Why does the professor tell the students about Cezanne's marriage?

    (A) To focus on Cezanne's personal life

    (B) To say why Cezanne and his father reconciled

    (C) To explain why Cezanne's painting style changed

    (D) To mention why Cezanne produced fewer works

5   What can be inferred about Cubism?

    (A) It is an art movement from the twentieth century.

    (B) It became popular worldwide in the 1890s.

    (C) The most important Cubist artist was Picasso.

    (D) It was a form of Realist art that was invented.

6   Listen again to part of the lecture. Then answer the question.
    What does the professor mean when he says this: 🎧

    (A) Cezanne's art improved as he got older.

    (B) Cezanne was the greatest artist in history.

    (C) The best art Cezanne made was in the 1890s.

    (D) He believes that Cezanne's art was great.

02-64

Listen to part of a conversation between a student and a basketball coach.

1 What problem does the student have?

    (A) He has a class that interferes with basketball.

    (B) His grades are too low for him to play basketball.

    (C) He cannot participate in a basketball tournament.

    (D) He injured his leg, so he cannot play basketball.

2 What is the student going to do on Friday afternoon?

    (A) Take a bus trip

    (B) Play a basketball game

    (C) Get treatment for his injury

    (D) Have a job interview

3 What does the coach suggest to solve the student's problem?

    (A) He will talk to the student's professor.

    (B) The team bus will wait for the student.

    (C) A coach can drive the student to the game.

    (D) The student can drive his own car.

4 What is the coach's opinion of the student?

    (A) The student is a valuable member of the team.

    (B) The student is letting his team members down.

    (C) The student is thinking only of himself.

    (D) The student needs to try harder.

5 What can be inferred about the student?

    (A) He wants to play professional basketball.

    (B) He will be able to play in the tournament.

    (C) Basketball is the most important thing to him.

    (D) He will return to the basketball team the next year.

Star Performer Word Files

- **allowance** (n) money that one is given on a regular basis

  Carmen's parents gave her an **allowance** every week.

- **author** (n) a writer

  Peter is the **author** of several children's books.

- **awkward** (adj) uncomfortable

  Mr. Thompson is **awkward** when he speaks to large groups of people.

- **border** (n) an edge

  The **border** of the painting is slightly damaged.

- **brilliant** (adj) very intelligent

  She is one of the most **brilliant** people I know.

- **classic** (adj) of the highest quality

  Here is a list of some **classic** songs you should listen to.

- **clip** (n) a short video from a movie, TV show, or something similar

  The students sometimes watch movie **clips** during class.

- **coin** (v) to make; to create

  Shakespeare **coined** a large number of words in English.

- **convey** (v) to express; to say; to communicate

  I want to **convey** my feelings as well as possible.

- **decorative** (adj) ornamental; pretty

  The shopping mall looked **decorative** because it was the holiday season.

- **ethnic** (adj) racial; tribal; relating to a particular group of people

  Sarah's favorite **ethnic** food is Brazilian.

- **experience** (v) to undergo; to go through

  You must **experience** this feeling to understand what it is like.

- **experiment** (v) to try; to do; to conduct a test

  Try to **experiment** with the chemicals to find the right combination.

- **fixed** (adj) unmoving; stationary

  The retired couple lives on a **fixed** income.

- **geometric** (adj) relating to geometry or shapes and figures

  Their paintings contain a large number of **geometric** shapes.

- **gesture** (n) a sign; a motion; body language

  That is a rude **gesture**, so you should not make it.

- **hang** (v) to put up or suspend on a wall

  Let's **hang** the painting on the wall above the sofa.

- **identical** (adj) alike; the same

  Identical twins look exactly alike.

- **impression** (n) a feeling about someone or something

  He made a good **impression** when he met the CEO.

- **inherit** (v) to receive something, such as money, after another person dies

  She will **inherit** a large amount of money from her parents.

- **intentionally** (adv) purposely

  That man **intentionally** pushed the boy down on the ground.

- **isolation** (n) the state of being alone

  The prisoner is kept in **isolation** as part of his punishment.

- **masterpiece** (n) a great work, often a person's best

  This movie is considered a **masterpiece** of cinema.

- **misunderstand** (v) to misinterpret

  Please do not **misunderstand** what I am saying to you.

- **partially** (adv) somewhat; partly

  They **partially** solved the question but could not completely answer it.

- **pen** (v) to write

  He **penned** more than 100 poems during his life.

- **oblige** (v) to obey; to follow; to make happy

  She **obliged** us by treating us to dinner.

- **over-the-top** (adj) exaggerated; too much

  Your **over-the-top** behavior is becoming annoying.

- **portray** (v) to show; to depict

  How was the politician **portrayed** by the media?

- **reconcile** (v) to make up with

  Emily and her mother **reconciled** after not speaking for many years.

- **ridicule** (v) to make fun of; to laugh at

  You should not **ridicule** a person for making a simple mistake.

- **scene** (n) a short part of a movie, play, or other performance

  In this **scene**, the name of the villain is revealed.

- **sew** (v) to stitch

  Eric quickly **sewed** the two pieces of cloth together.

- **shadow** (n) a shade; a dark image formed on the ground due to light

  Your **shadow** grows longer as the sun starts to set.

- **soft-spoken** (adj) quiet

  That **soft-spoken** man is the president of the company.

- **tragic** (adj) relating to something sad, unfortunate, or terrible

  It was **tragic** when the family was in a car accident.

- **vast** (adj) enormous; very large

  There are **vast** amounts of empty land in some countries.

- **vibrant** (adj) lively; animated

  These **vibrant** colors make the painting look more interesting.

- **viewpoint** (n) a perspective; a way of looking at something

  Look at the picture from another **viewpoint**.

- **villain** (n) a bad character; an evil person; an anti-hero

  The **villain** in the movie is defeated by the hero.

Vocabulary Review

Choose the word with the closest meaning to each highlighted word or phrase.

1 Her acting style was complimented by many people.
   (A) rehearsing
   (B) performing
   (C) speaking
   (D) playing

2 They are looking at a portrait hanging on a wall over there.
   (A) postcard
   (B) picture
   (C) cartoon
   (D) graphic

3 Mr. Davidson's approach is to try to solve problems immediately.
   (A) question
   (B) theory
   (C) job
   (D) style

4 They typically go on vacation for one week each year.
   (A) always
   (B) seldom
   (C) sometimes
   (D) normally

5 Did you note anything of interest in the story?
   (A) recognize
   (B) consider
   (C) determine
   (D) believe

6 She accurately answered the question and won the contest.
   (A) finally
   (B) correctly
   (C) eventually
   (D) fortunately

Match each word with the correct definition.

7 process   •   • (A) to come together in a group

8 realize   •   • (B) extreme sadness

9 gather   •   • (C) particularly

10 discuss   •   • (D) to be aware of; to know; to recognize

11 depression   •   • (E) a method of doing something

12 especially   •   • (F) to talk about

Part C

Experiencing the TOEFL iBT Actual Tests

Listening Section Directions

03-01

This section measures your ability to understand conversations and lectures in English.

The Listening section is divided into separately timed parts. In each part, you will listen to 1 conversation and 1 or 2 lectures. You will hear each conversation or lecture only **one** time.

After each conversation or lecture, you will answer some questions about it. The questions typically ask about the main idea and supporting details. Some questions ask about a speaker's purpose or attitude. Answer the questions based on what is stated or implied by the speakers.

You may take notes while you listen. You may use your notes to help you answer the questions. Your notes will not be scored.

If you need to change the volume while you listen, click on **Volume** at the top of the screen.

In some questions, you will see this icon: 🎧 This means that you will hear, but not see, part of the question.

Some of the questions have special directions. These directions appear in a gray box on the screen.

Most questions are worth 1 point. If a question is worth more than 1 point, it will have special directions that indicate how many points you can receive.

A clock at the top of the screen will show you how much time is remaining. The clock will not count down while you are listening. The clock will count down only while you are answering the questions.

Listening Directions

In this part, you will listen to 1 conversation and 2 lectures.

You must answer each question. After you answer, click on **Next**. Then click on **OK** to confirm your answer and go on to the next question. After you click on **OK**, you cannot return to the previous questions.

You may now begin this part of the Listening section. You will have **10 minutes** to answer the questions.

Click on **Continue** to go on.

03-03

1 Why does the student visit the professor?

    Ⓐ To arrange to change his major

    Ⓑ To speak with her about her class

    Ⓒ To get her to sign a form for him

    Ⓓ To ask where another professor is

2 What is the student interested in doing?

    Ⓐ Getting a different advisor

    Ⓑ Registering for a new class

    Ⓒ Finding out his next assignment

    Ⓓ Turning in a paper he wrote

3 What is the professor's attitude toward the student?

    Ⓐ She is interested in his opinion.

    Ⓑ She is considerate toward him.

    Ⓒ She is complimentary of his idea.

    Ⓓ She is impatient with him.

4 What can be inferred about the student?

    Ⓐ He has just starting attending the school.

    Ⓑ He gets good grades in most of his classes.

    Ⓒ He has studied with Professor Owens before.

    Ⓓ He has not met Professor Jackson yet.

5 Listen again to part of the conversation. Then answer the question.
What can be inferred from the student's response to the professor?

    Ⓐ The professor's classes are popular with students.

    Ⓑ The student regularly speaks with the professor.

    Ⓒ The class the professor teaches is for graduate students.

    Ⓓ The professor teaches classes with few students.

03-04

Zoology

6 What aspect of mosquitoes does the professor mainly discuss?

    (A) The features of their bodies

    (B) The way that they reproduce

    (C) The types of living conditions they prefer

    (D) The harm that they cause people

7 What does the proboscis do?
Click on 2 answers.

    (A) Puts an enzyme in a victim's blood

    (B) Makes a victim's blood thinner

    (C) Removes blood from a victim

    (D) Causes a victim's wound to bleed a lot

8 According to the professor, why do mosquitoes drink blood?

    (A) To give their eggs nutrients

    (B) To provide themselves with food

    (C) To act as a substitute for water

    (D) To give to their larvae

9 What comparison does the professor make between the anopheles mosquito and the culex mosquito?

Ⓐ What they usually feed on

Ⓑ Where in the world they live

Ⓒ How many people they kill

Ⓓ What diseases they spread

10 What is the professor's opinion of the malaria vaccine?

Ⓐ He trusts it enough to get it.

Ⓑ He is pleased that it was approved.

Ⓒ He does not think it works well.

Ⓓ He claims it has some side effects.

11 Listen again to part of the lecture. Then answer the question.
What is the purpose of the professor's response?

Ⓐ To tell the student to give more information

Ⓑ To say that the student is correct

Ⓒ To ask the student to try again

Ⓓ To encourage the student to guess

03-05

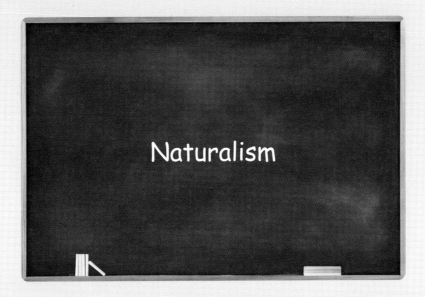

Naturalism

12 What is the main topic of the lecture?

Ⓐ The works of some major Naturalist artists

Ⓑ The differences between Naturalist and Romantic artists

Ⓒ The paintings of Jean-Francois Millet

Ⓓ The role of photography in Naturalism

13 Why does the professor mention Realism?

Ⓐ To show how it influenced some artists

Ⓑ To say that it is another term for Naturalism

Ⓒ To compare it with the Impressionist movement

Ⓓ To state that it is a word she prefers to use

14 What was the most famous painting made by Gustave Courbet?

Ⓐ *The Haymakers*

Ⓑ *The Gleaners*

Ⓒ *The Fisherman's Children*

Ⓓ *A Burial at Ornans*

15 What will the professor probably do next?

    Ⓐ Collect the students' homework

    Ⓑ Show some more slides to the class

    Ⓒ Dismiss the class for the day

    Ⓓ Ask the students for their opinions

16 Listen again to part of the lecture. Then answer the question.
Why does the professor say this?

    Ⓐ To change the topic

    Ⓑ To give a definition

    Ⓒ To make a comparison

    Ⓓ To explain a key point

17 Listen again to part of the lecture. Then answer the question.
What can be inferred about the professor when she says this?

    Ⓐ She expects the students to have their books in class.

    Ⓑ *The Gleaners* is one of her favorite works of art.

    Ⓒ She thinks the making of the painting is interesting.

    Ⓓ She forgot to bring a slide of the painting to class.

Listening Section Directions

03-06

This section measures your ability to understand conversations and lectures in English.

The Listening section is divided into separately timed parts. In each part, you will listen to 1 conversation and 1 or 2 lectures. You will hear each conversation or lecture only **one** time.

After each conversation or lecture, you will answer some questions about it. The questions typically ask about the main idea and supporting details. Some questions ask about a speaker's purpose or attitude. Answer the questions based on what is stated or implied by the speakers.

You may take notes while you listen. You may use your notes to help you answer the questions. Your notes will not be scored.

If you need to change the volume while you listen, click on **Volume** at the top of the screen.

In some questions, you will see this icon: 🎧 This means that you will hear, but not see, part of the question.

Some of the questions have special directions. These directions appear in a gray box on the screen.

Most questions are worth 1 point. If a question is worth more than 1 point, it will have special directions that indicate how many points you can receive.

A clock at the top of the screen will show you how much time is remaining. The clock will not count down while you are listening. The clock will count down only while you are answering the questions.

Listening Directions

In this part, you will listen to 1 conversation and 2 lectures.

You must answer each question. After you answer, click on **Next**. Then click on **OK** to confirm your answer and go on to the next question. After you click on **OK**, you cannot return to the previous questions.

You may now begin this part of the Listening section. You will have **10 minutes** to answer the questions.

Click on **Continue** to go on.

03-08

1 Why does the student visit the student activities office?

    (A) To find out when the parade is

    (B) To purchase tickets for an event

    (C) To ask about getting some supplies

    (D) To request to take part in the parade

2 What does the student give the woman?

    (A) A bill

    (B) A form

    (C) A check

    (D) A list

3 Why does the woman tell the student to contact Mark McNeil?

    (A) To receive permission to make a purchase

    (B) To learn more about a part-time job

    (C) To get some items that he wants

    (D) To receive help on building a float

4 What is the student's attitude toward the woman?

    (A) He wishes she would do more to help him.

    (B) He appreciates her assistance very much.

    (C) He likes that she orders everything he needs.

    (D) He is unhappy that she will not give him some items.

5 Listen again to part of the conversation. Then answer the question.
What does the woman imply when she says this: 🎧

    (A) The student needs to get approval for a purchase.

    (B) Some items the student wants are not available.

    (C) There is not enough time to order a few items.

    (D) She cannot order everything the student wants.

03-09

History

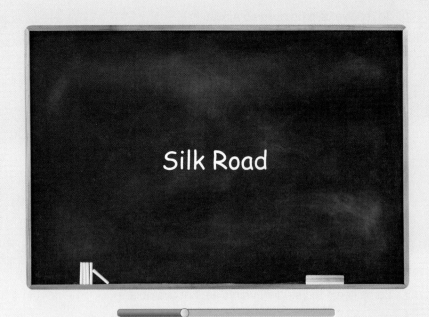

Silk Road

6   What aspect of the Silk Road does the professor mainly discuss?

    Ⓐ The reason that it got its name

    Ⓑ The routes that it followed

    Ⓒ The effects animals had on it

    Ⓓ The dangers travelers faced on it

7   Why does the professor explain the origins of the Silk Road's name?

    Ⓐ To stress the road's connection with China

    Ⓑ To mention that the name is relatively new

    Ⓒ To prove that silk was often transported on it

    Ⓓ To name some places where the routes went

8   What is the professor's opinion of the Silk Road?

    Ⓐ It was unsafe for lone travelers.

    Ⓑ It was the greatest achievement of the ancient world.

    Ⓒ It took too long to travel on.

    Ⓓ It was not well marked in enough places.

9 What does the professor imply about trade on the Silk Road?

   Ⓐ The majority of it took place between China and India.

   Ⓑ It cost too much money for most merchants to engage in.

   Ⓒ There was too little trade before Alexander the Great.

   Ⓓ More trade goods went to the West than to the East.

10 In the lecture, the professor describes a number of facts about the Silk Road. Indicate whether each of the following is a fact about the Silk Road.
Click in the correct box for each sentence.

	Fact	Not a Fact
1 The Silk Road ran from the Mediterranean Sea to China.		
2 Parts of the Silk Road went over mountains.		
3 Only caravans were permitted to travel on the Silk Road.		
4 Alexander the Great ordered the construction of the Silk Road.		

11 Listen again to part of the lecture. Then answer the question.
What does the professor mean when he says this: 🎧

   Ⓐ Deserts take a long time for most people to cross.

   Ⓑ There are fewer deserts in the north than in the south.

   Ⓒ Too many merchants died while traveling on the Silk Road.

   Ⓓ It was dangerous for merchants to travel across deserts.

03-10

Astronomy

12 According to the professor, why did people begin searching for Pluto?

    Ⓐ They wanted to become famous by discovering a new planet.

    Ⓑ Neptune's changing orbit made them think there was another planet.

    Ⓒ There were rumors that there were ten planets in the solar system.

    Ⓓ The effects of Uranus's gravity proved the existence of Pluto.

13 What does the professor imply about the discovery of Pluto?

    Ⓐ It proved the solar system was bigger than was originally thought.

    Ⓑ It made people much more interested in astronomy.

    Ⓒ It failed to increase astronomers' knowledge of the universe.

    Ⓓ It would have happened faster with better equipment.

14 How does the professor organize the information about the discovery of Pluto that she presents to the class?

    Ⓐ By covering the events in chronological order

    Ⓑ By focusing on the role of Clyde Tombaugh

    Ⓒ By encouraging the students to contribute to her lecture

    Ⓓ By quoting passages mentioned in the textbook

15 Based on the information in the lecture, do the statements refer to Percival Lowell or Clyde Tombaugh?

Click in the correct box for each sentence.

	Percival Lowell	Clyde Tombaugh
1 He was the person who discovered Pluto.		
2 He helped fund the search for Pluto.		
3 He studied Mars before getting interested in the search for Pluto.		
4 He utilized a special machine to analyze photographs of the sky.		

16 Listen again to part of the lecture. Then answer the question.
What does the professor imply when she says this: 🎧

Ⓐ She mentioned dwarf planets in a previous lecture.

Ⓑ She does not enjoy talking about the major planets.

Ⓒ She believes the students should pay closer attention.

Ⓓ She wants the students to answer her question.

17 Listen again to part of the lecture. Then answer the question.
Why does the professor say this: 🎧

Ⓐ To describe the surface of Pluto

Ⓑ To talk about two of her students

Ⓒ To clarify a term that she used

Ⓓ To note why little is known about Pluto

MEMO

TOEFL® MAP

Listening

New TOEFL® Edition

Basic

Answers, Explanations, and Scripts

TOEFL® MAP Listening

New TOEFL® Edition

Listening

Basic

Answers, Explanations, and Scripts

 DARAKWON

Part A

Understanding Listening Question Types

Question Type | 01 Gist-Content

Exercises with Gist-Content Questions   p.12

Exercise 1   C

At the beginning of the lecture, the professor states, "So the Industrial Revolution totally changed the Western world." Then, he gives some examples of some changes that happened during the Industrial Revolution.

Exercise 2   A

The student mentions that her grade on a test was low, so she wants to do an extra assignment. The professor says that it is possible, but he needs to think about what kind of work she can do. So they are mostly talking about how the student can improve her grade.

Exercise 3   C

The professor mostly talks about Andy Warhol during the lecture.

Exercise 4   A

When the employee asks the student what is wrong with his room, he answers, "There's no bed in my room."

Question Type | 02 Gist-Purpose

Exercises with Gist-Purpose Questions   p.16

Exercise 1   C

When the student first starts talking to the professor, he asks, "Can I talk to you about today's lecture?"

Exercise 2   A

The student asks, "Do all snakes rely on venom?" The professor then responds by describing the constriction method that some snakes use to kill their prey.

Exercise 3   D

The student asks the professor why she wants to see her. The professor responds by saying, "It's about your midterm exam."

Exercise 4   C

The student says, "I'm here to change rooms," when the employee asks her why she is at the office.

Question Type | 03 Detail

Exercises with Detail Questions   p.20

Exercise 1   C

The student tells the professor that she had some car problems. The professor mentions that the student was late for class. The student was obviously late because of her car problems.

Exercise 2   A, C

About pottery, the professor says, "It can be used to hold various items or for display purposes."

Exercise 3   B

When talking about the application for the scholarship, the professor tells the student, "First, you have to write an essay."

Exercise 4   D

The professor states, "Yet they both have stripes. Interestingly, it's for the same reason: camouflage." He also comments that the animals use their stripes "to hide from one another."

Question Type | 04 Understanding the Function of What Is Said

Exercises with Understanding the Function of What Is Said Questions   p.24

Exercise 1   B

When the professor answers, "Not really," she is disagreeing with what the student just said.

Exercise 2   B

The woman declares, "That's going to be hard to manage," when the student asks for some copies of his transcript on the same day. She implies that the student will probably not get the copies until later.

Exercise 3   C

The student asks the professor, "Is there anything I can do to improve my grade in this class?" When he tells her about the study groups, she asks him for more information about them. So she is trying to improve her grade in the class.

Exercise 4   A

When the professor states that she does not want to talk about what they can learn from fossils yet, she is indicating to the students that she wants to discuss something else instead of that topic.

Exercises with Understanding the Speaker's Attitude Questions

p.28

Exercise 1 B

While talking about various types of alternative energy, the professor states, "They have many advantages. But they aren't perfect. Each type of alternative energy has drawbacks as well."

Exercise 2 D

The professor notes, "They also traded with cultures near the Mississippi River. Impressive, isn't it? After all, the Mississippi was quite distant from where the Anasazi mainly lived." In saying that the Mississippi is distant from the Anasazi's home and that their trading with people in that region was impressive, the professor implies that the Anasazi traveled a remarkable distance.

Exercise 3 A

The woman says, "I'd be glad to help you." She is also friendly to the student while she speaks, so she is quite helpful.

Exercise 4 A

When the professor tells the student that his suggestion is not good enough, the professor is indicating that he dislikes the student's proposal.

 Question Type | 06 Understanding Organization

Exercises with Understanding Organization Questions

p.32

Exercise 1 B

The professor mentions the dates 1492, 1502, 1513, and 1519 in that order, so he discusses the events in chronological order.

Exercise 2 D

The professor says, "And look at the slide here." He also pauses several times during the lecture. This indicates that he is showing some other slides to the students.

Exercise 3 C

The woman asks the student why he wants a new dorm room. Then, the student describes what is wrong with his current housing situation. So he is talking about his room to explain why he wants to move to another place.

Exercise 4 B

The professor says, "First, it's an excellent conductor of electricity." So he mentions electricity to note that gold is a good conductor of it.

 Question Type | 07 Connecting Content

Exercises with Connecting Content Questions

p.36

Exercise 1 C

The professor mentions that the Milky Way is a spiral galaxy. Then, he states, "There are countless spiral galaxies throughout the universe." So it can be implied that the shape of the Milky Way is not unusual.

Exercise 2 A

The professor talks about how the cactus and the mesquite tree both have long roots that help them absorb water from the ground.

Exercise 3 D

When the student asks about his chances of winning a scholarship, the professor responds, "They're pretty good. I know all of the students applying. And you're the most qualified." So the likely outcome is that the student will receive the scholarship if he applies for it.

Exercise 4 C

When talking about ancient Greek vases, the professor mentions, "Fortunately, thousands of them have survived to the present day. That should tell you about the quality of those vases." So she implies that the vases were very well made since they have survived for so long.

 Question Type | 08 Making Inferences

Exercises with Making Inferences Questions

p.40

Exercise 1 D

The professor states, "After the Third Punic War, Rome was the only remaining major power in the Mediterranean region." Thus it can be inferred that Carthage lost the war since Rome was the only remaining power in that area.

The employee says, "Ah, there's one more thing. It costs twenty-five dollars per semester to join the gym." Since the student indicates that she wants to work out, she will most likely pay her membership fee first and then go to the gym to exercise.

The professor states, "A lot of art critics really disliked the Impressionists. In fact, they didn't think that the Impressionists' works were real art. I totally disagree with them." By disagreeing with the art critics, the professor implies that he believes that the works of the Impressionists were real art.

The student shows the professor that he made a mistake on her test grade. The professor looks at the test and then says, "I sincerely apologize." By saying that, the professor implies that he will change the student's test grade to the proper number.

Part B

Building Background Knowledge of TOEFL Topics

● Chapter | 01 **Life Sciences 1** • Conversations

Mastering Question Types with Lectures & Conversations A

p.44

[TYPES 1–4]

| TYPE 1 (D) | TYPE 2 (B) |
| TYPE 3 (A) | TYPE 4 (B) |

Script　02-01

M Professor: The monarch butterfly is unique among butterflies. It performs a two-way migration each year. Monarch butterflies live in North America. Those in cold northern regions migrate every fall and spring. They either fly to California or Mexico when they migrate. Some monarch butterflies fly around 5,000 kilometers. They average about 100 kilometers per day on their journey. Impressive, isn't it . . . ? They may take up to two months to reach their destination. That's similar to some birds.

W Student: Why exactly do they migrate?

M: Well, uh, the main reason is that they can't survive in cold temperatures. Indeed, the butterflies cluster together to stay warm on their trip. They only fly during the day. At night, tens of thousands of them may rest in the same tree to help them stay warm. Year after year, they fly the same routes. They also rest in the same areas. And their final destination doesn't change either. Later, in spring, they return north.

But the same monarchs don't return north. The lifespan of a monarch butterfly is typically, uh, about two months. However, those butterflies alive in fall enter a phase called diapause. That's D-I-A-P-A-U-S-E. Butterflies in diapause can live for up to seven months. But they don't reproduce until the spring. When spring comes, they mate, reproduce, and die. After that, a new generation is born. These butterflies head north to the exact places where their parent butterflies lived. No one's aware of how these butterflies know where to go. But there are some interesting theories.

TYPE 1　[Gist-Content Question]

The professor mostly focuses on how monarch butterflies migrate to avoid cold temperatures.

TYPE 2 [Connecting Content Question]

The professor states, "Some monarch butterflies fly around 5,000 kilometers. They average about 100 kilometers per day on their journey. Impressive, isn't it? They may take up to two months to reach their destination. That's similar to some birds."

TYPE 3 [Understanding Organization Question]

The professor remarks that monarch butterflies live for about two months. He then mentions diapause and explains that butterflies in that state can live for up to seven months.

TYPE 4 [Understanding Attitude Question]

When talking about how far monarch butterflies may migrate, the professor asks, "Impressive, isn't it?"

♪ Checking Listening Accuracy

1 **T**   2 **F**   3 **T**   4 **T**

[TYPES 5–8]

TYPE 5 Ⓓ   **TYPE 6** Ⓒ
TYPE 7 Ⓐ   **TYPE 8** Ⓑ

Script 02-02

W Professor: When a seed germinates, it develops roots and soon becomes a seedling. Later, it grows larger and becomes a mature plant. Generally, seeds need soil, water, oxygen, and sunlight to grow. However, getting seeds to germinate is not as simple as burying them in the ground and pouring water on them. Okay, that does work for many seeds. But other seeds require special conditions to germinate.

Many seeds are dormant. That means they require specific conditions before they can germinate. One of the most common conditions is cold weather. In lots of places, seeds lie dormant in the ground during winter. So they do not germinate until spring. But what do you do if you want to plant some of these seeds in summer? You need to stratify them. Stratification is the process of changing the temperature of seeds to get them to germinate. How? Well, most people put their seeds in the fridge for a month or two. After that, the seeds are ready to germinate. The seeds of apple, peach, and pear trees must be cold stratified. So must many other plants.

Other seeds require heat stratification. Some species of eucalyptus have seeds that remain dormant until they're exposed to great heat. This can happen during forest fires. Why is that? It's simple. You see, the fires typically burn mature trees during dry seasons. But seeds buried in the ground are exposed to heat from the fires. This makes them

germinate. So new trees grow and replace the ones burned by the fires.

TYPE 5 [Gist-Purpose Question]

The professor states, "Many seeds are dormant. That means they require specific conditions before they can germinate." Then, she describes stratification and explains it as a way to get seeds to germinate.

TYPE 6 [Detail Question]

The professor states, "The seeds of apple, peach, and pear trees must be cold stratified."

TYPE 7 [Making Inferences Question]

The professor says, "Some species of eucalyptus have seeds that remain dormant until they're exposed to great heat. This often happens during forest fires." She then adds, "You see, the fires typically burn mature trees during dry seasons." So she implies that eucalyptus trees live in areas with dry conditions.

TYPE 8 [Understanding Function Question]

First, the professor talks about the cold stratifying of seeds. Then, she says, "Other seeds require heat stratification," and she explains the process. So she is contrasting heat stratification with cold stratification.

♪ Checking Listening Accuracy

1 **T**   2 **T**   3 **F**   4 **T**

[TYPES 9–12]

TYPE 9 Ⓑ   **TYPE 10** Ⓒ
TYPE 11 Ⓒ   **TYPE 12** Ⓓ

Script 02-03

M Student: Professor Jenkins, did you hear about those changes the school just made?

W Professor: You're talking about the new requirements for graduation, right, Eric . . . ? Sure. I've seen them. I was actually, uh, on the committee that recommended them.

M: You were? But, uh, why didn't you tell me about them?

W: What do you mean?

M: [12]Well, next year, I'm going to have to change my entire schedule. I'll have to take an extra science class and a language class. **That is going to ruin my entire semester.**

W: Eric, you need to relax for a moment. Calm down, please. You don't have to take those classes.

M: I don't? Why not?

W: These changes only apply to freshmen and sophomores. You, on the other hand, are going to graduate after you finish one more year of school. So these changes don't apply to you. That means you can keep your regular schedule.

TYPE 9 [Gist-Purpose Question]

The student goes to the professor and talks about a change that has been made in the school's graduation requirements. He is unhappy about this change, so he is complaining about it.

TYPE 10 [Detail Question]

The professor tells the student, "These changes only apply to freshmen and sophomores." So the new graduation requirements do not apply to all of the students.

TYPE 11 [Making Inferences Question]

The student talks to the professor about his class schedule. He also comments that she should have told him about the changes earlier. These are topics that students would speak with their advisors about. So it can be inferred that the professor is the student's advisor.

TYPE 12 [Understanding Function Question]

When the student declares, "That is going to ruin my entire semester," he is indicating how upset he is. His tone of voice also shows that he is not pleased with the situation.

✓ Checking Listening Accuracy

1 T   2 F   3 F   4 T

Mastering Topics with Lectures B1   p.47

1 Coral: ☑1, ☑3   Zooxanthellae ☑2, ☑4   2 Ⓑ   3 Ⓐ

`Script & Graphic Organizer` 02-04

W Professor: Okay, now I want to examine an unusual life form called coral. You've all heard of coral reefs, right? And many of you may think they're a kind of rock. Right . . . ? But that's not right. In actuality, coral is a living organism. It's found primarily in tropical waters because it can only survive in a certain temperature range. It also grows best in shallow water since it needs sunlight to survive. Coral simply cannot grow more than fifty meters below the surface.

What coral does is, uh, it secretes calcium carbonate. This lets the coral attach itself to the reef. Then, the calcium carbonate hardens, which increases the size of the reef. In this way, coral reefs can expand.

M Student: Professor Jones, how does coral survive? I mean, er, what does it eat?

W: [3]Good question, Jake. Coral gets its nutrients from zooxanthellae. **That's a long word, so I wrote it up on the board here . . .** That's how you spell it. Zooxanthellae are single-cell organisms that live with the coral. They use photosynthesis to get their nourishment. But get this . . . They create extra nutrients. Coral lives off these nutrients. Now, if the zooxanthellae die, the coral starts dying, too. Dying coral loses its color and turns white. We call this coral bleaching. If new zooxanthellae aren't introduced into the ecosystem, the entire reef will rapidly die.

There are several factors that can cause zooxanthellae and coral reefs to die. The biggest reason is pollution. Chemicals enter the ocean from runoff from farms and harbor areas. This puts too many nutrients in the water. As a result, algae blooms—when too many algae grow simultaneously—form. The algae absorb all of the oxygen in the ocean, which kills the zooxanthellae. What else . . . ? Let's see . . . Ah, coral mining is a big problem. Miners use explosives to rip out coral to use for homes, fish tanks, and jewelry. Additionally, sometimes the water gets too warm. The coral can't adjust, so it dies. This may happen during an El Nino period. Let me show you how that happens now.

Coral

Characteristics:	Zooxanthellae:
- Is a living organism	Singled-celled organisms that live with coral; use photosynthesis; create many nutrients; coral use the leftover nutrients
- Lives in tropical waters	
- Grows best in shallow water	
- Needs sunlight	
- Cannot grow more than fifty meters below the surface	**What Kills Coral Reefs:**
- Secretes calcium carbonate	Pollution from farm and harbor runoff; coral mining rips out coral; warm water because of El Nino
- Calcium carbonate lets it create coral reefs and expand	

1 [Connecting Content Question]

According to the professor, "Dying coral loses its color and turns white." She also mentions that coral "grows best in shallow water since it needs sunlight to survive." As for zooxanthellae, "They use photosynthesis to get their nourishment." They are single-cell organisms as well.

2 [Making Inferences Question]

At the end of her lecture, the professor states, "This may happen during an El Nino period. Let me show you how that happens now." So she will probably discuss the effects of El Nino on coral reefs next.

3 [Understanding Attitude Question]

When the professor states that "zooxanthellae" is a long word so she wrote it on the board, she implies that it is difficult for the students to spell, so they may need help with it.

♪Listening Comprehension

1 c	2 a	3 d	4 b

Mastering Topics with Lectures B2　　　p.48

1 Ⓓ	2 Ⓑ	3 Ⓐ

Script & Graphic Organizer 02-05

M Professor: Fungi comprise one of the five kingdoms of organisms. People often think of them as plants. But that is erroneous thinking. Fungi and plants are, in fact, quite different. The main difference is that fungi don't undergo photosynthesis like plants do. In addition, the structures of the cell walls of fungi and plants are, well, different. Plants have cellulose while fungi have chitin. Chitin is a form of glucose. It's also the substance that the hard outer shells of many insects are made of. That's interesting, huh?

One example of a fungus is the mushroom. You often see mushrooms growing on the ground in a forest. But what you see is just a part of the fungus. We call that the "fruit." Much of the fungus, however, remains hidden. It's underground or buried within a tree trunk.

Fungi grow all around the world. They thrive in damp, dark places. Forest floors are one common place. They also grow well on dead trees. Fungi are useful to their ecosystems in that they help break down dead organic matter. This enables nutrients that benefit plants to enter the soil. Because of that, many fungi have symbiotic relationships with plants. They provide nutrients for plants while also getting to live in the plants' roots. It's a convenient relationship that helps both organisms.

People have discovered that fungi have many uses. In lots of countries, mushrooms, uh, are an important food source. Yeast is another type of fungi. Yeast, of course, is used to make bread and many types of, er, alcoholic beverages. People also use fungi to make certain medicines. For instance, penicillin, which can treat infections, comes from a fungus.

On the other hand, many fungi are poisonous. They cannot be eaten or used for anything. Other fungi are parasites that harm both plants and animals. Some fungi cause minor and major diseases in humans. Some of you may have gotten athlete's foot before. Anyone . . . ? Well, anyway, it's a painful itching of the feet. A fungus causes athlete's foot. Believe me. It's something you definitely don't want to get.

Fungi

Characteristics:	*How They Benefit People:*
- *Are different from plants*	*People often eat mushrooms;*
- *Do not undergo photosynthesis*	*use yeast to make bread and alcohol; can make medicines such as penicillin*
- *Have chitin in their cell walls*	
- *Can be mushrooms*	*How They Harm People:*
- *Grow in dark, damp places*	*Some are poisonous; cannot*
- *Break down dead organic matter*	*be eaten or used; may cause minor or major diseases; can cause athlete's foot*
- *Have many symbiotic relationships with plants*	

1 [Gist-Content Question]

The professor spends the majority of the lecture describing the characteristics of fungi.

2 [Detail Question]

About fungi, the professor notes, "They thrive in damp, dark places."

3 [Understanding Organization Question]

When the professor discusses athlete's foot, he states, "Some fungi cause minor and major diseases in humans. Some of you may have gotten athlete's foot before. Anyone? Well, anyway, it's a painful itching of the feet. A fungus causes athlete's foot." So he talks about it in order to show how fungi may be harmful.

♪Listening Comprehension

1 d	2 b	3 c	4 a

Mastering Topics with Conversations B3　　　p.49

1 Ⓓ	2 Ⓑ	3 Ⓓ

M Dining Services Employee: Good afternoon, miss. Is there something that I can help you with today?

W Student: I hope so. I, uh, I have a q-q-question about my meal plan. You're the person to talk to about that, right?

M: That is correct. I handle meal plans here. So, um, what exactly do you want to know?

W: Well, I'm a freshman here at the school. So I had to purchase the meal plan that gives me twenty meals a week.

M: That's right. It's a school requirement that all freshmen buy that plan. That way, uh, we can make sure that you students are getting enough to eat.

W: Uh, yeah. Sure. I understand that. But, uh, there's a big problem. You see, I only eat about ten to twelve meals a week on campus. That means my meal plan is a huge waste of money for me. So my question is . . . Can you, um, can you make any exceptions to the rule?

M: Possibly. Why do you eat so few meals at the cafeteria?

W: [3]The main reason is that my parents live in town. I have a dorm room, but I go home for dinner a lot. **The food's better there than at the cafeteria.** And I'm always home on the weekend. So I don't need twenty meals. And to be honest, the meal plan is too expensive as well.

M: Since you're eating at home, we can make an exception for you. What meal plan are you interested in?

W: I'm not sure. Could you show me my options, please?

Service Encounter

Reason for Visiting:	Result:
Wants to discuss her current meal plan	Is told that all freshmen must buy a meal plan for twenty meals a week

Student's Request:	Man's Response:
Wants a different meal plan since she often eats at home	Agrees to her request and asks her which meal plan she wants

1 [Gist-Purpose Question]

The student goes to the dining services office to talk with the man about getting a different meal plan since she is unhappy with the one that she currently has.

2 [Detail Question]

The student mentions that she is a freshman and has the meal plan that gives her twenty meals a week. The man responds by saying, "It's a school requirement that all freshmen buy that plan."

3 [Understanding Function Question]

The student is making a joke when she mentions that the food at her home is better than the food at the cafeteria.

Listening Comprehension

1 a   2 c   3 d   4 b

TOEFL Practice Tests C1   p.50

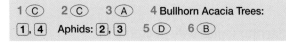

1 ⓒ   2 ⓒ   3 Ⓐ   4 Bullhorn Acacia Trees: ①, ④   Aphids: ②, ③   5 Ⓓ   6 Ⓑ

M Professor: Okay, class, let's turn our attention to another kind of relationship in the living world. I'm referring to something called symbiosis. [5]In symbiosis, one living organism has a close relationship with another living organism. Most of the time, the relationship is beneficial. **But that's not always the case.** Now, many times, one organism needs the other to survive. If one organism were absent, one—or both—would die. We call this obligate symbiosis. Oh . . . I know these terms are difficult. But look at page 57 of your books . . . You'll find these terms listed there. Okay . . . ? Now, there is also something called facultative symbiosis. In this relationship, the survival of one organism does not depend on the other one it has a relationship with.

Let me give you some examples. There's one animal that has numerous symbiotic relationships with other organisms. It's, uh, the ant. Ants have formed symbiotic relationships with, well, with plants, other insects, and fungi.

For instance, in Central America, the bullhorn acacia tree grows. This tree has hollow thorns. The ants live in its thorns. When other insects visit the acacia tree . . . to feed on its leaves perhaps . . . the ants come out and attack them. In return, the ants get nutrients from parts of the tree. Okay, another one . . . In the Amazon Rainforest, lemon ants protect lemon ant trees. The lemon ants build their nests in the trees. Then, they proceed to sting all of the nearby plants. Their stingers contain an acid that kills the plants. By killing the other plants, they eliminate the lemon ant trees' competitors. So the lemon ant trees become bigger and greater in number. The ants, meanwhile, benefit by getting large areas for them to build their nests.

W Student: [6]Sir, what about aphids? According to the textbook, ants and aphids help each other. How do they do that?

M: **Ah, yes, I was about to get to that.** Like I mentioned, ants have relationships with other insects. The aphid is a great example. Aphids are insects that eat plant sap. In turn, they produce a sweet nectar called honeydew. Ants love eating honeydew. Here is how their relationship works . . . The aphids allow the ants to eat the honeydew directly from their bodies. In return, the ants protect the aphids from predators such as beetles. Some scientists have observed ants carrying aphids. Why . . . ? Well, ants sometimes move aphids to new feeding places. Aphids are smaller than ants, so the ants merely pick them up and transport them. By the way, some ants have similar relationships with mealybugs and various caterpillar species that also produce honeydew.

Finally, some species of ants have relationships with fungi. The best relationship to explain concerns the leaf-cutter ant of South America. This ant is like a, um, a fungi farmer. You see, uh, the ants bring plant matter to the fungi. This provides the fungi with a food source. The ants even seem to know which food sources the fungi can eat and which ones are poisonous. In addition, the ants protect the fungi from pests. The fungi then produce nutrients that the leaf-cutter ants feed on.

Now, these relationships that I just described are all examples of facultative symbiosis. There's no reason to believe that the ants or other organisms would die without one another's help. However, the nature of their relationships makes all of them much stronger.

1 [Gist-Content Question]

The professor mostly talks about symbiotic relationships between ants and other organisms. He focuses on how these relationships affect both the ants and the other organisms involved.

2 [Detail Question]

The professor states, "Now, there is also something called facultative symbiosis. In this relationship, the survival of one organism does not depend on the other one it has a relationship with."

3 [Understanding Organization Question]

In his lecture, the professor first describes what symbiosis is. Then, he gives several examples of symbiotic relationships between various organisms.

4 [Connecting Content Question]

According to the professor, bullhorn acacia trees provide ants with some nutrients. They also grow in Central America, so that is where their relationship with ants takes place. As for aphids, the ants protect them in return for honeydew, which the ants eat.

5 [Understanding Function Question]

The professor notes that most symbiotic relationships are beneficial. However, he then says, "But that's not always the case." He is implying that some symbiotic relationships can be harmful.

6 [Understanding Attitude Question]

When the professor exclaims, "I was about to get to that," after the student asks him a question, he means that he is going to discuss the topic that the student just asked him about.

TOEFL Practice Tests C2   p.52

1 Ⓐ   2 Ⓑ   3 Ⓐ   4 Ⓑ   5 Ⓓ

Script 02-08

W1 Student: Good afternoon, Professor Burns. Do you have a few minutes to chat with me?

W2 Professor: I sure do, Amy. Please come on in and have a seat . . . So, um, what's on your mind today? [5]Is this something concerning our class?

W1: Well, uh, yes. Actually . . . um, that's exactly why I am here.

W2: **Go on.**

W1: Well, I want to talk to you about the class project we have to do.

W2: Hmm . . . Remind me again, please. What's your topic? I can't remember because, well, there are just too many students in that class.

W1: I was hoping to do my project on parrots. I had planned to do it on their habitats and their feeding habits. I already submitted a paper explaining the topic. You approved it, too. That was sometime around two weeks ago.

W2: So then, uh, what's the problem? You can't find enough research material? I have tons of material on parrots if you need some.

W1: Oh, no. There is plenty of information about parrots in the library. I've found several books about them. It's just . . .

W2: Yes?

W1: Well, uh . . . I was thinking of changing my topic. You see, I just got a job interning at the city zoo. I started last week. They have me working in the reptile house. It's totally amazing. I mean, uh, I get to see all kinds of snakes, alligators, and crocodiles up close and personal. You wouldn't believe how great it is.

W2: Let me guess. You want to do your project on reptiles now, right?

W1: Exactly. What do you say to that?

W2: Honestly, um, I recommend against it. I have two reasons. First, the project is due in two weeks. So it will be hard to start doing research on a new topic. Second, there are already three students in the class doing their projects on reptiles. You're the only one working on parrots. I like to see some diversity in my students' projects. So I'd prefer for you to stay with parrots.

W1: Oh. I see.

W2: Don't be too upset, Amy. There's always next year. I'm sure you'll find a way to do a project on reptiles sometime in the future.

1 [Gist-Purpose Question]

In the middle of their conversation, the student tells the professor, "I was thinking of changing my topic." That is the reason why the student visits the professor.

2 [Detail Question]

The student says to the professor, "I was hoping to do my project on parrots."

3 [Making Inferences Question]

At the end of the conversation, the professor remarks, "Don't be too upset, Amy. There's always next year." When she mentions, "There's always next year," she implies that the student is not a senior since she has at least one more year of school to attend.

4 [Understanding Attitude Question]

The student asks the professor what she thinks of her new topic. The professor responds, "Honestly, um, I recommend against it." So the professor dislikes the new topic.

5 [Understanding Function Question]

When a person says, "Go on," that person means that the other speaker should continue talking.

1	Ⓐ	2	Ⓒ	3	Ⓐ	4	Ⓒ
5	Ⓑ	6	Ⓓ	7	Ⓐ	8	Ⓓ
9	Ⓔ	10	Ⓑ	11	Ⓒ	12	Ⓕ

● Chapter | **02** **Life Sciences 2** • Conversations

Mastering Question Types with Lectures & Conversations A

p.58

[TYPES 1–4]

TYPE 1 Ⓒ

TYPE 2 Skin: ①, ④   White Blood Cells: ②, ③

TYPE 3 Ⓓ   **TYPE 4** Ⓑ

Script   02-09

W Professor: People, animals, plants, and fungi all get diseases. Pathogens cause them. Pathogens are things such as, uh, bacteria and viruses. They enter living things and cause them to get sick and, uh, sometimes, to die. But living things have defenses against pathogens. These defenses are found in their immune systems. There are two types of immune systems: innate and adaptive. First, let's examine the innate immune system.

An innate immune system in a living thing is always active. It's an organism's first line of defense against diseases. Let's think about humans, shall we? The skin is our first defense. How . . . ? Well, it prevents many things from entering the body. In addition, the mucus in the nose prevents airborne foreign bodies—many of which are harmful—from entering the body. What else . . . ? There are defenses in the body as well. For instance, both the stomach and the intestines produce acids. Some of them are able to remove pathogens from the food we eat.

There's another important defense inside the body. These are white blood cells. When pathogens enter the body, white blood cells move to fight them. It's like, uh, like they're soldiers fighting an invading army. The white blood cells go where the pathogens are. They attack the pathogens and try to remove them from the body. As you can guess, they're extremely useful. Now, how about some innate systems in other animals and plants? Let me give you some specific examples of them.

TYPE 1 [Gist-Content Question]

For the majority of the lecture, the professor explains how the innate immune system works.

TYPE 2 [Connecting Content Question]

According to the professor, the skin is the body's first line of defense, and it also keeps foreign bodies out. As for white blood cells, they fight pathogens inside the body. The professor also compares them to soldiers when she says, "When pathogens enter the body, white blood cells move to fight them. It's like, uh, like they're soldiers fighting an invading army."

TYPE 3 [Understanding Organization Question]

The professor tells the class, "There's another important defense inside the body." Then, she explains what white blood cells do. So she talks about them to describe one of the defenses inside the body.

TYPE 4 [Understanding Attitude Question]

About white blood cells, the professor states, "As you can guess, they're extremely useful." So she thinks that they benefit the body.

✔ Checking Listening Accuracy

1 T   2 T   3 F   4 T

[TYPES 5–8]

TYPE 5 (A)   **TYPE 6** (C)

TYPE 7 (B)   **TYPE 8** (B)

Script 02-10

> **M Professor**: Okay, so we've discussed the mosquito's appearance and life cycle. Now, let's cover what mosquitoes are most famous for . . . sucking blood. Mosquitoes suck blood from various animals. You see, uh, a mosquito has a long feeder appendage in its mouth. The appendage penetrates an animal's skin. Then, the mosquito sucks the animal's blood. Interestingly, only females suck blood. The blood they get enables them to reproduce.
>
> **W Student**: How so?
>
> **M**: Proteins in the blood they suck help them produce the eggs they lay. So they don't use the blood as food. For food, both female and male mosquitoes usually eat nectar from plants.
>
>   Tragically, mosquitoes kill more people than any other creature on the Earth. Their bites don't kill though. But the diseases that mosquitoes carry do. [8]Millions of people die every year from malaria, dengue fever, yellow fever, and other diseases that

mosquitoes carry. When mosquitoes bite people, they transmit whatever diseases they happen to be carrying. Each year, more than two million people die from mosquito-carried diseases. **That's a big number, huh?**

>   Unfortunately, controlling mosquitoes is difficult since they breed and spread rapidly. They lay their eggs in stagnant water, like, uh, in swamps. So draining these areas can control them. Insecticides—you know, insect killers—can also eliminate them. DDT is one such insecticide. It's highly effective, but it's banned in many countries. Some people claim that DDT harms certain animals. Still, in countries that use DDT, there are fewer deaths by diseases transmitted by mosquitoes.

TYPE 5 [Gist-Content Question]

Most of the lecture is spent describing what problems mosquitoes cause people.

TYPE 6 [Detail Question]

The professor remarks, "Interestingly, only females suck blood. The blood they get enables them to reproduce."

TYPE 7 [Making Inferences Question]

The professor mentions, "It's highly effective, but it's banned in many countries. Some people claim that DDT harms certain animals. Still, in countries that use DDT, there are fewer deaths by diseases transmitted by mosquitoes." So it can be inferred that DDT kills many mosquitoes that carry diseases.

TYPE 8 [Understanding Function Question]

When the professor asks, "That's a big number, huh?" he is emphasizing just how many people die from diseases carried by mosquitoes.

✔ Checking Listening Accuracy

1 F   2 T   3 T   4 F

[TYPES 9–12]

TYPE 9 (D)   **TYPE 10** (A)

TYPE 11 (A)   **TYPE 12** (C)

Script 02-11

> **W Student**: Good afternoon. I've got a big problem, and I really need your assistance.
>
> **M Computer Services Office Employee**: Uh, okay. What's the matter? Did your computer break down or something?
>
> **W**: No, not that. I can't log into my school email

account. There's some kind of problem. You see, I know the password. But it still won't let me log into my account.

M: Ah. I think I might know why. How long have you been using the same password?

W: I don't know. At least a year, I guess. Why?

M: There's a new regulation in place. All passwords on school email accounts have to be changed every three months. You must not have done that. ¹²So the system won't let you log in.

W: What? **That's the silliest idea I've ever heard.** Who decided to implement that idea?

M: The school administration did. Now, would you like me to show you how you can access your account?

TYPE 9 [Gist-Purpose Question]

When the man asks the student what her problem is, she answers, "I can't log into my school email account."

TYPE 10 [Detail Question]

The man tells the student, "All passwords on school email accounts have to be changed every three months. You must not have done that."

TYPE 11 [Making Inferences Question]

At the end of the conversation, the man asks, "Now, would you like me to show you how you can access your account?" So he will probably fix the student's problem by telling her what she needs to do.

TYPE 12 [Understanding Function Question]

When the student remarks that the new policy is silly, she is indicating that she disagrees with it.

Checking Listening Accuracy

1 F	2 T	3 T	4 T

Mastering Topics with Lectures B1   p.61

1 Ⓑ	2 Ⓐ	3 Ⓒ

Script & Graphic Organizer 02-12

W Professor: Spiders produce a sticky substance that's like silk. They use this substance to make webs. Special glands in the spider's body produce the silk. It's mostly made of proteins. It's strong, lightweight, and practically invisible. The main purpose of a spider's web is to catch food for the

spider. Spiders mostly eat insects. Since their webs are difficult to see, insects often crawl onto or fly into them. Then, the insects get stuck. Spiders typically stay at one edge of their webs. They can feel the vibrations from insects trying to free themselves after getting stuck. Spiders, unlike insects, can crawl on their webs without getting stuck. So they can then capture the insects and eat them.

There are several different kinds of spider webs. Here are a few of them. Let's look . . . ³This . . . is an orb web. Notice how it's shaped like a circle. **It looks sort of like, uh, a wheel with spokes.** You know, like on a bicycle. Right . . . ? The orb web is one of the most common types of spider webs. Spiders often build them vertically between tree branches. So insects fly straight into them.

Next, is the sheet web . . . See it here . . . ? Spiders build these webs between blades of grass or between the branches of shrubs and trees. The sheet is horizontal. Above it are many silk threads. These threads cross each other and form a net. When an insect hits one of the threads, it falls onto the sheet web and gets stuck. That makes it easy prey for the spider.

Here's a third type . . . We call this a tangled web. It's common indoors, like, uh, in the corner of a room. It's basically just a tangled mess of silk threads. It has, uh, obviously, no specific pattern. There are other types of webs, but those are the three primary ones.

Now, did any of you notice the, uh, decorations in some of the webs I showed you? Yes, spiders decorate their webs. I've got a few pictures of these decorations for you right here.

Spider Webs

Characteristics:
- *Made of a substance that is like silk*
- *Are mostly protein*
- *Are strong, lightweight, and almost invisible*
- *Are used to catch food for spiders*
- *Can be crawled on by spiders but not by other insects*

Orb Webs:
Are shaped like circles; are common types of webs; are often built vertically between tree branches

Sheet Webs:
Are between blades of grass or branches of shrubs and trees; are horizontal; threads form a net

Tangled Webs:
Are common indoors; are tangled messes of silk threads; have no specific patterns

1 [Understanding Organization Question]

When the professor begins talking about spider webs, she says, "Let's look." Then, she pauses many times while she is speaking about spider webs. When she pauses, she is pointing out pictures on slides that she is showing to the class.

2 [Making Inferences Question]

At the end of the lecture, the professor notes, "Yes, spiders decorate their webs. I've got a few pictures of these decorations for you right here." So she is probably going to talk about spider web decorations.

3 [Understanding Function Question]

The professor is making a comparison when she talks about a wheel with spokes when discussing orb webs.

◢ Listening Comprehension

1 d   **2** a   **3** c   **4** b

Mastering Topics with Lectures B2   p.62

1 Ⓐ   **2** Ⓐ, Ⓓ   **3** Ⓒ

`Script & Graphic Organizer` 02-13

M Professor: The largest animals ever were the dinosaurs. We know about their sizes thanks to the fossils that we've found. Accordingly, we've learned that dinosaurs varied in size. Some were rather small. Others were, oh, human-sized creatures. And a few were the size of a house or even bigger. So . . . why were some dinosaurs so enormous? There are three major theories.

First, dinosaurs lived when there was plenty of vegetation on the planet. Remember that the Earth was much warmer millions of years ago. Plants thrived back then. So, uh, plant-eating dinosaurs, some say, could eat as much as they wanted to. This made some of them become huge. Naturally, this benefitted carnivorous dinosaurs since they had bigger animals to hunt. They too grew bigger.

This leads to the second theory. According to it, some dinosaurs became so big in order to defend themselves against predators. Bigger animals could fight back against the bigger predators. Imagine, for instance, being hit by the tail of a brontosaurus. That would have caused damage even to the most fearsome predators.

The third theory depends upon dinosaurs being coldblooded animals. Warm-blooded animals, as you know, can control their body temperatures. Cold-blooded animals cannot. Their body temperatures depend on two things: the air temperature and the amount of heat they absorb from the sun. If dinosaurs were cold blooded, then size was an advantage. Their big bodies could absorb lots of heat from the sun all day long. Since they were so big, their bodies would cool slowly at night. So their bodies could maintain the same temperature all the time. Question?

W Student: I'm curious . . . How could dinosaurs support such enormous bodies?

M: Ah, good question. Mostly, they had large bones and lots of muscles. So they were very strong. Large dinosaurs likely evolved and developed the capability to support their body mass. [3]In addition, fossil remains show that some dinosaur bones were hollow, like, uh, those of birds. Some scientists believe that dinosaurs could somehow pump air into these hollow bones. This would have made it easier for them to stand. **It's an interesting theory, but it hasn't been proven yet.**

The Sizes of Dinosaurs

First Theory:	Second Theory:	Third Theory:
- Was much vegetation on the planet	- Dinosaurs needed to grow big to defend themselves from big predators	- Dinosaurs were cold blooded
- Plant-eating dinosaurs could eat much	- Big dinosaurs such as the brontosaurus could defend themselves	- Size was an advantage
- So they grew very big		- Could absorb lots of heat
- Carnivorous dinosaurs grew big from eating plant eaters		- At night, it would take a long time for their bodies to cool

1 [Gist-Content Question]

At the beginning of the lecture, the professor says, "Why were some dinosaurs so enormous? There are three major theories." Then, he spends the rest of the lecture discussing these three theories.

2 [Detail Question]

The professor tells the class, "First, dinosaurs lived when there was plenty of vegetation on the planet. Remember that the Earth was much warmer millions of years ago."

3 [Understanding Attitude Question]

When the professor says that the theory has not been proven yet, it can be inferred that he is not convinced that the theory is correct.

1 b   2 a   3 d   4 c

Mastering Topics with Conversations B3   p.63

1 Ⓑ   2 Ⓓ   3 Ⓓ

Script & Graphic Organizer 02-14

M Professor: Good afternoon, Sheila. Thanks for arriving on time. Why don't you come in and have a seat?

W Student: Hello, Professor Daniels. What can I do for you? You didn't indicate why you want to see me in your email.

M: Ah, right. Well, it's about your missing assignments.

W: Huh? What missing assignments? I turned in the midterm paper, and I took the two exams. I don't think I have missed any assignments.

M: On the contrary, you haven't submitted any of the weekly online assignments. You're the only student who hasn't done that.

W: Um . . . I'm really sorry, but I have no idea what you're talking about.

M: I discussed it on the first day of class. I made it clear to the class that the online assignments are important. They're supposed to be emailed to me by Friday at 5:00 PM. But you haven't done that even once.

W: Oh, I think I see the problem. [3]I didn't start this class until the second week of the semester. Remember? So I never knew about that. And there's nothing about online assignments on the syllabus.

M: **Oh, yeah, you're right about that.** Okay, uh . . . here, take this paper. It explains what you should do. Finish all of the assignments by next Monday, please. Do that, and you won't be penalized.

W: Thanks so much, Professor Daniels. I really appreciate it.

Office Hours

Reason for Contacting Student:	Professor's Response:
To discuss some work that she has not turned in	Says he talked about online assignments on the first day of class
Student's Response:	Professor's Solution:
Does not know what the professor is talking about	Says the student can submit the missing assignments by next Monday

1 [Gist-Purpose Question]

When the student asks why the professor wants to see her, he says, "Well, it's about your missing assignments."

2 [Detail Question]

About the online assignments, the professor states, "I made it clear to the class that the online assignments are important. They're supposed to be emailed to me by Friday at 5:00 PM."

3 [Understanding Attitude Question]

The student says, "And there's nothing about online assignments on the syllabus." Then, the professor agrees by responding, "Oh, yeah, you're right about that."

1 b   2 d   3 a   4 c

TOEFL Practice Tests C1   p.64

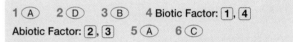

1 Ⓐ   2 Ⓓ   3 Ⓑ   4 Biotic Factor: ①, ④
Abiotic Factor: ②, ③   5 Ⓐ   6 Ⓒ

Script 02-15

W1 Professor: [5]Okay. **Would everyone take a seat please? We have a busy day and need to start at once . . .** All right. Today's lecture is about ecosystems. First, I'd like to give you some general information about them. After that, we're going to examine some of the world's ecosystems in depth. To begin, uh, what is an ecosystem? Anyone . . . ?

W2 Student: It's a community of organisms living together, isn't it?

W1: That's a good start, Leslie. And you're right. An ecosystem includes the organisms that live in a particular area. However, that is not all it includes. An ecosystem is a combination of the living and nonliving things in a specific area. We call the living things the biotic factors. These come from the five kingdoms of organisms. Uh, you know . . . animals, plants, fungi, protists, and monera. Now, what about the nonliving things? What do we call them . . . ? Leslie, do you know?

W2: Aren't those abiotic factors?

W1: Well done, Leslie. You must have done your reading last night. Leslie is correct, class. The abiotic factors include all the nonliving things in an ecosystem. What are some of these factors . . . ?

Hmm . . . Let's see . . . Soil, water, air, sunlight, minerals, and climate are the primary abiotic factors.

Okay, now what kind of an area can be an ecosystem? Well, that depends. Some people consider the planet to be one giant ecosystem. I suppose they're right. But I prefer to work on a smaller scale. We can divide the majority of ecosystems into water and land ecosystems. For water, well, the ocean is an ecosystem. So are rivers, lakes, ponds, and streams. But we can think on a smaller scale, too. In an ocean, a coral reef forms a unique ecosystem. As for land, there are countless types of ecosystems. Speaking broadly, there are desert, forest, plain, and jungle ecosystems. Naturally, there are many other types, too. And please remember this: Ecosystems vary in size. They can be huge, like, uh, the Sahara Desert or the Amazon Rainforest. But there are also microecosystems. These are tiny places. Think about, uh, a home garden. Or think even smaller. A tree or a puddle of water can be a microecosystem as well.

Next . . . What makes an ecosystem healthy? A couple of things. Typically, healthy ecosystems contain a diversity of life. Again, don't just think about animals. I'm referring to a diversity of life from all five kingdoms. Second, healthy ecosystems are often in balance with one another. What does that mean? Okay . . . The life in an ecosystem has various relationships. For instance, let's see . . . Here's part of how a forest ecosystem works . . . The sun shines on the forest, so plants grow. Large numbers of organisms depend on these plants for food. For instance, deer, rabbits, and squirrels eat various plants. Insects thrive thanks to the nectar that flowers produce. Then, other animals, you know, uh, carnivores . . . meat eaters . . . These animals eat the herbivores, uh, the plant eaters. When these animals die, their bodies often decompose. This enriches the soil. This enables the plants to grow better.

[6]That's just a small example of some of what goes on in an ecosystem. As you can see, there's a balance. When an ecosystem is in balance, everything is fine. But, uh, what happens when an ecosystem gets out of balance? Let's find out.

1 [Understanding Attitude Question]

After the student asks her first question, the professor comments, "That's a good start, Leslie." After the student asks her second question, the professor says, "Well done, Leslie. You must have done your reading last night." In both cases, she is praising the student, so the professor is being complimentary to the student.

2 [Understanding Organization Question]

The professor states, "We can divide the majority of ecosystems into water and land ecosystems. For water, well, the ocean is an ecosystem. So are rivers, lakes, ponds, and streams. But we can think on a smaller scale, too. In an ocean, a coral reef forms a unique ecosystem. As for land, there are countless types of ecosystems. Speaking broadly, there are desert, forest, plain, and jungle ecosystems." So she names some types of ecosystems found on land and in the water.

3 [Detail Question]

The professor claims, "A tree or a puddle of water can be a microecosystem as well."

4 [Connecting Content Question]

According to the professor, biotic factors include monera and plants, which are from the five kingdoms of organisms. As for abiotic factors, they include climate and sunlight, which are both nonliving factors.

5 [Understanding Function Question]

When the professor tells the students to sit down and says, "We have a busy day and need to start at once," she is indicating that she wants to begin teaching the class.

6 [Making Inferences Question]

When the professor comments, "That's just a small example of some of what goes on in an ecosystem," she is implying that her description of an ecosystem is incomplete.

TOEFL Practice Tests C2 p.66

1 (B) 2 (D) 3 (A) 4 (B) 5 (A)

Script 02-16

W Student: Hello. Good afternoon. My name is Alice Hopewell. I'm a student here at the university. I wonder if you have any positions available for volunteers.

M Museum Staff Member: For volunteers? What exactly do you mean?

W: Well, uh, here at the school, we have to do some volunteer work before we can graduate. It's kind of annoying, but it's a requirement. Anyway, uh, my major is Archaeology. And I thought that it would be logical for me to volunteer at the museum. It's right on campus. And it would be an interesting job, too. Um, volunteering here would be great for me. Oh, and, of course, I'd also be able to help you out.

M: Ah, I see what you mean.

W: So, um . . . is it possible for me to do some volunteer work here? I don't need to work too many hours. I was thinking about doing three or four hours a week this semester. Perhaps I could come in on the weekend on Saturday or Sunday.

M: Hmm . . . I suppose we could use an extra volunteer or two here. There is always some kind of work that needs to get done.

W: Great. What kind of work do you need?

M: It's nothing too big. Mostly, it's filing and cleaning. [4]It's pretty boring stuff actually. I don't know if it will really help you too much regarding your major.

W: **Oh. I see . . .** Well, I guess I can do that.

M: Great.

W: But, uh, is it also possible to do some different kind of work in the future?

M: Such as . . . ?

W: Well, like I mentioned, my major is Archaeology. And I know the museum has a big collection of ancient relics. Is there any way that, uh, I can do some work with them?

M: [5]Perhaps . . . But you'll need to show me that you're a good worker first. After I get to know you, I'll give you some better assignments. You need to, uh, work your way up.

W: That makes sense. **In that case, why don't I get started right now?** What would you like for me to do?

M: That's the spirit. Come on and follow me. I'll show you something you can do for me right now.

1 [Gist-Purpose Question]

As soon as the student greets the museum employee, she states, "I wonder if you have any positions available for volunteers."

2 [Detail Question]

The student suggests, "Perhaps I could come in on the weekend on Saturday or Sunday."

3 [Making Inferences Question]

The student asks, "In that case, why don't I get started right now?" Then, the employee tells her to follow him so that he can show her what to do. So she is probably going to start working for the man.

4 [Understanding Function Question]

The student says, "Oh. I see," in response to the employee's comment about the work that he wants her to do. She is showing her disappointment when

she says this. Her tone of voice also expresses disappointment.

5 [Understanding Attitude Question]

When the student declares that she wants to get started immediately, it can be inferred that she is willing to work hard.

Vocabulary Review   p.70

1	D	2	C	3	A	4	A
5	C	6	D	7	E	8	D
9	A	10	B	11	F	12	C

● Chapter | 03 Social Sciences 1 • Conversations

Mastering Question Types with Lectures & Conversations A   p.72

[TYPES 1–4]

| TYPE 1 | C | TYPE 2 | B |
| TYPE 3 | C | TYPE 4 | A |

Script 02-17

M Professor: All of you, of course, can read. There was a time, however, when you couldn't. Yet you all learned. Do you remember how you did that? There are several methods teachers use to, uh, teach reading. You probably learned by using a combination of them.

There are four main methods of teaching reading. The first—and most common—is the phonics method. Here's how teachers use phonics. First, they teach their students the alphabet. So the students learn the letters and which sounds each one makes. The instructors also teach the students how letters can blend together. Then, they often show the students sentences with similar sounds. For example, uh . . . The cat sat on the hat . . . How now brown cow . . . Or how about this one . . . ? There's a mouse in the house. You remember those, right? Well, as students learn more sounds, they learn more words. This helps them improve their vocabulary level. Soon, students who use the phonics method are able to read new words and sound them out for themselves. I think you can see why this method is so successful.

That's the first method. But, like I said, there are three more ways. The next is the look-and-say method. This basically teaches children to recognize words and to remember how to say them. This involves a lot of memorization. Flashcards are often used to accomplish this. You probably used this method in the past as well, right?

TYPE 1 [Gist-Content Question]

The professor mentions that there are four main methods of teaching reading, but he only describes two of them in his lecture.

TYPE 2 [Connecting Content Question]

About the phonics method, the professor mentions, "Well, as students learn more sounds, they learn more words. This helps them improve their vocabulary level. Soon, students who use the phonics method are able to read new words and sound them out for themselves." So it is likely that a student who uses the phonics method will be about to teach him or herself many new words.

TYPE 3 [Understanding Organization Question]

During the lecture, the professor goes into detail on two different types of learning methods.

TYPE 4 [Understanding Attitude Question]

After describing the phonics method, the professor states, "I think you can see why this method is so successful."

✓ Checking Listening Accuracy

1 T   2 F   3 F   4 T

[TYPES 5–8]

TYPE 5 D	**TYPE 6** B
TYPE 7 A	**TYPE 8** A

Script 02-18

M Professor: We all know that the capital of the United States is Washington, D.C. However, when America first became a country, Washington didn't even exist. Back then, Philadelphia was the logical choice as the new country's capital.

W Student: Why Philadelphia? Why not Boston, New York, or even, uh, Charleston?

M: For several reasons . . . First, Philadelphia had a roughly central location in the U.S. at that time. It had also been a focal point of the American Revolution. The Continental Congress had met there

before the war. And several major events took place there. So, uh, why is Washington the capital and not Philadelphia . . . ? Mostly because of a riot in Philadelphia in 1783. Congress was meeting there when some soldiers disrupted the proceedings. The soldiers demanded payment for their service during the war. But Congress had no money. It asked the government of Pennsylvania to protect it. But the government refused. Congress promptly left Philadelphia. So that, um, ruled out Philadelphia.

Congress realized it couldn't rely on the states to defend it. Thus the members of Congress decided to create an entirely new area, called the District of Columbia. Several states competed for the right to host the district. Ultimately, Congress decided on a stretch of land between Virginia and Maryland. Like Philadelphia, it was near the geographical center of the country. The necessary land was given to the federal government. Construction on the new capital then began. And that's how Washington, D.C. became our capital. Let's look at its design now.

TYPE 5 [Gist-Content Question]

The professor mostly focuses on the reasons why Washington, D.C. is the capital of the United States.

TYPE 6 [Detail Question]

The professor declares, "Back then, Philadelphia was the logical choice as the new country's capital."

TYPE 7 [Making Inferences Question]

At the end of the lecture, the professor says, "And that's how Washington, D.C. became our capital. Let's look at its design now." So he will continue talking about Washington, D.C.

TYPE 8 [Understanding Function Question]

When the student asks about the choice of Philadelphia as the American capital, she is indicating that she does not know about Philadelphia's history.

✓ Checking Listening Accuracy

1 T   2 F   3 T   4 F

[TYPES 9–12]

TYPE 9 B	**TYPE 10** A
TYPE 11 B	**TYPE 12** D

W Student: Hello. I made a reservation to play squash on one of the courts at 3:30. My name is Sarah Watkins. Which court should I play on?

M Gymnasium Employee: Hello. I'm terribly sorry, but I don't think you can play on any of the courts now.

W: Why not? Are they being cleaned or something?

M: No, it's not that. You see, uh, the school's squash team is using them. They have practice now.

W: That can't be right. The team always practices from 5:00 to 7:00 each evening.

M: Ah, the coach wants them to practice a lot this week. There's a big tournament coming up soon. So he wants to make sure everyone on the team is ready.

W: [12]Well, that doesn't seem fair to me. After all, the courts are supposed to be for everyone to use. They aren't only for the members of the team to play on.

M: **I completely understand what you mean.** But there's nothing I can do to help you.

TYPE 9 [Gist-Purpose Question]

The student asks the man, "Which court should I play on?"

TYPE 10 [Detail Question]

The man tells the student, "You see, uh, the school's squash team is using them. They have practice now."

TYPE 11 [Making Inferences Question]

The student mentions that the squash team usually practices from 5:00 to 7:00. Then, the man says, "Ah, the coach wants them to practice a lot this week. There's a big tournament coming up soon. So he wants to make sure everyone on the team is ready." So the man implies that the squash team is practicing more than usual this week.

TYPE 12 [Understanding Function Question]

When the student complains that the situation is not fair, the man responds by saying, "I completely understand what you mean." So he agrees with the student that it is not fair to her.

✏ Checking Listening Accuracy

1 T   2 F   3 F   4 F

Mastering Topics with Lectures B1   p.75

1 Ⓐ   2 Ⓐ   3 Ⓓ

W Professor: There's a branch of psychology called cognitive psychology. It deals with how living things learn. Has anyone ever heard of Edward Tolman . . . ? No? Well, he was crucial in the formative years of cognitive psychology. That was in the early twentieth century by the way. Tolman is most famous for his studies with rats and mazes. He used them to prove that animals can learn and produce something called a, um, a cognitive map.

Here's what Tolman did . . . He put some rats in a maze. First, he used rats that were hungry. He placed food at one end of the maze. Then, he started the rats from the other end. The rats ran through the maze and eventually found the food. After that, he conducted another test. Tolman put the food in the same place. But he started the rats from a different point. Still, the rats found the food.

M Student: [3]That makes sense. I mean, uh, the rats were hungry. So it's natural that they found the food.

W: **Yes, I see your point. But here's what Tolman did next . . .** He tried the same experiment with some different groups of rats. At first, all the rats that entered the maze were hungry. But there was no food waiting for them at the end. Nevertheless, the rats completed the maze. The next time, they completed it even faster. Finally, Tolman rewarded one group of rats with food at the end. He noticed that this group of rats finished the maze even faster than the others. Then, a few days later, he rewarded another group with food at the end. He got the same results. The rats had learned the maze. They had remembered it with or without food.

Tolman claimed that the rats had made a cognitive map. They understood where to turn each time. And they improved their performance in the maze every time. They even learned when there were no rewards involved. To Tolman, this showed that it wasn't an urge such as hunger that drove them to learn. It was something else.

Tolman's Rats

Tolman's Experiment:

- *Put some rats in a maze*
- *Put food at the other end*
- *Let the rats run through the maze and find the food*
- *Put the rats at another starting point*
- *Saw that the rats were still able to find the food*

Results with No Food for Rats:

The rats completed the maze faster each time

Results with Food for Rats:

The rats finished even faster than before

Tolman's Theory:

The rats made a cognitive map; learned even when there were no rewards for them

1 [Gist-Content Question]

During the lecture, the professor focuses on how Tolman conducted his experiments with rats.

2 [Connecting Content Question]

The professor compares how quickly the rats that got food and those that did not get food finished the maze.

3 [Understanding Function Question]

The professor says, "I see your point." However, she then counters with, "But here's what Tolman did next." Thus she implies that she is going to tell the student why his idea is incorrect.

♪ Listening Comprehension

1 d   2 c   3 a   4 b

Mastering Topics with Lectures B2   p.76

1 Fact: ③, ④   Not a Fact: ①, ②   2 Ⓐ   3 Ⓓ

Script & Graphic Organizer   02-21

W Professor: You've all seen hieroglyphics. Hieroglyphics was used by the ancient Egyptians to write with. It's based on pictograms. However, for centuries, no one knew how to read it. Then, in 1799, some French soldiers in Napoleon's army discovered the Rosetta Stone in Egypt. It was part of a wall in an old fort in the town of Rosetta. It was originally located in an ancient temple. But it was later moved to the fort. [3]The Rosetta Stone had some writing on it. The writing was in three languages. One was ancient Greek. One was Demotic . . . **Uh, that's an ancient Egyptian language.** And the other was hieroglyphics. All three languages contained the same information. It was a decree issued by some

priests in 196 B.C. It was about the new pharaoh of Egypt, Ptolemy the Fifth. The priests declared that Ptolemy had been chosen to rule. And they said that they would honor Ptolemy with a feast each year.

The text on the Rosetta Stone became the key to understanding ancient Egyptian hieroglyphics. Scholars started to compare the three writings. They understood the ancient Greek very well. The second writing, Demotic, was less well known. But some scholars came to understand it. Eventually, after much work, scholars started to decipher what the picture symbols in hieroglyphics meant. Two men were involved in most of the important translation work.

The first was Thomas Young, an Englishman. In 1814, he made the first major discovery. He realized that the three texts contained the same information. He found about eighty words in the Demotic and hieroglyphic texts that were similar to words in ancient Greek. For example, the name Ptolemy was Greek. It appears several times in all three texts. Young was able to figure out which symbols in Demotic and hieroglyphics represented the name Ptolemy. The other scholar was a Frenchman. His name is Jean-Francois Champollion. In 1822, he produced an alphabet for hieroglyphics based on the Rosetta Stone inscriptions. Later, he made a grammar and a dictionary for hieroglyphics.

The Rosetta Stone

The Rosetta Stone:

- *Was discovered in Rosetta, Egypt, in 1799*
- *Had text in three languages: ancient Greek, Demotic, and hieroglyphics*
- *Was a decree by some priests in honor of a new pharaoh*
- *Was the key to understanding hieroglyphics*

Thomas Young:

Made the first major discovery in 1814; realized that all three texts contained the same information

Jean-Francois Champollion:

Produced an alphabet of hieroglyphics in 1822; made a grammar and dictionary for hieroglyphics

1 [Detail Question]

According to the professor, it took scholars many years to decipher the Rosetta Stone. She also says, "The first was Thomas Young, an Englishman. In 1814, he made the first major discovery." However, the Rosetta Stone was found in a fort, not in an ancient Egyptian temple. And Latin was not one of the three languages found on the Rosetta Stone.

2 [Understanding Organization Question]

The professor covers the story of the Rosetta Stone and its translation in chronological order.

3 [Understanding Attitude Question]

The professor mentions Demotic and then comments, "Uh, that's an ancient Egyptian language." When she says that, she is implying that she believes the students do not know what Demotic is.

Listening Comprehension

1 a   **2** d   **3** c   **4** b

Mastering Topics with Conversations B3   p.77

1 Ⓑ   **2** Ⓐ   **3** Ⓐ

`Script & Graphic Organizer` 02-22

> **M Student**: Excuse me. Could you please give me a hand? I'm looking for a book that I know the library has. However, I can't find it on the shelves.
>
> **W Librarian**: That's peculiar. Do you have the title of the book?
>
> **M**: I sure do. It's called *Applications in Economic Theory*. I found the book on the library's computer system, but . . .
>
> **W**: Let me look it up for you . . . Okay. It seems like the library has two copies of that book.
>
> **M**: Awesome. Where are they?
>
> **W**: Hold on a minute. You didn't let me finish. We have two copies of that book. But, um, I regret to say that both are currently checked out.
>
> **M**: That's no good. I've got to read that book over the weekend. It's part of my homework assignment for a class. Do you know when the books will get returned?
>
> **W**: Sorry, but I have no idea about that. If I were you, I wouldn't count on someone returning it to the library. You might want to consider purchasing it as an electronic book. I see that you have an e-reader with you.
>
> **M**: Ah, yeah. That's a good idea. But, uh, it might be kind of expensive.
>
> **W**: Perhaps. But e-books are usually cheaper than actual books. You also don't seem to have any other options. I'm sorry that I can't help you out any more than that.

Service Encounter

Reason for Visiting:	Result:
Is looking for a book that the library has	Is told that both copies of the book are currently checked out

Student's Response:	Librarian's Response:
Says that he needs the book to complete a homework assignment	Suggests that the student purchase an electronic book

1 [Gist-Content Question]

The student asks, "Could you please give me a hand? I'm looking for a book that I know the library has. However, I can't find it on the shelves."

2 [Understanding Attitude Question]

The librarian apologizes to the student because the book that he wants is not currently available at the library. Her tone of voice also indicates that she is being sincere. So it can be inferred that she feels bad about not being able to help the student.

3 [Making Inferences Question]

The librarian recommends that the student buy the book for his e-reader. She also says that the book will not be expensive and that he does not have any other options. So the student will probably purchase the book for his e-reader.

Listening Comprehension

1 c   **2** b   **3** d   **4** a

TOEFL Practice Tests C1   p.78

`Script` 02-23

> **M Professor:** Customer loyalty is something that all companies desire. Loyal customers will use a company's products for years and years. They will constantly shop at the same store, too. So how do companies and stores create customer loyalty? Mostly, um, they keep their customers happy. There are several ways to do this. Of course, providing excellent products and services is the best method. There are others though. Treating customers well is another effective way. For instance, companies and stores can do this by providing loyal customers with, well, let's think . . . free offers, coupons, long warranties, low-interest rates on purchases, rebates, and even VIP treatment.

Let me give you an example. Think of a computer shop. These days, almost everyone has a computer at home. But computers get old, break down, and become obsolete. So customers need to upgrade or replace them. But there are many brands of computers and computer accessories, right? And there are many computer shops as well as online vendors. So how can a computer shop keep its customers loyal . . . ? Well, first, it can offer items for free. For instance, the shop could offer a free printer when a customer purchases a computer. It could also provide customers with coupons for free services, such as, uh, upgrades. The shop could offer a warranty that lasts for several years. And it might even give a customer a rebate. Uh, you know, reduce the price of the computer. Yes, Dianne? You have a question?

W Student: An observation mostly. As a customer, all of these things sound great. I get more services and products for less money. But won't these special offers cost the computer shop lots of money? How does it make a profit?

M: That's an outstanding question, Dianne. Let me see . . . In the short term, you're correct. The computer shop will lose money. However, this changes over the long term. Why is that? Well, a happy customer can easily become a lifelong customer. The money a customer spends at the shop in the future will more than offset any free products he or she receives. How so . . . ? Well, the customer—let's call him Mr. Smith—who bought the computer will appreciate the service at the shop. So in the future, anytime Mr. Smith needs a computer-related product, what's he going to do . . . ? That's right. He's going to visit that same computer shop. He'll get all of his software, his hardware, his computer games, his accessories— everything computer related—from that shop. Do you see what I mean?

W: [6]I think so. You mean that the computer shop will lose money when it sells the computer. But it will make more money by selling the customer other products.

M: I couldn't have said that any better myself. Basically, to make a profit, the store must lose a bit of money first. However, once that shop has a loyal customer, it has many advantages. First, of course, is the customer himself. Mr. Smith is going to spend money there. But he's also going to tell his friends about that shop. After all, he's a loyal customer now. Mr. Smith's recommendations are going to give that computer shop more customers. So that's another major reason that companies and stores love loyal customers. Let's consider the effects of this after we take a short break. All right?

1 [Gist-Content Question]

During his lecture, the professor focuses on a number of ways that companies can develop customer loyalty.

2 [Detail Question]

The professor states, "It could also provide customers with coupons for free services, such as, uh, upgrades." He also notes, "And it might even give a customer a rebate. Uh, you know, reduce the price of the computer."

3 [Understanding Organization Question]

During much of the lecture, the professor asks questions. But he does not expect the students to answer the questions. Instead, he answers the questions himself.

4 [Connecting Content Question]

The professor states, "However, once that shop has a loyal customer, it has many advantages." He also mentions, "But he's also going to tell his friends about that shop. After all, he's a loyal customer now. Mr. Smith's recommendations are going to give that computer shop more customers. So that's another major reason companies and stores love loyal customers." The professor therefore implies that customer loyalty is of great importance to places of business.

5 [Making Inferences Question]

At the end of the lecture, the professor tells the class, "Let's consider the effects of this after we take a short break." So he is going to give the students a break next.

6 [Understanding Attitude Question]

When the professor states, "I couldn't have said that any better myself," he means that he totally agrees with what the student just said.

TOEFL Practice Tests C2 p.79

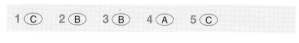

1 Ⓒ 2 Ⓑ 3 Ⓑ 4 Ⓐ 5 Ⓒ

Script 02-24

M Professor: Ah, Mary. Thank you for coming by my office. I appreciate that.

W Student: No problem, sir. You told me after class that you wanted to see me. So, uh, here I am.

M: Yes. I want to talk about your presentation. You were scheduled to give your class presentation last Tuesday. However, you missed both our Tuesday and Thursday class. What happened?

W: Oh, uh, sorry, sir. I was sick and couldn't come to class.

M: You were sick?

W: Yes, sir. I had a bad cold. ⁴I'm just now getting over it. Anyway, I went to the doctor, and he told me to stay in bed. I have a note from him. I can show it to you if you want.

M: **Yes, I'm going to have to see it.** Otherwise, you will lose points for not giving your presentation on the assigned date.

W: I understand. The note's in my dorm room. I'll bring it to you later today. Is that all right?

M: That will be fine. I'll be in my office until five thirty this evening. Be sure to come back and show it to me by then.

W: I will. Thank you, sir. Er, is that all you wanted to discuss with me, sir?

M: We're not quite yet done, Mary. You still have to give your presentation.

W: Oh, right.

M: Let me see . . . Today is Tuesday. We have class in two days. Why don't you give your presentation then? I believe only one student is scheduled for Thursday. We will have enough time in class for you to give yours as well.

W: Well, uh, actually . . . I don't think I'm quite yet ready to give my presentation. After all, I was sick last week. So I haven't had a chance to complete it. How about next Tuesday?

M: Mary, you have known about this presentation for more than one month. I think that is plenty of time to prepare. Plus, you only need to speak for about ten minutes. ⁵I'm sorry, but I cannot give you any more time. **I'm sure you'll do fine though. So don't get too worried about it.**

W: Yes, sir. I understand. I'll do my best. I'll see you in a couple of hours with my note.

1   [Gist-Purpose Question]

The professor says to the student, "You were scheduled to give your class presentation last Tuesday. However, you missed both our Tuesday and Thursday class. What happened?"

2   [Detail Question]

Because the student missed class, she could not give a class presentation.

3   [Detail Question]

The professor tells the student, "I'll be in my office until five thirty this evening. Be sure to come back and show it to me by then." He is talking about her note from the doctor indicating that she was sick.

4   [Understanding Function Question]

When the professor comments, "Yes, I'm going to have to see it," he is indicating that he does not believe the student when she says that she was sick.

5   [Making Inferences Question]

The professor tells the student, "I'm sure you'll do fine though," when talking about her presentation. So the professor implies that he is confident in the student's ability to do well on her presentation.

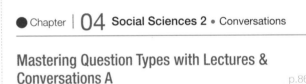

Vocabulary Review   p.84

1	Ⓓ	2	Ⓐ	3	Ⓐ	4	Ⓓ
5	Ⓒ	6	Ⓑ	7	Ⓒ	8	Ⓕ
9	Ⓑ	10	Ⓔ	11	Ⓓ	12	Ⓐ

● Chapter | 04 Social Sciences 2 • Conversations

Mastering Question Types with Lectures & Conversations A   p.86

[TYPES 1–4]

TYPE 1 Ⓐ   TYPE 2 Ⓐ

TYPE 3 Ⓒ   TYPE 4 Ⓓ

Script 02-25

W Professor: The Mayans were a group of people who lived in Central America. They developed an advanced civilization. It lasted for . . . Excuse me. It lasted for many centuries. Its high point was between the years 200 and 900. The Mayans are famous for a number of things . . . They built many city-states. These were like small countries. Naturally, the center of each was a city. Farms surrounded these cities and supported them with food. Mayan cities also contained exceptional works of architecture. The ruins of some buildings can be seen today. There are both large palaces and stepped pyramids.

The Mayans had a writing system and literature. But they didn't use paper. Odd, no? Instead, they wrote on stone, wood, and tree bark. Lots of writing was done on the insides and outsides of their temples and palaces. They also formed books from tree bark. Sadly, few of these books have survived to the present day.

M Student: What happened to them?

W: Well, first, the heat and wet weather of the jungle destroyed many. But Spanish conquerors got most of them. They actively sought to destroy the Mayans' written records. Fortunately, other objects, including Mayan works of art, have survived. We can see some of this art on the stones of their temples and palaces. [4]The Mayans were excellent pottery makers as well. They created figures of stone, clay, and wood. And they even made some objects out of metal. **But there are few extant examples of any metal devices.**

TYPE 1 [Gist-Content Question]

The professor talks about many different aspects of Mayan civilization during her lecture.

TYPE 2 [Connecting Content Question]

The professor notes, "Fortunately, other objects, including Mayan works of art, have survived. We can see some of this art on the stones of their temples and palaces." So it can be inferred that Mayan temples and palaces were decorated with both art and writing.

TYPE 3 [Understanding Organization Question]

The professor mentions that few of the Mayans' books remain today. She then states, "But Spanish conquerors got most of them. They actively sought to destroy the Mayans' written records."

TYPE 4 [Understanding Attitude Question]

The professor says, "There are few extant examples of any metal devices." She means that most Mayan metal objects have not survived to the present day.

Checking Listening Accuracy

1 T   2 F   3 F   4 T

[TYPES 5-8]

TYPE 5 Ⓐ   **TYPE 6** Ⓐ
TYPE 7 Ⓑ   **TYPE 8** Ⓓ

Script 02-26

W Professor: You've all probably heard about zoning laws. But many people are confused about what they are. So I'd like to cover them now. Local governments, such as cities and counties, typically pass zoning laws. They regulate how people use the land in certain parts of the city or country.

Think about our city for a moment. It's divided into various districts. Some are commercial while others are residential. This isn't accidental; it's intentional. The city developed this way because of zoning laws. You see, in the commercial district, there are businesses. And in the residential district, there are houses and apartments. You can't open a factory in the residential district. And you can't erect an apartment building in the commercial district. You can't do these things because of zoning laws.

There are actually quite a number of zones. As I just stated, there are residential and commercial zones. There are also industrial, agricultural, and recreational zones. Industrial zones are for factories and other manufacturers. Agricultural zones are for farms. And recreational zones are for parks, lakes, and sporting facilities.

So why do we need these zones? Well, think of it like this. [8]Would you like a factory located right next to your house? How about a huge farm next to the shopping mall downtown? Or what about a big warehouse with lots of trucks next to the park . . . ? **Yeah. That's what I thought.** And that's why we have zoning laws. They keep various buildings or businesses out of places where they don't belong.

TYPE 5 [Gist-Content Question]

The professor mainly discusses the purposes of zones and why cities and counties have them.

TYPE 6 [Detail Question]

The professor notes, "Local governments, such as cities and counties, typically pass zoning laws."

TYPE 7 [Making Inferences Question]

The professor claims, "And recreational zones are for parks, lakes, and sporting facilities." Since a stadium is a sporting facility, it can be inferred that it would be in a recreational zone.

TYPE 8 [Understanding Function Question]

The professor asks two questions and then pauses. Then, she says, "Yeah. That's what I thought." By saying that, she is implying that she knows what the answers to her questions are since the answers are obvious.

Checking Listening Accuracy

1 F   2 T   3 F   4 T

TYPE 9 Ⓒ   TYPE 10 Ⓐ, Ⓒ
TYPE 11 Ⓓ   TYPE 12 Ⓓ

Script 02-27

M Student: Hello. Are you the person in charge of the biology lab?

W Laboratory Assistant: Yes, I am. Is there something you need? Are you a student? You're early for your lab. It doesn't start for thirty minutes.

M: Uh . . . Well, I'm a student, but I'm not in your lab class.

W: Oh . . . All right. Then what can I do for you?

M: I'm looking for a job. I'm double-majoring in Chemistry and Biology. And I really want a lab job. There aren't any available in the chemistry labs though. So, uh, how about here?

W: Well, I suppose we could always use an extra worker. I know it would help me out a lot.

M: [12]So I'm hired? That's great.

W: **Slow down a little.** Why don't you tell me about yourself first? I need to make sure you're qualified.

TYPE **9** [Gist-Purpose Question]

When the laboratory assistant asks how she can help the student, he responds by saying, "I'm looking for a job."

TYPE **10** [Detail Question]

The student mentions, "I'm double-majoring in Chemistry and Biology."

TYPE **11** [Making Inferences Question]

The laboratory assistant notes, "Well, I suppose we could always use an extra worker. I know it would help me out a lot." When she says this, she is implying that she has a lot of work in the laboratory.

TYPE **12** [Understanding Attitude Question]

By telling the student, "Slow down a little," the laboratory assistant is indicating that she is not going to hire him yet since she needs to know more about him.

Checking Listening Accuracy

1 T   2 T   3 T   4 F

Mastering Topics with Lectures B1   p.89

1 Ⓒ   2 Ⓐ   3 Short-Term Marketing: [1], [4]   Long-Term Marketing: [2], [3]

Script & Graphic Organizer 02-28

M Professor: Let's discuss marketing for a moment. First, what is marketing? It's basically the process of trying to get people interested in a business. There are many ways to engage in marketing. And most businesses do it. After all, they want to increase their customer base. That will enable them to improve their revenues and profits. Now, uh, businesses may engage in both short-term and long-term marketing.

Short-term marketing is a plan for any period of time from one day to one year. Businesses have several options available for this type of marketing. These include sales and promotions as well as discounts to specific groups of people. For instance, a back-to-school sale by a clothing store is aimed at students. Many stores also offer discounts to members of the military. Businesses often send representatives to attend professional events such as trade shows, too. Those events are designed to let companies promote their products to potential customers.

And what about long-term marketing? Obviously, this is for planning that will take longer than one year. Most companies don't think too far into the future. But five to ten years is reasonable for many businesses. They want to make sure that their messaging stays current by changing with the times. They also want to figure out ways to retain the customers they have and to find new ones.

How do they do this? One way is that big companies may hire a public relations firm. In addition, almost every business today uses social media. They may also pay search engines such as Google to optimize their placement in searches. This happens when people do searches for subjects related to the businesses.

Now, uh, I should mention one thing about social media. It can be used for both short-term and long-term marketing. For instance, a business may announce a special sale or promotion on its social media accounts. That's short-term marketing. However, we normally consider social media to be long-term marketing. The reason is that most businesses use social media to promote themselves for many years. This is, of course, an extensive process. Any questions . . . ?

Marketing

Short-Term Marketing	Long-Term Marketing:
- Lasts from one day to one year	Lasts more than one year; public relations firm; social media; optimize placement on search engines like Google
- Sales and promotions	
- Back-to-school sale for students	
- Discounts to military members	**Social Media:**
- Send representatives to trade shows	Can be short- and long-term marketing; special sale or promotion is short-term; promoting selves for years is long term
- Promote products to potential customers	

1 [Detail Question]

The professor tells the class, "Businesses often send representatives to attend professional events such as trade shows, too. Those events are designed to let companies promote their products to potential customers."

2 [Making Inferences Question]

The professor mentions that long-term marketing lasts for more than one year. Then, the professor states, "One way is that big companies may hire a public relations firm." So the professor implies that some companies may use public relations firms for a long time.

3 [Connecting Content Question]

According to the professor, special sales and promotions are connected to short-term marketing. As for long-term marketing, it involves the extensive use of social media as well as the optimized use of product placement.

♪ **Listening Comprehension**

1 c   2 a   3 d   4 b

Mastering Topics with Lectures B2   p.90

1 ⒟   2 ⒞   3 Internet Advertisements: ②, ④
Television Commercials: ①, ③

Script & Graphic Organizer   02-29

M Professor: For years, TV advertisements and print advertisements dominated the advertising industry. Yes, TV commercials and newspaper and magazine ads were expensive. But for most advertisers, the money they spent was worth it. People were watching television and reading newspapers and magazines. Times are changing though. Television

is still the biggest segment for advertisers. Yet that won't last for much longer.

Instead, the Internet will overtake both TV and print marketing very soon. There are several reasons for this. First is the Internet's growing popularity. Today, the number of people who surf the Internet is enormous. In the 1980s, few people owned personal computers. Nowadays, most households have at least one type of computer. More people are using the World Wide Web every year. People are also getting their news from the Internet. That's making print newspapers and magazines less popular. People are watching TV programs and movies on the Internet, too. So as you can see, there's a growing audience available to Internet advertisers.

Another important reason is cost. Making and airing a television commercial can cost a huge amount of money. For local TV, it might be thousands of dollars. And for national TV, it can cost hundreds of thousands of dollars. In some cases, advertisers spend millions of dollars to run thirty-second commercials on highly rated TV shows or sports broadcasts. But it's much less expensive to advertise on the Internet. Internet advertisements are typically cheap to make. Many times, they merely provide a link to a company's website. They don't cost that much either. Some Internet advertisements cost a few hundred dollars or even less to place on another website. The most expensive ads rarely require more than several thousand dollars.

Finally, companies can advertise to specific groups on the Internet. All sorts of people watch TV or read newspapers and magazines. So an advertisement for, uh, baby products might not appeal to most of the audience or readers. However, a company advertising baby products on the Internet can buy ad space on websites that parents with babies often visit. This lets the advertiser get more value from its money.

Internet Advertising

TV and Print Media Ads:	Internet Ads:
- Dominated the advertising industry in the past	- Will overcome TV and print marketing soon
- TV is biggest segment for advertisers today	- More people are using the Internet nowadays
- TV commercials can be very expensive	- Is cheap to make Internet ads
- Some advertisements might not appeal to all of the audience or readers	- Can advertise to specific groups on the Internet

1 [Gist-Content Question]

The professor mostly focuses on the various benefits of Internet advertising in his lecture.

2 [Understanding Organization Question]

The professor emphasizes the advantages of Internet advertising by comparing it with other forms of advertising, such as TV commercials and advertisements in print media.

3 [Connecting Content Question]

According to the professor, Internet advertisements can be targeted to a specific audience and are usually cheap. As for television commercials, they can cost millions of dollars. And they were once worth the money that advertisers spent on them.

Listening Comprehension

1 b   2 a   3 d   4 c

Mastering Topics with Conversations B3   p.91

1 Ⓒ   2 Ⓐ   3 Ⓑ

Script & Graphic Organizer 02-30

W Student: Professor Garvey, I need to talk to you about our homework assignment. Uh, the one that's due next week.

M Professor: Sure. That's not a problem. What exactly would you like to talk about?

W: Well, I've decided to write on *A Midsummer Night's Dream*. It's my favorite play by Shakespeare, so that's why I chose it.

M: Ah, that's one of my favorite plays as well. So tell me . . . What about the play do you intend to write? Are you going to look at the fairy aspect of it?

W: No, but that's a good topic. Uh, I was thinking of exploring the historical context of the play. I know it's not a history like some of Shakespeare's other works. But, uh . . . I thought it would be an interesting approach. And unique, too.

M: I agree. It would be interesting, but . . .

W: But what?

M: Well, you only have to write a two-page essay. This is a short assignment. I don't think that's enough space to write about the historical context of that play. And I would prefer that you focus on either the theme or the symbolism used in the work. I think I mentioned that in class. You can write lots

of fascinating things about the symbolism in *A Midsummer Night's Dream*.

W: ³Yes, that's true. All right. Maybe I can develop my idea into a longer paper. . . **Hey. I might be able to use it in your Shakespeare class next semester.**

M: That's good thinking. And you're probably right.

Office Hours

Reason for Visiting:
Wants to discuss a paper she is writing

Professor's Response:
Asks her exactly what she is going to write about

Student's Response:
Wants to look at the historical background of a Shakespeare play

Professor's Comment:
Wants her to write on another topic since it is only a two-page paper

1 [Gist-Purpose Question]

When the professor asks the student what she wants to talk about, she responds, "Well, I've decided to write on *A Midsummer Night's Dream*. It's my favorite play by Shakespeare, so that's why I chose it." So she is telling him about an assignment that she is doing.

2 [Understanding Attitude Question]

The professor rejects the student's proposal, so her paper topic is unacceptable to him.

3 [Understanding Function Question]

When the student mentions the professor's Shakespeare class in the next semester, she is implying that the professor will be her teacher again in the future.

Listening Comprehension

1 b   2 d   3 a   4 c

TOEFL Practice Tests C1   p.92

1 Ⓐ   2 Ⓓ   3 Ⓑ   4 Ⓒ   5 Ⓒ   6 Ⓓ

Script 02-31

W Professor: Nowadays, we take food for granted. When we're hungry, we have options. We can go to a supermarket. We can go to a restaurant. Or we can simply order food for delivery. We live in an age when we don't have to think much about where our next meal is coming from. Or, uh, if we will actually get to eat. We're very fortunate because this wasn't always the case.

In ancient times, food was always on people's

minds. Famines were common. Many people were undernourished. People frequently starved to death. So getting food was a primary element to preventing the collapse of society. Think about it like this . . . Most food is grown. But most regions only have one or two growing seasons. It also takes time to grow food. It can take weeks or months for plants and trees to produce food. But numerous problems can happen to the food supply. For instance, bad weather and diseases can kill crops or reduce the amount that gets harvested. Harvested food can spoil. In addition, pests such as rats and mice can ruin it.

As you can probably guess, preserving the food that farmers grew was a key to power in ancient times. Some empires became powerful simply because they kept their populations fed all year long.

M Student: Which places are you thinking of, Professor Carter?

W: Well . . . Mesopotamia, Egypt, Greece, and Rome are all good examples. In these four places, grain was the main source of food. The people in these civilizations used grain to make both bread and beer. Grain was popular because it has many advantages over vegetables, fruits, and meats. First, grain doesn't spoil as easily as other foods. You see, grain gets harvested when it's dry. It's also stored dry. Since it contains less moisture, the chances of it spoiling are lower. As a result, it can be stored for long periods of time.

These ancient societies also had large granaries. These were usually enclosed buildings. Typically, the government operated these granaries. The rulers knew the importance of keeping the grain supply safe. So the granaries were very well guarded. They had to be protected from people and pests. And they had to be sheltered from the rain and other sources of water. Here's something interesting as well: Grain was often given to the people for free. This was especially true in cities. [6]Rome, for example, gave free grain—usually wheat or barley—and cooking oil to the citizens of the city. This kept the people both fed and happy. **So they were less likely to, uh, you know, cause any trouble.**

Having a year-round food supply greatly helped ancient societies. As civilization developed, there were many people who weren't farmers. For instance, there were administrators, soldiers, priests, and scholars. These people all needed food. Armies especially required food. Hungry armies can't fight and are more likely to disobey their generals. If you look at the history of the four empires I just mentioned, you'll notice that they often experienced

trouble when there were problems with the food supply. I'd like to give you a few examples now. That way, you'll understand more clearly what I'm talking about.

1 [Gist-Content Question]

The professor focuses on the importance of food in ancient societies.

2 [Gist-Purpose Question]

The professor talks about different options for eating that modern-day people have. Then, she says, "We're very fortunate because this wasn't always the case."

3 [Detail Question]

When talking about grain, the professor notes, "As a result, it can be stored for long periods of time."

4 [Understanding Organization Question]

The professor mentions that the granaries were well protected. Then, she explains the purpose that they filled and why having enough grain was important to ancient societies.

5 [Making Inferences Question]

At the end of the lecture, the professor comments, "I'd like to give you a few examples now. That way, you'll understand more clearly what I'm talking about." So she is going to continue discussing the current topic.

6 [Understanding Function Question]

The professor implies that some people revolted when there was no food when she mentions, "So they were less likely to, uh, you know, cause any trouble."

TOEFL Practice Tests C2 p.94

1 (B)   2 (D)   3 (A)   4 (B)   5 (A)

`Script` 02-32

W Housing Office Employee: Greetings. Is there something I can do for you today?

M Student: I hope there is. I'm here because of my school transcript.

W: Er . . . I'm sorry, but I think you're in the wrong office. The Registrar's office handles transcripts. We only take care of housing in this office. You can get to the Registrar's office by going straight up the hill. It's located in the basement of Minor Hall.

M: Actually, um, I was just at the Registrar's office. The woman working there told me to come here.

W: That can't be right. This has to do with your transcript? Did she say why you should come here?

M: Uh, yes, she did. You see . . . I'm going to graduate this year. Right now, I need some copies of my transcript. I have to send them to potential employers. Uh, anyway, I went to the Registrar's office to get some printed. But, uh, they told me that I owed the school some money. The woman wouldn't print my transcript until I paid the money.

W: Ah, and this money you owe is connected to the housing office, right?

M: I guess. To be honest, I'm not really sure what the problem is. I mean, uh, I thought that I had paid all of my bills.

W: Why don't you give me your name and student ID? I'll check you out on our computer system.

M: Sure. My name is Matthew Crawford. That's C-R-A-W-F-O-R-D. And my student ID number is 32-019-1983.

W: [5]Okay . . . It's coming up on the screen now . . . Ah, you owe forty-five dollars for damage to your dorm room.

M: Damage? What damage?

W: Apparently, you broke some furniture in your room on . . . let me see . . . October 14 of last year. Do you remember that incident?

M: Oh, wait a minute . . . That was my roommate. He broke a chair and was supposed to pay the damage. So, um, how did I get stuck with the bill?

W: According to the information here, your roommate . . . Peter Johnson . . . paid forty-five dollars on November 10. I guess he left the other half for you to pay.

M: I can't believe it. He never even told me about that. I'm going to go and have a chat with him about this. Thanks so much for your assistance.

1 [Gist-Content Question]

The student visits the housing office because he has to pay some money that he owes before he can get some copies of his transcript.

2 [Detail Question]

The student states, "Right now, I need some copies of my transcript. I have to send them to potential employers."

3 [Understanding Attitude Question]

When the woman tells the student that his roommate only paid half the bill, he responds, "I can't believe it. He never even told me about that. I'm going to go and

have a chat with him about this." The student's tone of voice also indicates that he is very displeased with his roommate.

4 [Making Inferences Question]

The student mentions that his roommate broke a chair and was "supposed to pay the damage." So the student implies that his roommate should pay to replace the chair.

5 [Understanding Function Question]

The student's tone of voice indicates that he is very surprised by what the woman has just told him.

Vocabulary **Review**   p.98

1	Ⓐ	2	Ⓑ	3	Ⓓ	4	Ⓐ
5	Ⓒ	6	Ⓓ	7	Ⓑ	8	Ⓔ
9	Ⓒ	10	Ⓕ	11	Ⓓ	12	Ⓐ

● Chapter | **05 Physical Sciences 1** • Conversations

Mastering Question Types with Lectures & Conversations A   p.100

[TYPES 1–4]

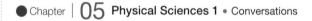

TYPE 1 Ⓑ

TYPE 2 Cause: [2], [3], [4]   Effect: [1]

TYPE 3 Ⓒ   TYPE 4 Ⓑ

Script 02-33

M1 Professor: Did any of you notice those strange greenish-colored lights in the sky last night . . . ? Anybody . . . ? Mark?

M2 Student: I did, sir. They were beautiful. But, uh, what were they?

M1: We call them the northern lights. But they're also called auroras. There are two types of auroras: those in the Northern Hemisphere and those in the Southern Hemisphere. In the north, we call them the aurora borealis. In the south, they're the aurora australis. Auroras appear as colorful streams of light in the sky in high northern and southern latitudes. They frequently occur during the months before or after the equinox. The equinox happens in March and September. That's when the planet is tilted so that it's neither pointed away from nor toward the sun.

So, uh . . . Why do auroras occur . . . ? They're the result of a reaction in the upper atmosphere. Solar winds hit the Earth's magnetic field. This may excite the oxygen and nitrogen atoms in the atmosphere. After some time, the atoms become relaxed. As they relax, the electrons in these atoms give off energy. This energy appears in the form of light. The color of the light depends on whether it comes from oxygen or nitrogen. In addition, the height in the atmosphere helps determine the colors that the light forms. And, um, just so you know . . . Oxygen usually emits a green or brownish-red light. Nitrogen typically gives off a red or blue light. Most auroras are green in color.

TYPE 1 [Gist-Content Question]

The professor talks mostly about the northern and southern lights, which are auroras.

TYPE 2 [Connecting Content Question]

According to the professor, auroras are caused by three things: nitrogen atoms getting excited, solar winds in the Earth's magnetic field, and electrons in oxygen atoms giving off energy. An effect of auroras is that green lights may appear in the sky.

TYPE 3 [Understanding Organization Question]

The professor states, "They frequently occur during the months before or after the equinox."

TYPE 4 [Understanding Attitude Question]

About the auroras, the student comments, "They were beautiful."

Checking Listening Accuracy

1 F   2 F   3 F   4 T

[TYPES 5–8]

TYPE 5 Ⓑ   **TYPE 6** Ⓒ

TYPE 7 Ⓒ   **TYPE 8** Ⓓ

Script 02-34

W Professor: It's common sense that some objects are harder than others. We refer to this characteristic as hardness. But what exactly is hardness . . . ? Let me tell you . . . It's the ability of a material to resist being damaged, scratched, or marred in any way. There's even a way to measure it. It's the Mohs Scale of Hardness. A German scientist . . . um, a mineralogist . . . named Friedrich Mohs came up with the scale in 1812. Here's how he made it . . . Mohs took ten different minerals. Then, he rated them from

one to ten based on their ability to withstand damage and to damage other materials. Talc received a rating of one. It's soft, is easily scratched, and can hardly damage anything. Diamond received a rating of ten. It's the hardest natural substance known to man.

The other objects on the scale that number from two to nine are . . . gypsum, calcite, fluorite, apatite, feldspar, quartz, topaz, and corundum. I see worried looks on your faces. Don't worry about writing them down. They're listed on page 234 of your text. Take a look. Now, what about the hardness of other objects? Hmm . . . It depends on which of the ten minerals can scratch them. For instance, your fingernails get a rating of 2.5 on the Mohs Scale. So talc and gypsum can't scratch them, but calcite can. What are some others? Let's see . . . Iron is rated between four and five. Glass is between six and seven. And steel is close to eight.

TYPE 5 [Gist-Purpose Question]

The professor focuses on the rating system for the Mohs Scale of Hardness.

TYPE 6 [Detail Question]

The professor remarks, "Then, he rated them from one to ten based on their ability to withstand damage and to damage other materials. Talc received a rating of one. It's soft, is easily scratched, and can hardly damage anything."

TYPE 7 [Making Inferences Question]

Since diamonds are the hardest substances known to man, it can be inferred that diamonds can scratch anything.

TYPE 8 [Understanding Function Question]

The professor states, "The other objects on the scale that number from two to nine are . . . gypsum, calcite, fluorite, apatite, feldspar, quartz, topaz, and corundum. I see worried looks on your faces. Don't worry about writing them down. They're listed on page 234 of your text. Take a look."

Checking Listening Accuracy

1 T   2 F   3 T   4 T

[TYPES 9–12]

TYPE 9 Ⓓ   **TYPE 10** Ⓑ

TYPE 11 Ⓓ   **TYPE 12** Ⓑ

M1 Student: Professor Chandler, could you take a look at this book for me, please?

M2 Professor: *A Study of Nature's Animals*. Ah, yes. I'm familiar with this book. Why do you ask?

M1: I'm planning to use this book for my research paper. [12]I wanted to make sure it's an acceptable reference. That's why I'm asking you.

M2: Yes. It's a good start.

M1: **A good start?** Er . . . What do you mean?

M2: Tom, this is a research paper. You need more than one source. This book will provide you with some great information. But you definitely need to find some more books from the library.

M1: Okay. I think I see what you mean. Thanks for the advice, sir. I guess I'll head over there now.

TYPE 9 [Gist-Purpose Question]

At the beginning of the conversation, the student asks the professor, "Professor Chandler, could you take a look at this book for me, please?"

TYPE 10 [Detail Question]

The professor tells the student, "But you definitely need to find some more books from the library."

TYPE 11 [Making Inferences Question]

At the end of the conversation, the student mentions, "I guess I'll head over there now." So he will probably visit the library next.

TYPE 12 [Understanding Function Question]

When the student asks, "A good start?" he does so in a confused tone of voice. He is confused by the professor's comment.

Checking Listening Accuracy

1 F   2 T   3 T   4 F

Mastering Topics with Lectures B1   p.103

1 Ⓐ   2 Heterogeneous Mixture: [1], [4]   Homogenous
Mixture: [2], [3]   3 Ⓒ

M Professor: I'd like to speak about mixtures now. [3]First, a mixture is not the same as a chemical compound. The atoms in a compound are bonded together and form a new substance. **You remember that, right?** For example, oxygen and hydrogen combine to form water. In a mixture, the items are combined yet don't unite chemically. For example, think of a salad. It contains many different vegetables, but they don't bond with one another. You can separate the individual parts of a salad. So a salad is a mixture, not a compound. There are two types of mixtures. They are heterogeneous and homogenous mixtures. They're different because of the way their individual parts combine and how they can be separated.

First, heterogeneous mixtures . . . They have different parts that we can easily see. Their parts are usually easy to separate. The salad I just mentioned is a good example of a heterogeneous mixture. Please note that it's not always easy to see the individual, um, components, of heterogeneous mixtures. Some contain particles so small that it's hard to tell they're separate. Milk is one example. It contains parts so small you can only distinguish them by using a microscope. So, uh, you can separate some heterogeneous mixtures by hand. Others require special machinery such as centrifuges.

As for homogenous mixtures . . . Well, we can separate them, but it's much more difficult. In a homogenous mixture, the parts appear to be uniform either in shade or substance. Salt dissolved in water, for instance, is a homogenous mixture. It is possible to separate the salt from the water since there's no chemical bonding. However, it's rather difficult.

W Student: How can you do it, sir?

M: By using heat. That evaporates the water, which leaves the salt behind. Or you could use filters. You force the water through a filter with extremely tiny holes. The water goes through, but the salt remains behind. So you can see that it's not easy. Oh, yeah . . . Air is another example of a homogenous mixture. We can separate its parts into nitrogen, oxygen, and several other minor gases.

Mixtures

Characteristics:

- *Some items are combined*
- *But the items do not unite chemically*
- *Can be like a salad*
- *May have many ingredients, but they do not bond with one another*
- *Are two types of mixtures*

Heterogeneous Mixtures:

Have different parts that are easy to see; are usually easy to separate; milk

Homogenous Mixtures:

Are more difficult to separate; appear uniform in shape or substance; salt dissolved in water

Separating Salt from Water:

Can evaporate water to leave salt behind; can pass water through a filter with very small holes

1 [Gist-Content Question]

During the lecture, the professor mostly discusses heterogeneous and homogenous mixtures.

2 [Connecting Content Question]

According to the professor, heterogeneous mixtures may often be separated by hand, and it is often easy to see their individual parts, such as those of a salad. As for homogenous mixtures, salt dissolved in water is an example of one. And its different parts often appear to be the same color.

3 [Understanding Function Question]

When the professor asks, "You remember that, right?" he implies that the class has already studied that particular topic.

Listening Comprehension

1 c   2 a   3 d   4 b

Mastering Topics with Lectures B2   p.104

1 Ⓓ   2 Fact: ②, ④   Not a Fact: ①, ③   3 Ⓑ

 Script & Graphic Organizer 02-37

W Professor: This winter has been rather cold. It almost feels like we're entering a new ice age . . . Now, don't laugh. That statement isn't as crazy as it seems. Yes, global warming is a, uh, hot topic these days. But more and more scientists are considering the possibility of global cooling occurring soon. This would result in the average temperatures on the Earth dropping. It has happened in the past. And it will happen again in the future.

The Earth is warm now, but that's not always the case. In the past, large parts of the planet were covered in ice. We call these periods ice ages. Note the plural . . . There wasn't just one ice age. There have been several. During the recent past, we experienced the Little Ice Age. It lasted almost 500 years from around, hmm . . . say 1300 to 1800. The ice pack in the Arctic Ocean grew larger and moved south. Glaciers in the European Alps and on Greenland grew bigger and advanced southward. Temperatures dropped all over the Northern Hemisphere. Winters were longer, summers were shorter, and summer rains were heavier. There were numerous famines since cold weather and rain frequently destroyed crops.

Why did this ice age and others like it happen? One theory claims that the Earth's orbit caused them. The Earth's orbit changes slightly over time, so the Northern Hemisphere receives less sunlight on those occasions. This reduces temperatures. It's possible that an orbital change caused the major ice ages. In case you're curious, the last such ice age happened around 20,000 years ago.

M Student: How often does the Earth's orbit change?

W: No one knows for sure. Scientists estimate it changes between every 20,000 to 50,000 years. There's also a second possible reason for global cooling. This relates to decreased solar activity. The appearance—or lack of—sunspots can affect temperatures here on the Earth. During the Little Ice Age, there were significantly fewer sunspots. For instance, in one thirty-year period, astronomers spotted a few dozen sunspots. Normally, they would have seen tens of thousands of them. With less solar activity, some believe, temperatures on the Earth decreased, thereby resulting in colder weather.

Global Cooling

The Little Ice Age:

- *From around 1300 to 1800*
- *The ice pack in the Arctic Ocean grew*
- *Glaciers expanded southward*
- *Temperatures in the Northern Hemisphere dropped*
- *Winters were longer*
- *Summers were shorter*
- *Summer rains were heavier*
- *Were many famines*

Why There Are Ice Ages:

- *The Earth's orbit changes over time*
- *The Northern Hemisphere gets less sunlight, so temperatures drop*
- *Solar activity decreases*
- *Fewer sunspots cause temperatures on the Earth to decrease*

1 [Understanding Attitude Question]

At the beginning of the lecture, the professor declares, "This winter has been rather cold. It almost feels like we're entering a new ice age. Now, don't laugh. That statement isn't as crazy as it seems. Yes, global warming is a, uh, hot topic these days. But more and more scientists are considering the possibility of global cooling occurring soon." So she thinks that global cooling could happen soon.

2 [Detail Question]

According to the professor, it is a fact that the Little Ice Age ended around 1800, and it is a fact that there was not enough food during it. However, there was not less rain in summer during it; there was more rain during summer. And temperatures in the Northern Hemisphere did not remain the same; they declined.

3 [Understanding Organization Question]

The professor states, "The appearance—or lack of—sunspots can affect temperatures here on the Earth." She then explains how sunspots can affect the temperatures on the Earth.

♪ **Listening Comprehension**

1 d   2 b   3 c   4 a

Mastering Topics with Conversations B3   p.105

| 1 | 2 | 3 Ⓑ |

`Script & Graphic Organizer` 02-38

M Student: Thank you for agreeing to meet me, Dean Watkins.

W Dean of Students: It's no problem at all, Mr. Parker. So . . . you want to start a new publication on campus. Is that correct?

M: Yes, ma'am. Mr. Foster at the student activities office liked my idea very much. But he informed me that you have to approve it first.

W: That's correct. First, um, what kind of magazine are you interested in founding?

M: I want something that provides in-depth analysis of global news.

W: Do you have any students willing to join you?

M: Yes, there are nine people who have expressed interest in writing for me. I can provide you with their names if you want.

W: That won't be necessary now. What about financing? After all, it's not cheap to publish a magazine.

M: I was hoping to publish it online. Uh, that would be cheaper than printing it, right?

W: Yes, but this project will still cost money. The school can't pay for everything. Hmm . . . Okay, let's do this. Provide me with a detailed budget for the first year by next Friday. And explain how you can raise funds for half that amount. Then, I can seriously consider giving your proposal the green light.

Service Encounter

Reason for Visiting:	Student's Response:
Wants to start a new publication on campus	Wants a magazine on global news; has nine students willing to write; wants to publish online to save money
Dean's Questions:	Dean's Decision:
Asks what kind of magazine the student will found; asks if other students will write; asks about paying for the magazine	Tells the students to make a budget and to figure out how to pay half of that money; can then consider approving the project

1 [Gist-Content Question]

The student and the dean mostly talk about a magazine that the student would like to start.

2 [Detail Question]

The student tells the dean, "I want something that provides in-depth analysis of global news."

3 [Making Inferences Question]

At the end of the conversation, the dean tells the student, "Provide me with a detailed budget for the first year by next Friday." So it can be inferred that the student will meet the dean next week.

♪ **Listening Comprehension**

1 d   2 c   3 a   4 b

TOEFL Practice Tests C1   p.106

| 1 Ⓑ | 2 Ⓓ | 3 Ⓐ | 4 Ⓒ | 5 Ⓓ | 6 Ⓑ |

`Script` 02-39

M Professor: All right . . . Now that we've discussed the sun, let's examine the planets. There are eight major planets. We once said there were nine, but

Pluto has been downgraded to a dwarf planet. Astronomers divide the eight planets into two types: Terran and Jovian planets. The Terran planets are Mercury, Venus, Earth, and Mars. The Jovian planets are Jupiter, Saturn, Uranus, and Neptune. Terran and Jovian planets are different in several significant ways.

First and foremost are their sizes . . . The Terran planets are small. [5]Earth is the largest Terran planet while Jupiter is the biggest Jovian. **But Jupiter is 300—yes, 300—times the size of Earth.** Consider for a moment how big that is . . . Next, the planets differ in their closeness to the sun. The Terran planets are closer to the sun. The Jovians, obviously, are farther from the sun. As a result, temperatures on the Terran planets are much higher. The Jovians, meanwhile, are extremely cold. In addition, as you would expect, the Terran planets orbit the sun much more quickly than the Jovians. For instance, Mercury orbits the sun in around eighty-eight days. Neptune, on the other hand, completes one orbit in almost 165 years.

The Terran and Jovian planets also have different compositions. The Terran planets are hard and rocky. They have hard surfaces and are denser than the Jovians. The Jovians are not very dense at all. Instead, they're, uh . . . they're giant gas balls. We actually call them gas giants. That's a common term for them.

There are two more major differences. The Jovian planets all have rings around them. Saturn's are the most spectacular, but all four Jovians have rings. Don't forget that fact. These rings are mostly comprised of ice crystals and pieces of rocks. The Terran planets lack rings. The Jovian planets also have many moons. Saturn has more than eighty large and small moons. Jupiter, Uranus, and Neptune have numerous moons as well. The Terran planets have few natural satellites. Mercury and Venus have none. Earth has one while Mars has two.

W Student: How come there are two totally different types of planets in the solar system? I don't get it. What happened?

M: The answer, Lisa, concerns the formation of the solar system. The main theory states that the solar system began as a spinning disk. This disk contained many elements in the form of dust. These elements collided and then combined. Over time, they grew larger and formed planets. Heavy metals, such as iron and nickel, formed the planets' dense inner cores. Yes, despite being gas giants, even the Jovian planets are thought to have solid inner cores.

Finally, why are some planets rocky while others are gaseous? That's connected to their temperatures. The temperatures closer to the sun were higher. As the sun formed, it gave off heat. The heat prevented nearby elements from freezing and forming ice particles. But this didn't happen on the planets far from the sun. [6]So, um, large amounts of ice formed on them. This greatly increased these planets' sizes. Then, these icy-rocky planets began gathering gases. We don't exactly know how or why that happened though. **That's a topic for another lecture anyway.** Now, I'd like to complete our overview of the solar system by moving on to the smaller bodies. Let's start with the dwarf planets.

1 [Gist-Purpose Question]

The professor's lecture is about the various characteristics of the major planets.

2 [Understanding Organization Question]

During his lecture, the professor compares and contrasts different aspects of the Terran and Jovian planets.

3 [Connecting Content Question]

The professor notes, "For instance, Mercury orbits the sun in around eighty-eight days. Neptune, on the other hand, completes one orbit in almost 165 years."

4 [Detail Question]

The professor responds to a question by saying, "The answer, Lisa, concerns the formation of the solar system. The main theory states that the solar system began as a spinning disk."

5 [Understanding Function Question]

The professor makes the comment about the sizes of Jupiter and Earth in order to compare the two of them.

6 [Making Inferences Question]

When the professor comments, "That's a topic for another lecture anyway," he is letting the class know that he does not want to discuss that topic right now but that he will talk about it at a later time.

TOEFL Practice Tests C2   p.108

Script 02-40

M Professor: Denise, please come in. I'm so glad you dropped by. You received my email, didn't you?

W Student: Yes, sir. I did. You mentioned something

about the article I wrote for the school's music journal. Um, I hate to ask, but . . . um, was there something wrong with it?

M: Well, overall, I'd say your article was well written. You have a way with words, Denise. You have great promise as a writer.

W: Thank you for the compliment, sir. But, well, I'm guessing there's still a problem with it. Am I right?

M: Yes, I'm afraid you are. Let me see how I can explain this . . . Again, let me stress that I liked the article a lot. It was a great piece of expository writing.

W: Expository writing? What do you mean by that?

M: Ah, you're not familiar with the term. Basically, expository writing is a type of writing that explains or describes something.

W: Oh, yeah. Sure. That's what I wrote.

M: Yes, it was. But that's the problem, Denise. You see, uh, I was hoping this article would be a piece of critical writing. In other words, I wanted you to put your own opinion in the writing.

W: Oh. I didn't realize that. But, uh . . . how exactly am I supposed to do that? Oh, no. Wait a minute. Am I going to have to rewrite my entire paper?

M: No, no, no. Not at all . . . Well, you're going to have to rewrite some portions of it. But you definitely don't have to redo the entire thing.

W: That's a relief . . . Okay, um, so how do I do this critical writing essay? Can you explain it to me, please?

M: It's not too complicated. Just insert your personal thoughts throughout the essay. Don't simply write about the Classical Period. Instead, write how you feel about the various composers and their works. Let your readers know your opinion. That's all there is to it.

W: All right. I think I can do that. At least I'll give it a try. But could you please look over my work as soon as I finish it? I'd like to get your opinion. That way, I can make sure I've done it properly.

M: It would be my pleasure. Can you get it to me in two days? We have a deadline coming up soon.

W: I'll do my best. I'll get started on it right away.

1 [Gist-Purpose Question]

The professor asked to see the student because he wants to talk about a paper that the student wrote for the school's music journal.

2 [Detail Question]

The student wrote the paper for the school's music journal.

3 [Understanding Attitude Question]

The professor compliments the student as a writer by telling her, "Well, overall, I'd say your article was well written. You have a way with words, Denise. You have great promise as a writer." He clearly believes her writing is outstanding.

4 [Detail Question]

The professor tells the student, "You see, uh, I was hoping this article would be a piece of critical writing."

5 [Understanding Function Question]

At the end of the conversation, the student remarks, "I'll get started on it right away." So she will probably rewrite her paper next, especially since the professor wants to see it in two days.

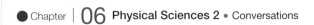

Vocabulary **Review**   p.112

1	(D)	2	(A)	3	(B)	4	(D)
5	(C)	6	(A)	7	(A)	8	(F)
9	(E)	10	(B)	11	(D)	12	(C)

● Chapter | **06** **Physical Sciences 2** • Conversations

Mastering Question Types with Lectures & Conversations A   p.114

[TYPES 1–4]

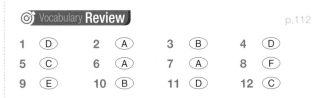

TYPE **1** (B)

TYPE **2** Organic Compounds: [1], [2], [3]   Inorganic Compounds: [4]

TYPE **3** (A)   TYPE **4** (D)

Script   02-41

W Professor: [4]Okay. Today's our first class. I'd like to begin with some important definitions. **We're going to use these terms all semester, so pay close attention.** To begin with, chemistry is basically the study of matter. Matter is everything that makes up the universe. In this class, we're going to study the various elements and how they interact with one another. Sometimes they unite. When two or more elements unite, we call them compounds.

Now, uh, the study of chemical compounds is divided into two main branches of chemistry: organic chemistry and inorganic chemistry. Organic chemistry is the study of compounds that contain the element carbon. This basically covers, well, uh . . . It covers all living things. Carbon is an element all living organisms have in common. As for inorganic chemistry, it's the study of non-carbon-based compounds.

There are five differences between organic and inorganic compounds. Listen carefully to these. First, there are more than ten million carbon compounds. That's ten times the number of inorganic compounds.

M Student: Why are there so many carbon compounds?

W: Hmm . . . Mostly because carbon bonds easily with other elements. It can also form complex groups. Got it . . . ? Okay, second . . . Uh, organic compounds melt and boil at lower temperatures than inorganic compounds. Third, organic compounds don't dissolve in water as easily as inorganic compounds. Fourth, organic compounds catch fire more easily than inorganic compounds. However, inorganic compounds conduct heat and electricity more easily. Finally, organic compound reactions take place at slower rates than do inorganic compound reactions.

TYPE 1 [Gist-Content Question]

The professor mostly talks about organic and inorganic compounds in her lecture.

TYPE 2 [Connecting Content Question]

According to the professor, organic compounds include all living organisms, boil at lower temperatures, and bond easily with other elements. As for inorganic compounds, they are less common than organic compounds.

TYPE 3 [Understanding Organization Question]

The professor lists the characteristics of organic compounds when she discusses them with the class.

TYPE 4 [Understanding Attitude Question]

When the professor tells the class to "pay close attention," she is indicating that she is about to give them some information that is important. That is why she wants them to listen closely.

♪ Checking Listening Accuracy

1 T   2 F   3 T   4 T

[TYPES 5–8]

TYPE 5 Ⓒ   **TYPE 6** Ⓑ

TYPE 7 Ⓓ   **TYPE 8** Ⓑ

Script 02-42

M Professor: Erosion happens primarily due to wind, water, and ice. It often alters the appearance of the land. It is the force that created the Grand Canyon and Niagara Falls. Those two places took incredibly long times to form. Other changes, however, can happen much more quickly. After all, erosion can take place over a few years, months, weeks, or even days. And some erosion can have dramatic effects on agriculture.

Yes, that's right. Farmers can suffer a great deal due to erosion. You've all heard about the Dust Bowl of the 1930s, haven't you? In the 1920s, farmers plowed millions of acres of soil in the Great Plains in the United States. Uh, that's in states such as Oklahoma and Kansas. However, there was a drought, so the land dried up. Crops couldn't grow because there wasn't any water. Then, the wind blew away the valuable topsoil. Obviously, that had a tremendous negative effect on farmers.

You see, uh, when the wind blows away the topsoil, the land loses its fertility. So no more crops grow on it. This has happened in many places around the world and during different time periods. The Dust Bowl is just one example of many. But the results are always the same . . . The topsoil is eroded . . . Farmers cannot grow crops anymore . . . [8]Mass migrations take place as farmers move elsewhere . . . The affected region takes many years—sometimes decades—to recover from erosion. **And that's why we need to practice sustainable farming.** Let me tell you a few methods that farmers can use to prevent erosion.

TYPE 5 [Gist-Purpose Question]

The professor talks about the manner in which erosion caused the Dust Bowl to happen.

TYPE 6 [Detail Question]

The professor states, "You see, uh, when the wind blows away the topsoil, the land loses its fertility."

TYPE 7 [Making Inferences Question]

The professor states, "This has happened in many places around the world and during different time periods. The Dust Bowl is just one example of many." So it can be inferred that the Dust Bowl was not a unique event in history.

TYPE 8 [Understanding Function Question]

The professor talks about erosion causing problems. Then, he states, "And that's why we need to practice sustainable farming." So the professor implies that it is possible to prevent erosion from happening.

✎ Checking Listening Accuracy

1 T   2 T   3 T   4 F

[TYPES 9–12]

TYPE 9 Ⓒ	**TYPE 10** Ⓐ, Ⓓ
TYPE 11 Ⓑ	**TYPE 12** Ⓑ

Script 02-43

W Student: [12]Hello. I have a problem with the washing machines in my dormitory.

M Housing Office Employee: **You, too?** Okay. What is the problem you have with them?

W: They're a lot different from the old ones. And not in a good way. First, they're too small. I can't fit very many clothes into these washing machines.

M: Yeah. You're not the first person to tell me that.

W: And they're more expensive. It used to cost a dollar per load. Now, it costs a dollar fifty. How come?

M: The price of electricity has gone up. So we had to raise the prices. Otherwise, we would lose money.

W: And what about the size of the machines?

M: I'll talk to my boss about that. We might be able to get some larger ones for the dorms. I'll do my best to solve that problem. No one seems happy with the size of the washers.

TYPE 9 [Gist-Purpose Question]

At the beginning of the conversation, the student tells the man, "I have a problem with the washing machines in my dormitory."

TYPE 10 [Detail Question]

The student complains that the washing machines cost a dollar fifty to use instead of a dollar like they did in the past. She also states that the washing machines "are too small."

TYPE 11 [Making Inferences Question]

The student is definitely unhappy with the current situation of the washing machines in her dormitory.

TYPE 12 [Understanding Function Question]

When the man asks, "You, too?" it can be inferred that he has heard the same complaint several times from other students.

✎ Checking Listening Accuracy

1 T   2 T   3 F   4 T

Mastering Topics with Lectures B1   p.117

1 Cause: ②, ③ Effect: ①, ④   2 Ⓒ   3 Ⓒ

Script & Graphic Organizer 02-44

W Professor: Recently, a group of scientists unearthed some dinosaur fossils in Antarctica. Surprised . . . ? Well, it sounds odd, doesn't it? After all, uh, most scientists believe dinosaurs were cold-blooded animals. If so, then how could they have survived in Antarctica? They would have frozen to death, right . . . ? Well, the truth of the matter is that Antarctica wasn't always cold. In fact, it wasn't always in its current position at the bottom of the Earth. It has actually moved around several times throughout our planet's history.

To begin with, I need to explain how it moved. The Earth's crust—its topmost part—isn't one gigantic piece of land. Instead, it's formed of many large and small pieces that fit together. We call these pieces plates. The theory that describes their movement is called plate tectonics. Under the crust is the mantle. Part of the mantle is solid, but much of it isn't. It's not a liquid either. It's more like a, uh . . . well, a slow-moving oozing substance. And the mantle is incredibly hot. This heat creates convection waves. These waves cause the mantle to move the plates on the crust. As a result, the landmasses on the surface are constantly moving. At one time, all of them . . . including Antarctica . . . were connected.

There was once a supercontinent formed by Antarctica, Australia, South Africa, South America, and India. How do we know this? Well, researchers have found similar fossils of plants and animals in all of these regions. Currently, Antarctica is covered in ice. But it was once a tropical region with diverse plant and animal life. Then, it started moving south. Over a period of millions of years, it made its way to the Polar Regions. It's been there since around twenty-five million years ago.

M Student: So the cold weather there killed the dinosaurs?

W: No. The dinosaurs were extinct long before ice ever covered Antarctica. But the ice did succeed in killing most of the other plants and animals living there. They simply couldn't adapt. Today, only those very few plants and animals able to survive in such cold weather live in Antarctica.

Antarctica

Plate Tectonics:	Effects on Antarctica:
- The Earth's crust is made of many plates	- Has moved many times in the past
- The plates sit on the mantle	- Was once part of a supercontinent
- Much of the mantle is a slow-moving oozing substance	- Was joined to other landmasses
- The mantle's heat creates convection waves	- Was once a tropical area
- The waves make the plates move	- Is now covered with ice
	- Are few plants and animals living on it

1 [Connecting Content Question]

According to the professor, the facts that the Earth's crust is made of many plates and that the Earth's mantle creates convection waves are both causes of the movement of Antarctica. As for the effects of the movement of Antarctica, that continent is currently at the bottom of the Earth, and India became separated from it in the past.

2 [Detail Question]

The professor tells the students, "But the ice did succeed in killing most of the other plants and animals living there."

3 [Making Inferences Question]

The professor states, "But it was once a tropical region with diverse plant and animal life." Since the professor also notes that fossils have been found in Antarctica, it can be inferred that some of these fossils are those of tropical creatures.

♪ Listening Comprehension

1 d   2 b   3 a   4 c

Mastering Topics with Lectures B2   p.118

1 Ⓐ   2 Ⓓ   3 Ⓒ

`Script & Graphic Organizer` 02-45

M Professor: Sir Isaac Newton, the famous English scientist, is most famous for his work on the principles of gravity and the laws of motion. But did you also know that he worked with light . . . ? Okay. I see a few heads nodding. That's good. Newton

researched the different components of the light spectrum. He wrote a book on it called *Opticks*. He published it in 1704. The book described many of the experiments he conducted on light.

[3]Newton began working on optics while he was teaching at Cambridge in the 1650s. **No. Sorry. I meant the 1670s.** Yes. That's right. Anyway, uh, he used various objects to bend, or refract, light. These objects included lenses, glasses of water, and prisms. He observed that white light changed colors as it passed through these objects. Some people believed that the objects produced the colors. But Newton had a different theory. He thought that the colors were always present. People simply couldn't see them. However, when white light passed through a translucent object, the light showed its true colors, so to speak. This belief became Newton's basic theory of color.

Newton said that there were seven colors in the light spectrum. These colors are red, orange, yellow, green, blue, indigo, and violet. He believed that the different colors were made of particles of color. Yet Newton wasn't exactly correct. As we know today, light is composed of wavelengths of different ranges. Each color has a different wavelength that's visible to the eye. Despite this one obvious mistake, Newton's theory of light is still considered a significant advancement of science.

Newton also tried to use his work on light to create a better telescope. He knew that a telescope with a lens would distort the colors of the images it observed. So he made a telescope with a mirror, which gathered the light. This is the reflecting telescope. Some people call it a Newtonian telescope since he invented it. Today, reflecting telescopes are among the largest and best telescopes used to observe images.

Sir Isaac Newton

Sir Isaac Newton:	Newton's Experiments with Light:	The Newtonian Telescope:
- Was an English scientist	- Used objects to bend light	- Wanted to make a telescope with a mirror
- Worked on gravity and the laws of motion	- Thought colors were always present in light	- Would not distort colors
- Did work on light	- Discovered the seven colors of the spectrum	- Is called the reflecting telescope
- Wrote a book called Opticks	- Believed colors were made of particles	- Are some of the largest and best telescopes today
- Was published in 1704		

1 [Gist-Content Question]

The professor focuses his lecture on the research that Sir Isaac Newton did on light.

2 [Understanding Organization Question]

The professor mentions the reflecting telescope to remark that Newton invented it because of his work on light.

3 [Understanding Function Question]

When the professor says, "No. Sorry. I meant the 1670s," he is correcting himself because he just misspoke.

Listening Comprehension

1 a   2 c   3 d   4 b

Mastering Topics with Conversations B3   p.119

1 Ⓒ   2 Ⓐ   3 Ⓒ

Script & Graphic Organizer   02-46

W Professor: Overall, I think your rough draft looks fine. Just make a few changes to it. And then you should have an A paper.

M Student: Great, Professor Dyson. Thanks for your assistance.

W: It's my pleasure. Come anytime you need more help, Brad.

M: I appreciate your saying that. Oh, uh . . . If you don't mind, there's one more thing I'd like to speak about with you. Do you have a few more moments?

W: Sure. Sure. I have an empty schedule this afternoon. What else do you want to discuss?

M: Well, uh . . . I was considering applying to be a teaching assistant in the Philosophy Department. I'd love to be the TA for your Introduction to Philosophy class next year. I know you usually have three or four TAs. So . . . do you, uh, think you could recommend me for one of those positions?

W: Hmm . . . Did you know that TAs are almost always graduate students, Brad?

M: They are? Oh . . . I had no idea.

W: Yes, they are. So, uh, I could recommend you for the position. But I don't think you'd get it. There are a lot of grad students here in the Philosophy Department. And they would all get an opportunity to be TAs before you.

M: Oh, that's okay. I didn't know. But thanks for explaining the situation to me. I appreciate it.

Office Hours

Student's Request:	Professor's Response:
Wants to be a teaching assistant in the professor's philosophy class	Says that most TAs are graduate students

Student's Response:	Professor's Comment:
States that he did not know that about TAs	Says that graduate students should get the first opportunity to be TAs

1 [Gist-Content Question]

The student and the professor are mostly talking about how the student wants to be a teaching assistant in one of her classes.

2 [Understanding Attitude Question]

Since the student wants to become a teaching assistant in a Philosophy course, it can be inferred that his major is Philosophy.

3 [Making Inferences Question]

The professor asks the student, "Did you know that TAs are almost always graduate students, Brad?" When she mentions this and says that he will not get a chance to become a TA, it can be inferred that the student is currently an undergraduate.

Listening Comprehension

1 c   2 a   3 b   4 d

TOEFL Practice Tests C1   p.120

1 Ⓒ   2 Ⓑ   3 Ⓓ   4 Ⓓ   5 Climate Change:
③   Landscape: ①, ②   Humans: ④   6 Ⓑ

Script   02-47

W Professor: Today, I think we'll begin class by finishing our talk about river systems. The last time, I spoke about how rivers are formed. Today, I want to discuss why rivers sometimes disappear. For the most part, well, uh, they simply dry up. This could be a seasonal occurrence. For instance, some rivers in deserts only flow during brief periods when rain falls. Yet other rivers actually dry up permanently. There are several reasons why this may happen. First, changes in the local climate can dry up a river. Additionally, changes in the landscape can cause a river to stop flowing and then to dry up. Finally, humans can cause rivers to disappear.

Climate change is a constant on the Earth. Sometimes it's hot, and sometimes it's cold. Rivers are water, which can evaporate. When the temperature is high, this can happen quickly. North Africa is one place where this has happened. Experts believe that many rivers used to flow through North Africa. But, over time, the region's climate changed. Rain fell less often, and the temperatures rose, so many rivers dried up. Then, the area became a desert. Today, we call it the Sahara Desert. This has happened in Australia, too. There are signs of former rivers in the dry, dusty outback that makes up much of that continent.

The landscape can also dry up rivers. The types of rocks and, uh, soil around a river are important. Some rocks and soil allow water to seep through them very easily. Some rivers simply, uh, sink into the ground. They just, well, they disappear before they reach a lake, sea, ocean, or larger river. Some rivers also get cut off. This happens when the land around them changes. For instance, a volcano may erupt, thereby disrupting the flow of a river. Earthquakes can cause sudden changes to the land as well. Over long periods of time, mountains can rise and interrupt the path of a river. Some rivers also carry too much silt. This can cause the river to get blocked. The water may find a way around the blockage, which keeps the river flowing. Or, instead, it could get blocked permanently. When this happens, the blocked river frequently dries up.

Finally, humans can cause rivers to dry up. For example, large dams block river flows. The water from rivers is used to make electricity, to irrigate crops, and to provide drinking water for nearby people. All over the world, water gets diverted from rivers to large cities. Millions of people depend on this water. But overuse can cause these rivers to vanish. Sometimes a larger disaster may occur. In southern Russia, several rivers were blocked by dams in the past. The water was diverted to use for large agricultural projects. The overuse of water caused these rivers to disappear. Today, this enormous area is a barren wasteland. It's unable to support either crops or people.

M Student: [6]Could a large river like the Nile or the Amazon dry up?

W: Hmm . . . **I suppose it's possible.** But it's not going to happen immediately unless there's some sort of drastic change to the planet. However, over time—meaning millions of years—it's possible that even our greatest rivers will cease to exist.

1 [Gist-Content Question]

The professor mostly talks about the various ways in which rivers can dry up and disappear.

2 [Detail Question]

The professor comments, "Rivers are water, which can evaporate. When the temperature is high, this can happen quickly. North Africa is one place where this has happened."

3 [Understanding Organization Question]

The professor first notes how rivers may dry up, and then she goes into detail on each way that it can happen.

4 [Making Inferences Question]

The professor notes that natural methods can dry up "over time." But when she talks about human causes, such as dams, she implies that they can make rivers dry up quickly.

5 [Connecting Content Question]

According to the professor, rain falling less often in a region is an example of how climate change may cause a river to dry up. An erupting volcano and silt blocking a river's flow are two examples of how the landscape may cause a river to dry up. And a dam blocking a river is an example of how humans may cause a river to dry up.

6 [Understanding Attitude Question]

When the professor declares, "I suppose it's possible," she does so with a skeptical tone of voice. She admits the possibility, but she indicates that she doubts that either the Nile or the Amazon will dry up.

TOEFL Practice Tests C2   p.122

1 Ⓒ   2 Ⓐ   3 Ⓑ   4 Ⓓ   5 Ⓑ

Script   02-48

M1 Student: Excuse me. I need to talk to someone about these tickets that I got.

M2 Parking Office Employee: Of course. You're here to pay your fines, right? I can do that for you. Are you going to pay in cash or with a check?

M1: Neither. I'm here to protest both of these two tickets. It's totally unfair that my car got ticketed.

M2: What makes you say that?

M1: Okay. Let me tell you what happened.

M2: Go ahead. I'm listening.

M1: I live in one of the dorms here on campus. I'm in Taylor Hall. So I am supposed to park my car in parking lot number 2. That's pretty much the only place on campus where I park. I only use my car to drive between school and my home.

M2: Uh, so how did you get a ticket then if you were parked in lot number 2? You obviously have permission to park there.

M1: That's what I'm about to tell you. Now, last Thursday, I saw a notice at the entrance to parking lot 2. According to it, the school was going to do some maintenance in the parking lot. Oh, and it mentioned that the parking lot was going to be closed.

M2: Yes. I remember that.

M1: Anyway, I asked the security guard what to do. He told me to park my car in lot number 5. That's the place right next to Edison Hall. So, uh, I drove my car there and parked my car. That's when the problem began.

M2: Oh?

M1: Yes. I left my car there overnight. When I went back on Friday morning, there were two tickets on my car. Each one was for fifty dollars. I'm sorry, but I just don't have that kind of money. And it's not my fault either. The guard told me to go there. His name's Daryl Smith by the way. Uh, you know, if you want to confirm my story with him. He'll back me up.

M2: No. There's no need to do that. I can go ahead and waive these fines.

M1: Seriously? You mean you can do that?

M2: Sure. I've gotten two similar complaints today. It's obviously not your fault you got these tickets. Now, let me go onto the computer. I can remove them from your record. This will take just a minute.

1 [Gist-Content Question]

The student announces, "I'm here to protest both of these two tickets."

2 [Detail Question]

The student mentions, "Anyway, I asked the security guard what to do. He told me to park my car in lot number 5."

3 [Understanding Function Question]

When the employee says, "I've gotten two similar complaints today. It's obviously not your fault you got these tickets," he is letting the student know that he believes the student's story.

4 [Understanding Attitude Question]

The employee is polite and listens to everything that the student has to tell him about his situation.

5 [Understanding Organization Question]

The student notes, "His name's Daryl Smith by the way. Uh, you know, if you want to confirm my story with him. He'll back me up." The student is letting the employee know the name of a person who can confirm the truth of his story.

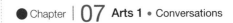 Vocabulary **Review**   p.126

1	Ⓐ	2	Ⓒ	3	Ⓐ	4	Ⓓ
5	Ⓑ	6	Ⓒ	7	Ⓒ	8	Ⓐ
9	Ⓕ	10	Ⓑ	11	Ⓔ	12	Ⓓ

● Chapter | 07 **Arts 1** ● Conversations

Mastering Question Types with Lectures & Conversations A   p.128

[TYPES 1–4]

TYPE **1** Ⓑ   TYPE **2** Ⓓ
TYPE **3** Ⓐ   TYPE **4** Ⓑ

 Script 02-49

W1 Professor: What did you think of that music? Julie, how did you like it?

W2 Student: I loved it. It sounded . . . uh, well . . . it sounded like it was folk music or something.

W1: That's a good way of putting it. Actually, it kind of was folk music. You just listened to some of Bela Bartok's music. Bartok was an important musician and composer in the twentieth century. He was an outstanding pianist from a young age. One reason for this, uh, aside from his talent, is that he spent much of his early life at home. While there, he mostly listened to his mother play the piano. This obviously greatly influenced him since he was composing music before he turned ten.

But Bartok's piano playing isn't my primary interest today. Instead, I want to focus on his fascination with folk music. Around 1904, Bartok began conducting research on Hungarian folk music. He learned that a great amount of Hungarian folk music had been influenced by gypsies. Gypsies were a group of people who lived in the Southeastern European area.

Intrigued, Bartok began investigating the origins of folk music. He eventually published his research on the folk music of the region. That included music from Hungary as well as Romania and Slovakia. Hungarian folk music also influenced his own compositions. This resulted in much of Bartok's music being both personal and nationalistic. Here . . . Let's listen to some more. See if you can hear what I'm talking about.

TYPE 1 [Gist-Content Question]

The professor notes, "Instead, I want to focus on his fascination with folk music."

TYPE 2 [Connecting Content Question]

The professor states, "He learned that a great amount of Hungarian folk music had been influenced by gypsies. Gypsies were a group of people who lived in the Southeastern European area. Intrigued, Bartok began investigating the origins of folk music. He eventually published his research on the folk music of the region. That included music from Hungary as well as Romania and Slovakia." Since Romania and Slovakia are in the same region as Hungary, it can be inferred that some of the music from those two places was also influenced by gypsies.

TYPE 3 [Understanding Organization Question]

The professor comments, "While there, he mostly listened to his mother play the piano. This obviously greatly influenced him since he was composing music before he turned ten."

TYPE 4 [Understanding Attitude Question]

When the professor asks the student how she liked the music that they just heard, she responds, "I loved it."

♪ Checking Listening Accuracy

1 T	2 T	3 T	4 F

[TYPES 5–8]

TYPE 5 Ⓓ	**TYPE 6** Ⓑ
TYPE 7 Ⓑ	**TYPE 8** Ⓐ

Script 02-50

W Professor: Today, we're going to examine murals. A mural is simply a painting on a wall, floor, or ceiling. A mural can be done in the realistic, stylized, or abstract style. It's up to the muralist really. As a general rule, a mural is much larger than other types of paintings. I think the reason is obvious. After all, there's more room on a wall than on a piece of

canvas. Additionally, artists often use murals to relate stories, to support causes, and to make tributes to some aspect of their culture. Ah, here's something important: Some people mistakenly believe that murals are located on the outsides of buildings. They're not. They're on the insides. Yes?

M Student: [8]Are murals an old or a new art form?

W: Quite old. The earliest murals have been found in caves dating back to, um, prehistoric times. **That's about as old as it gets.** Prehistoric people likely made these murals for religious reasons. But we're not positive about that. As for other famous murals . . . A large number of Roman murals were found in the ruins of Pompeii. Pompeii was, of course, the city swallowed whole when the volcano Vesuvius erupted. The Renaissance masters also showed a great deal of creativity in the murals that they created. And there have even been several famous murals painted in the twentieth century. Now that I've given you a quick overview of murals, let's look at some of them. Would someone get the lights, please?

TYPE 5 [Gist-Purpose Question]

The professor mostly gives the students some facts about murals in her lecture.

TYPE 6 [Detail Question]

The professor states, "A mural is simply a painting on a wall, floor, or ceiling."

TYPE 7 [Making Inferences Question]

At the end of the lecture, the professor remarks, "Now that I've given you a quick overview of murals, let's look at some of them. Would someone get the lights, please?" Since they are turning out the lights, it is highly likely that the professor is going to show some slides to the students.

TYPE 8 [Understanding Function Question]

When the professor mentions, "That's about as old as it gets," when talking about murals being found in caves dating to prehistoric times, she implies that murals are some of the oldest types of art that humans have made.

♪ Checking Listening Accuracy

1 F	2 T	3 F	4 T

[TYPES 9–12]

TYPE 9 Ⓓ	**TYPE 10** Ⓓ
TYPE 11 Ⓑ	**TYPE 12** Ⓓ

M Professor: Lisa, you've been late for the last three classes. What's going on? You've never done anything like this in previous semesters.

W Student: I'm sorry, Professor Jackson. I meant to talk to you earlier, but I've been really busy.

M: Okay . . . So what's the problem?

W: It's my internship. I started one at a consulting firm downtown two weeks ago. I'm supposed to finish at 1:00. But, uh, sometimes my boss keeps me late.

M: And that's why you're arriving late for class?

W: [12]Yes, sir. I'm not sure what to do. I can't leave early, or I might lose my position. And that would hurt my chances of getting hired when I graduate.

M: **Okay, I get it.** Just try to get to class on time from now on. And if you arrive late, enter the room quietly without making a fuss.

W: Right. I'll be sure not to disturb the class again. Thanks, sir.

TYPE 9 [Gist-Content Question]

The student and the professor are mostly discussing why she has been late for class recently.

TYPE 10 [Detail Question]

The student tells the professor, "It's my internship. I started one at a consulting firm downtown two weeks ago."

TYPE 11 [Making Inferences Question]

The student tells the professor, "I'll be sure not to disturb the class again," so it can be inferred that the student caused a problem in a recent class.

TYPE 12 [Understanding Function Question]

When the professor says, "Okay, I get it," he is indicating that he understands the student's problem.

Checking Listening Accuracy

1 F   2 T   3 F   4 T

Mastering Topics with Lectures B1   p.131

1 Ⓐ   2 Ⓒ   3 Ⓑ

M Professor: World War I had a tremendous effect on people. You can clearly see this in the literature written after it. It's also true of the art world. We can see this in the Dada Art Movement, also known as Dadaism.

Dadaism originated in Europe during World War I. It was a cultural movement in both art and literature. A group of artists and intellectuals in Switzerland started it. They had moved to Switzerland, which was neutral, to escape the war. These people were furious with modern society. They simply couldn't understand how such a violent war ever could have started. So they expressed their feelings through artistic means. The result was that they created absurd pieces of, uh, non-art.

W Student: Non-art? What's that?

M: Yeah, it sounds strange, doesn't it? Well, the Dadaists claimed that modern society had shown them that art had no meaning. So that's why they created non-art. They also called it anti-art.

Anyway, in 1916, Dadaism became an actual art movement. Now, about that non-art . . . Basically, these non-artists, as they called themselves, created works that were slightly obscene or humorous, contained visible puns, and involved everyday objects. For instance . . . Marcel Duchamp made one outrageous work of, er, non-art. He took a copy of the *Mona Lisa* and painted a mustache on her. Then, he scribbled obscenities at the bottom. He also made a sculpture that he called *Fountain*. It was simply a urinal that he signed with a fake signature.

W: That's disgusting. And it's definitely not art either.

M: Well, Melissa, you're not alone in thinking that. The public at that time wasn't amused by the Dadaists. Many, in fact, were repulsed by them. Both members of the public and the art community expressed their displeasure with the Dadaists. But this only encouraged the Dadaists to continue making their non-art. The movement even expanded. It spread throughout Europe and even crossed the Atlantic Ocean and made it to the United States. However, by the early 1920s, it had disappeared. Yet it had one lasting influence: It influenced many later trends in the visual arts, particularly Surrealism.

The Dada Art Movement

Characteristics:	Marcel Duchamp:
- Originated in Europe during World War I	Drew a mustache on the Mona Lisa and wrote obscenities on it; displayed a urinal with a fake signature called Fountain
- Artists were furious about the war and its violence	
- Created pieces of non-art	**Reactions to Dadaism:**
- Made obscene and humorous works	The public and art critics disliked it; were not amused by the Dadaists; expressed their displeasure with the Dadaists
- Works had puns	
- Works used everyday objects	

1 [Gist-Purpose Question]

The student asks the professor what non-art is, so the professor explains it to answer her question.

2 [Detail Question]

The professor tells the class, "They simply couldn't understand how such a violent war ever could have started. So they expressed their feelings through artistic means. The result was that they created absurd pieces of, uh, non-art."

3 [Understanding Attitude Question]

About Dadaist art, the student exclaims, "That's disgusting. And it's definitely not art either." She clearly does not feel that they produced real art.

♪ Listening Comprehension

1 b   2 c   3 a   4 d

Mastering Topics with Lectures B2   p.132

1 ⒟   2 ⒞   3 ⒝

Script & Graphic Organizer   02-53

M Professor: Frederic Remington is easily the most famous painter of the American West. Remington hailed from the East. But he spent much of his early adulthood in the West. Later, he returned east to take up art. He mostly drew images of the American West. Soon, he was hired to draw and paint images for popular magazines such as *Harper's Weekly and Colliers*.

Ah, I should mention that Remington was born in 1861. So he worked in the late nineteenth and early twentieth centuries. At that time, the people in the East were fascinated with the American West. Remington wisely sold himself as an expert on the American West. In actuality, many of his stories about his life in the West were false. But they were outstanding advertisements for himself. People regarded his work as examples of the real West. And, of course, he had spent many years there. So despite his exaggerations, he did know what he was talking about.

[3]Most of Remington's works involved people and animals. **Much of it is simply brilliant.** Take a look here . . . and here . . . and here . . . He created outdoor scenes like this one . . . images of cowboys and soldiers on their horses like this . . . and this . . . Many times, the people in his paintings were fighting either the weather or Native Americans. Like in this picture . . . Remington also created works of Native Americans themselves . . . Nice, isn't it? Strangely, women rarely appear in his works. And even though his works are mostly outdoor scenes, he didn't focus on the landscape. Instead, his specialty was depicting the people and animals of the West. He illustrated them with great detail. As you can see here . . . and here . . . many of his scenes involve movement and action. Remington also created many realistic works of horses in motion. Here's one of my favorites . . .

Virtually all of Remington's works are paintings or illustrations for magazines and books. Yet here's his best-known work . . . It's a sculpture, one of the few he ever made. See the cowboy on a wild horse as it bucks and bounces.

Frederic Remington

Remington's Life:	Remington's Artwork:
- Was born in 1861	- Focused on people and animals
- Spent much of his early adulthood in the West	- Made outdoor scenes
- Returned to the East later	- Painted cowboys and soldiers fighting the weather or Indians
- Sold himself as an expert on the American West	- Did not focus on the landscape
- Many stories about himself were false	- Scenes often involve movement or action
- Drew and painted for magazines	- Made some sculptures

1 [Gist-Content Question]

The professor focuses on the characteristics of the art that Frederic Remington produced.

2 [Understanding Organization Question]

The professor shows a lot of slides of Remington's artwork while describing various aspects of it to the students.

3 [Understanding Function Question]

When the professor comments that much of Remington's work is "simply brilliant," he is giving his opinion of Remington's paintings.

♪ **Listening Comprehension**

1 d　　　2 b　　　3 c　　　4 a

Mastering Topics with Conversations B3　　p.133

1 Ⓒ　　　2 Ⓓ　　　3 Ⓐ

Script & Graphic Organizer 02-54

> **M Financial Aid Office Employee**: Welcome to the financial aid office. How may I be of assistance to you today?
>
> **W Student**: Uh, hi. I'm here because, uh, well, I need some help with my tuition. I heard about the tuition increase for next semester. That's going to be too much for me to pay. I might have to quit school.
>
> **M**: Okay. Can you give me some details about your current economic status?
>
> **W**: Uh . . . Such as what?
>
> **M**: Well, do you currently receive any financial aid? For example, do you have any scholarships or loans?
>
> **W**: No, I don't have any of those. Right now, I'm paying full tuition. But my parents told me that they can't afford to pay for my tuition next semester.
>
> **M**: Is there any special reason why they said that? I mean, um . . . is your family experiencing some financial hardship? Did one or both of your parents lose their jobs?
>
> **W**: No, not at all. They're still working. But I have two younger brothers. They're twins. And they start college next semester. So my parents can't afford to pay for three kids in college at the same time.
>
> **M**: Ah, that makes sense. Okay. We can probably help you out. Fill out these forms. And bring them back here by next Friday.
>
> **W**: Great. Thanks for your assistance. You've been a really big help.

Service Encounter

Reason for Visiting:	Employee's Question:
Needs some help with her tuition	Asks the student about her current financial situation

Student's Response:	Employee's Comment:
Says that her twin brothers are starting college, so her parents cannot pay full tuition	The school will probably be able to provide some assistance for the student

1 [Gist-Purpose Question]

The student tells the man, "They're still working. But I have two younger brothers. They're twins. And they start college next semester. So my parents can't afford to pay for three kids in college at the same time." She explains her family situation to explain why she needs financial aid to continue going to school.

2 [Detail Question]

The student states, "Right now, I'm paying full tuition." So she is paying all of her tuition.

3 [Making Inferences Question]

The man tells the student, "We can probably help you out." He implies that the student will probably receive some financial aid.

♪ **Listening Comprehension**

1 b　　　2 d　　　3 a　　　4 c

TOEFL Practice Tests C1　　p.134

1 Ⓒ　　2 Ⓑ, Ⓓ　　3 Ⓐ　　4 Ⓐ　　5 Ⓑ　　6 Ⓒ

Script 02-55

> **W Professor**: Two Frenchmen, Louis Daguerre and Joseph Niepce, invented photography in the 1830s. The process they created used a camera box and metal plates with chemicals on them. ⁶We call it a daguerreotype. That's D-A-G-U-E-R-R-E-O-T-Y-P-E. **I hope you all got that because I don't want to say it a second time. I might get it wrong.** Now, uh, this became the primary method for making photographs for around a decade. After that, other methods replaced the daguerreotype.
>
> **M Student**: How did the daguerreotype work?
>
> **W**: Good query. Let me tell you. Now, keep in mind that both Daguerre and Niepce were chemists. So it should come as no surprise that their method utilized chemicals. It was complicated, too. Listen to this . . . First, they coated a copper plate with silver. Then, they put the plate in the camera box. They opened a lens in the box. This exposed the plate to light. The typical exposure was long—around twenty minutes or so. The image the light made on the silver was a latent image. By that, I mean that it wasn't quite an

image. It had to be treated further in order to create one. Daguerre accidentally discovered that the fumes from heated mercury would expose the image on the silver plate. So he and Niepce did this to develop the plate and then produce a final image. After that, they put the plate into another chemical solution. This permanently fixed the image to the plate . . . Phew. That was a lot of steps, wasn't it?

The images they produced were the first photographs in history. Unfortunately for Niepce, he died in 1833. This was before the process was perfected. A few years later, in, uh . . . 1839 . . . Daguerre revealed their invention to the world. So most people consider 1839 the year when photography was invented. From France, the process spread around the world. It went first to England and the rest of Europe. Then, it moved to America. By the 1850s, photography reached Asia. But, like I said a moment ago, the daguerreotype was only used for about ten years.

M: Why is that, ma'am?

W: Mostly because of its limitations. First, the exposure time was too long. So it was impossible to capture many images. For instance, photographing people was difficult. After all, how'd you like to stand still for twenty minutes . . . ? Second, the image produced was fixed on the plate. But it was a single image. It couldn't be reproduced like modern negative film can. Third, it was easy to damage the image. Even though it was fixed on the plate, rubbing it—or even touching it—could remove the image. So all daguerreotype images had to be covered with glass to protect them. What else . . . ? Ah, the mercury it required . . . Mercury's a dangerous chemical. It's actually poisonous to humans. Some photographers are believed to have died due to constant exposure to mercury. Finally, some new photographic processes were developed. These perfected the daguerreotype method. The exposure time was reduced. Fewer chemicals were used. The images could be copied. There was no need to display them with glass. The daguerreotype's main legacy was that it was the first practical method of photography. It introduced the world to photographic images. And that has had an enormous impact.

1 [Gist-Content Question]

Before explaining how the daguerreotype worked, the professor states, "It was complicated, too." After completing her explanation, she states, "That was a lot of steps, wasn't it?" So she explains the process to show how complicated it was.

2 [Detail Question]

The professor mentions, "It was a single image. It couldn't be reproduced like modern negative film can." She also says, "Third, it was easy to damage the image. Even though it was fixed on the plate, rubbing it—or even touching it—could remove the image."

3 [Connecting Content Question]

The professor notes, "First, the exposure time was too long. So it was impossible to capture many images. For instance, photographing people was difficult. After all, how'd you like to stand still for twenty minutes?" So the likely outcome of taking a picture with the lens exposed for only five minutes is that the image will be unclear.

4 [Understanding Organization Question]

Before mentioning the specific changes that were made to the daguerreotype, the professor declares, "Finally, some new photographic processes were developed. These perfected the daguerreotype method." So she is telling the students what improvements were made to it.

5 [Understanding Attitude Question]

The professor states, "The daguerreotype's main legacy was that it was the first practical method of photography. It introduced the world to photographic images. And that has had an enormous impact." So she believes that it has an important global legacy.

6 [Understanding Function Question]

When the professor comments that she might spell the word incorrectly if she tries it again, she is implying that she has just spelled a difficult word for the students.

TOEFL Practice Tests C2 p.136

1 Ⓑ   2 Ⓓ   3 Ⓐ   4 Ⓒ   5 Ⓓ

Script 02-56

M1 Student: Greetings, Professor Lee. I just listened to your telephone message about ten minutes ago. [4]I came here from my dormitory as soon as I could.

M2 Professor: Thank you so much for the quick response, Todd. Why don't you have a seat right there? **You sound like you're breathing hard.**

M1: Thank you, sir. I'm all right. I'm just a little out of shape.

M2: Now, Todd . . . I have a question for you. Are you planning to stay here at school this summer? I know you did that last year. What about this year?

M1: Oh, yes. I like staying on campus during the

summer. I am going to take a history class this summer. It should be pretty fun. Um, why do you ask?

M2: Well, are you going to be looking for a job?

M1: Hmm . . . I'm most likely going to work at the library like I always do. I have a good job there.

M2: Oh, I see. Well, I have a job that I would like to offer you. I have several old interviews that are on tape. But they need to be transcribed. So I need someone to listen to the interviews and type all of the dialogue on them.

M1: Wow. That sounds like a lot of work.

M2: [5]Yes. It won't be easy to do. And I suppose it might get a little tedious at times.

M1: Uh, you're not really selling the job very well, sir.

M2: **I suppose not.** Anyway, the money isn't too bad. The job pays ten dollars an hour. And you can work as many hours as you need to finish the project. I got a grant from the school for this project.

M1: Well, I'll have to think about it. I really like my library job a lot.

M2: Okay. That's fine. You know, um, you could do both. Maybe you could just work on my project for one or two hours a day. And then you can still work at the library. It would take about two months to finish my project though.

M1: That's a possibility. When do you need an answer by?

M2: Tomorrow evening. Let me know by then, please.

1 [Gist-Content Question]

The student and the professor are discussing a job offer that the professor makes to the student.

2 [Detail Question]

In response to the professor's question, the student says, "I am going to take a history class this summer."

3 [Detail Question]

The professor tells the student, "Well, I have a job that I would like to offer you. I have several old interviews that are on tape. But they need to be transcribed. So I need someone to listen to the interviews and type all of the dialogue on them."

4 [Making Inferences Question]

The professor remarks, "You sound like you're breathing hard," after the student notes that he went to the professor's office as soon as he could. The professor

therefore implies that the student ran to get to his office.

5 [Understanding Function Question]

When the professor answers, "I suppose not," he is agreeing with the student that he is not doing well at convincing the student to take the job.

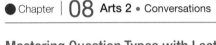 Vocabulary **Review**   p.140

1	Ⓒ	2	Ⓓ	3	Ⓑ	4	Ⓐ
5	Ⓒ	6	Ⓐ	7	Ⓐ	8	Ⓒ
9	Ⓕ	10	Ⓑ	11	Ⓓ	12	Ⓔ

● Chapter | **08** **Arts 2** • Conversations

Mastering Question Types with Lectures & Conversations A   p.142

[TYPES 1–4]

TYPE 1	Ⓐ, Ⓑ	TYPE 2	Ⓑ
TYPE 3	Ⓓ	TYPE 4	Ⓑ

Script 02-57

M Professor: Was this the face that launched a thousand ships and burnt the topless towers of Illium . . . ? Does anyone know who wrote those lines . . . ? Don't guess Shakespeare. It wasn't him. Anyone . . . ? No? Okay, those lines were written by Christopher Marlowe. They appear in his masterpiece *The Tragical History of Dr. Faustus*. It's often called *Dr. Faustus* for short.

   Marlowe himself had a somewhat tragic life. You see, he died when he was only twenty-nine years old. He was killed in a fight in a tavern. Supposedly, there was an argument about the bill. It's always sad when someone young dies. But it was a real tragedy in Marlowe's case. The reason is that if he had lived, we would be saying his name alongside Shakespeare's. He might have even become more famous than Shakespeare. He was that good.

   Marlowe was a brilliant man. He was well educated and graduated from college when he was just twenty years old. He penned his first play while he was a student. The title was *Tamburlaine the Great*. That play, by the way, had two separate parts. Marlowe would write several more plays before he died. These included *Dr. Faustus* and *The Massacre at Paris*.

   Now, before I continue . . . Let's watch a couple

of clips of Marlowe's plays being performed. Pay attention to the lines the performers speak. After we finish watching, I want you to give me your impressions. Here is a scene from *Dr. Faustus* . . .

TYPE 1 [Gist-Content Question]

The professor mostly focuses on the life and work of Christopher Marlowe.

TYPE 2 [Detail Question]

About Marlowe's death, the professor says, "Marlowe himself had a somewhat tragic life. You see, he died when he was only twenty-nine years old. He was killed in a fight in a tavern. Supposedly, there was an argument about the bill. It's always sad when someone young dies. But it was a real tragedy in Marlowe's case."

TYPE 3 [Understanding Organization Question]

The professor says, "He penned his first play while he was a student. The title was *Tamburlaine the Great*."

TYPE 4 [Understanding Attitude Question]

The professor makes many complimentary comments about Marlowe. He also says, "The reason is that if he had lived, we would be saying his name alongside Shakespeare's. He might have even become more famous than Shakespeare. He was that good."

Checking Listening Accuracy

1 T   2 F   3 F   4 F

[TYPES 5–8]

| **TYPE 5** (A) | **TYPE 6** (B) |
| **TYPE 7** (D) | **TYPE 8** (C) |

Script 02-58

M Professor: [8]When the twentieth century began, many artists were experimenting with abstract art. **As you should know, abstract art differs from realistic art.** In abstract art, objects are not portrayed exactly as they appear in reality. The first modern form of abstract art was created by two artists. They were Pablo Picasso and Georges Braque. I know you've all heard of Picasso. You might not have heard of Braque. The new art form they created was called Cubism.

W Student: Why is it called Cubism? Did Picasso call it that?

M: It wasn't Picasso who, uh, coined the name. Instead, it was a French art critic who did. The art critic described one of Braque's works as being

"full of little cubes." This led to the term Cubism. Cubism, uh, obviously, focused on geometric shapes such as cubes. It was partially inspired by some of the works of Paul Cezanne. However, much of the inspiration for Cubism came from elsewhere. Picasso and Braque got many ideas from African sculptures. If you look at, say, African art—especially tribal masks—you'll understand the connection between the two.

As for Cubism itself . . . Again, it relies on geometric shapes to create images. Cubist paintings also don't show an object from a fixed viewpoint. Instead, they show many views of an object in the same work. Cubism relies upon a combination of forms and colors to do this. Over time, two major styles of Cubism developed. Let's look at the first. It's called Analytical Cubism.

TYPE 5 [Gist-Purpose Question]

The professor mostly focuses on the origin of Cubism and what its main features are.

TYPE 6 [Detail Question]

The professor states, "It wasn't Picasso who, uh, coined the name. Instead, it was a French art critic who did."

TYPE 7 [Making Inferences Question]

The professor notes, "Over time, two major styles of Cubism developed." He therefore implies that not all Cubist works look the same since there are two major styles of it.

TYPE 8 [Understanding Function Question]

When the professor says, "As you should know," he is implying that they have already talked about abstract art in his class.

Checking Listening Accuracy

1 F   2 T   3 T   4 F

[TYPES 9–12]

| **TYPE 9** (D) | **TYPE 10** (A) |
| **TYPE 11** (D) | **TYPE 12** (C) |

Script 02-59

M Student: Excuse me. I'm looking for a book for one of my classes. But, uh, it doesn't seem to be on the shelves. At least I can't find it.

W Bookstore Employee: Really? Let me have the name of the book. I'll check it out on my computer.

M: Sure. It's this book here . . . Uh, the one that I

circled.

W: Okay . . . Let me type in the title . . . Hmm . . . According to the computer, it's all sold out. We ordered twenty copies, and they've all been purchased.

M: Twenty copies? But the class has forty students. Why didn't you order enough books?

W: [12]Nowadays, lots of students order their textbooks online. So we don't usually order many copies of some books. **Especially the expensive ones.**

M: Oh, that makes sense. I guess I should order this book online then, huh?

W: Yeah. That's exactly what I'd do. I'm sorry that we don't have it.

TYPE 9 [Gist-Purpose Question]

The student and the bookstore employee are discussing a book that the student is looking for but cannot find.

TYPE 10 [Detail Question]

The bookstore employee states, "Nowadays, lots of students order their textbooks online. So we don't usually order many copies of some books."

TYPE 11 [Making Inferences Question]

The student asks, "I guess I should order this book online then, huh?" the bookstore employee agrees with him. So the student will probably purchase the book online.

TYPE 12 [Understanding Function Question]

When the bookstore employee declares that the bookstore often doesn't order many copies of some books, "Especially the expensive ones," she implies that the textbook that the student is looking for is expensive.

♪ Checking Listening Accuracy

1 T   2 F   3 T   4 F

Mastering Topics with Lectures B1   p.145

1 Ⓓ   2 Ⓑ   3 Ⓑ

Script & Graphic Organizer   02-60

W Professor: I'm sure you all know what a quilt is. I remember my mother covering me with one on cold days to help keep me warm. But did you know this . . . ? Quilts are considered forms of art. In fact, many

people don't use them as bedding. Instead, they hang quilts on walls to display them. Interesting, isn't it?

Let me tell you a bit about quilts in general and how they're made. A quilt typically has three layers. The top layer is the decorative part. It's called the quilt top. The middle layer contains the soft, thick material. It's known as the batting. The third and final, um, bottom layer is the backing. It's often similar to the quilt top, but it's not, uh, not as decorative. The person making the quilt sews or stitches all three layers together. After the layers are brought together, the person adds borders to the quilt. This makes it whole. In the past, quilts were made by hand. However, nowadays, they're made by machines as well.

The process of making a quilt differs from place to place. Sometimes a quilt is made of three large pieces . . . uh, one for each layer. Other times, small blocks of the quilt are completed first. These small blocks each include a quilt top, batting, and backing. Then, the blocks are joined together to form one large quilt after the borders are added. Each block may contain identical, similar, or completely different images. In the past, people often gathered together to make quilts. These gatherings were called quilting bees. People made quilts at them, but they were also social events. Friends and family members used to gather and talk while they worked.

As for quilts as works of art . . . Well, they come in different forms. Some quilts portray historical events. In fact, some families make quilts that show their family history. Quilts may show national symbols. People in different cultures and ethnic groups have their own quilting styles. Essentially, uh, as you'll see in just a minute, there are as many styles and patterns as there are quilts.

Quilts

The Three Parts of Quilts:	How People Make Quilts:
- Top layer = the decorative part that is the quilt top	May make quilts from three large pieces; may use small blocks that are then sewn together
- Middle layer = has the soft, thick material and is called the batting	
- Bottom layer = is called the backing; is similar to the top but is not as decorative	**What Quilts May Show:** May portray historical events; may show a family's history; may show national symbols; may have many styles and patterns

1 [Detail Question]

The professor says, "The middle layer contains the soft, thick material. It's known as the batting."

2 [Understanding Organization Question]

The professor comments, "These gatherings were called quilting bees. People made quilts at them, but they were also social events."

3 [Making Inferences Question]

At the end of the lecture, the professor tells the class, "Essentially, uh, as you'll see in just a minute, there are as many styles and patterns as there are quilts." So she will probably show them some pictures of quilts next.

✓ **Listening Comprehension**

1 b   2 a   3 d   4 c

Mastering Topics with Lectures B2
p.146

1 Ⓐ   2 Ⓒ   3 Method Acting: ③, ④   The Acting Style before Method Acting: ①, ②

Script & Graphic Organizer 02-61

W Professor: I wonder if any of you have heard of Konstantin Stanislavski . . . No . . . ? That's too bad. I say that because he had a tremendous influence on the world of acting. Stanislavski was the director of the Moscow Art Theater and the author of numerous books on acting. He was also the founder of method acting. Yes, Tim?

M Student: I know about method acting. That's when actors use their own personal experiences to, uh, to essentially become the character they are playing, right?

W: That's correct. It doesn't matter what role the actor plays. He could be a hero or a villain. He really, well, tries to become that character.

Now, uh, before method acting became popular, performers used different acting methods. Basically, they used exaggerated gestures. They also made loud over-the-top exclamations. These let actors convey their intentions and emotions to their audiences. You might have seen this kind of acting in old movies from many decades ago.

Method actors, however, take a different approach. They portray their characters based on how they'd act in real life. So the actors try to, um, tap into their own feelings and experiences. This permits them to emotionally and psychologically understand the characters they're playing. So if small gestures,

pauses, or soft-spoken words can accurately portray a character . . . then that's what method actors do.

Over time, method acting became popular in the U.S. In 1931, the Group Theater began to use it. Elia Kazan was a member of the Group Theater. He would later direct *On the Waterfront*. It was a classic movie. And it provides an outstanding demonstration of method acting. If you haven't seen that movie, I highly recommend it.

In the 1940s and 1950s, more people began teaching method acting. Let's see . . . Lee Strasberg popularized it at his Actors' Studio in New York. Stella Adler taught method acting at the Actors' Group, also in New York. Which actors used this style? Well, there were many. Marlon Brando . . . James Dean . . . Montgomery Clift. As for more modern actors, method actors include Al Pacino, Dustin Hoffman, Paul Newman, and Robert De Niro.

Method Acting

Early Acting Methods:	Method Acting:	Method Acting Instructors:
- Used exaggerated gestures - Made loud over-the-top exclamations - Let actors convey their intentions and emotions to their audiences	- Actors use their own personal experiences to become the characters they're playing - Tap into their feelings - Emotionally and psychologically understand their characters	- Konstantin Stanislavski = founded method acting - Lee Strasberg = ran the Actors' Studio in New York - Stella Adler = taught at the Actors' Group in New York

1 [Gist-Purpose Question]

The professor describes the style of acting before method acting. Then, she states, "Method actors, however, take a different approach," before describing method acting. So she is contrasting the two styles.

2 [Understanding Attitude Question]

The professor comments, "He would later direct *On the Waterfront*. It was a classic movie. And it provides an outstanding demonstration of method acting. If you haven't seen that movie, I highly recommend it."

3 [Connecting Content Question]

According to the professor, in method acting, actors used their own experiences and tried to understand the characters they were playing. As for the acting style before method acting, actors used exaggerated gestures and made loud exclamations.

Listening Comprehension

1 b   2 d   3 c   4 a

Mastering Topics with Conversations B3   p.147

1 Ⓑ   2 Ⓒ   3 Ⓒ

Script & Graphic Organizer 02-62

W Student: Good afternoon. Excuse me, but are you Professor Stephenson?

M Professor: Yes, I am. How may I assist you today, young lady?

W: Well, my name is Denise Reed. I'm a student in the History Department here. I was trying to register for the seminar you're teaching next semester. That's the one on modern economic history. Uh, but when I tried to enroll, the man said that the class was full.

M: Ah, yes. That makes sense. You see, it's a seminar. So, um, only fifteen students are allowed to sign up for it.

W: Why do so few students take it?

M: Since it's a seminar, I expect lots of participation from the students. So I keep the number of students in the class low. That lets everyone get many opportunities to talk during class.

W: I see. Then, um . . . Is there anything I can do to get into your class?

M: ³You could sign up to be on the waiting list. That way, if anyone drops the class, you'll get the first chance to join. How does that sound to you?

W: **I guess that's better than nothing.** But I think I'm going to see if any other seminars are still open as well.

M: That's probably a good idea. The chances are very low that you'll actually get in my class. I'm terribly sorry about that.

Office Hours

Reason for Visiting:	Professor's Response:
Wants to enroll in the professor's seminar	Only allows fifteen students to take the class

Student's Question:	Professor's Response:
Asks why so few students are allowed in the class	Wants few students so that they can all talk during class

1 [Gist-Purpose Question]

The student visits the professor to discuss a seminar that he is teaching and which she wants to register for.

2 [Detail Question]

About the seminar, the professor remarks, "So, um, only fifteen students are allowed to sign up for it."

3 [Making Inferences Question]

When the student says, "I guess that's better than nothing," she implies that she will sign up for the waiting list.

Listening Comprehension

1 d   2 b   3 c   4 a

TOEFL Practice Tests C1   p.148

1 Ⓑ   2 Ⓑ   3 Ⓓ   4 Ⓒ   5 Ⓐ   6 Ⓓ

Script 02-63

M Professor: Before we move on to the twentieth century, we have to discuss one last artist from the nineteenth. I'm referring to Paul Cezanne of France. Here's a quick bio . . . Cezanne lived from 1839 to 1906. His father was a banker, so his family was well off. But like most artists, Cezanne experienced financial problems during his lifetime. His father wanted him to be a lawyer. Cezanne obliged him by studying law. Then, in the 1860s, Cezanne moved to Paris to focus on art. This angered his father. Nevertheless, Cezanne's father still gave him a small allowance to live on. Cezanne only remained in Paris for a short time though. Instead, he spent most of his time near his family home in southern France.

Let me show you some of Cezanne's works as I talk about him. Art historians consider Cezanne to be an Impressionist. Like most Impressionists, his work was misunderstood when he made it. In both Paris and the south of France, Cezanne's work was ridiculed. He mainly painted still lifes of fruit . . . portraits of family members . . . and himself . . . landscapes . . . and scenes with nude bathers . . .

Cezanne's personality greatly affected his paintings. He was often troubled by depression. He had few close friends. And he was also socially, um, awkward. His depression and feelings of isolation are evident in his early works. Heavy black lines, dark tones, and isolated figures are common. You can see what I mean here . . . Look at this portrait of his father in an armchair. It's from 1866. Here's a man reading a newspaper all alone. The background is partly in shadow. There are few bright colors. Notice the short, heavy brushstrokes . . . They're easy to see . . . This was a trademark of Cezanne's. Many of his other works from the 1860s have a similar look.

However, Cezanne's style changed. His later work is more colorful and vibrant. In the 1870s, he turned to landscapes. Take a look . . . He studied under the landscape artist Camille Pissarro. Here's a country scene. Notice the greens and blues . . . the reflections of the trees in the water . . . The brushstrokes are short but not as heavy or as easy to see as before. During this period, as you may have guessed, Cezanne was much happier. He got married and reconciled with his father. This was, perhaps, the happiest time of his life. His father even built a studio for Cezanne near the family home. When his father died in 1886, Cezanne inherited a vast sum of money.

[6]As he grew older, Cezanne became somewhat famous. **In the 1890s, people started to recognize his early paintings as great works of art . . . uh, which they were.** Around this time, Cezanne became interested in geometric shapes. He often saw objects in his paintings as cubes, cylinders, and triangles. Take a look at this work . . . It's one of his last paintings. Notice that it's a village scene with some trees and buildings. But the details are hard to distinguish. Note also the clear use of geometric patterns.

W Student: It reminds me of a Picasso.

M: Very good, Brenda. In fact, Cezanne is considered the father of the art movement known as Cubism. And that happens to be our next topic for the day.

1 [Gist-Content Question]

The main focus of the lecture is the life and work of Paul Cezanne.

2 [Detail Question]

The professor declares, "Art historians consider Cezanne to be an Impressionist."

3 [Gist-Purpose Question]

The professor says, "Cezanne's personality greatly affected his paintings." Then, he notes how Cezanne's work varied depending upon whether he was happy or sad.

4 [Understanding Function Question]

The professor tells the students about how Cezanne's work changed. Then, he comments, "During this period, as you may have guessed, Cezanne was much happier.

He got married."

5 [Connecting Content Question]

At the beginning of the lecture, the professor states, "Before we move on to the twentieth century, we have to discuss one last artist from the nineteenth." At the end of the lecture, he notes, "In fact, Cezanne is considered the father of the art movement known as Cubism. And that happens to be our next topic for the day." So it can be inferred that Cubism is an art movement from the twentieth century.

6 [Understanding Attitude Question]

When the professor says, "People started to recognize his early paintings as great works of art . . . uh, which they were," he is letting the students know that he believes that Cezanne's art was great.

TOEFL Practice Tests C2   p.150

1 (C)   2 (D)   3 (C)   4 (A)   5 (B)

Script 02-64

M1 Student: Coach Young, I need to have a word with you. It's kind of important.

M2 Basketball Coach: Sure, Jim. What's going on? Are you ready for the big tournament this weekend?

M1: Actually . . . I need to talk to you about the tournament. I, uh . . . I don't think I'll be able to go to it.

M2: What are you talking about? Are you hurt? No, you can't be. You look fine to me.

M1: No, sir. I'm not hurt. It's just that, well . . . We're leaving for the tournament in Wellborn this Friday at one in the afternoon, right?

M2: That's right. It's a four-hour bus ride. And our first game is at eight o'clock. So if we leave then, we'll get there in plenty of time. Uh . . . Wait a minute. Do you have a class then? I could talk to your professor if that's the problem.

M1: No, sir. All of my classes are in the morning.

M2: I'm really confused, Jim. What's the matter?

M1: As you know, I'm a senior, sir. And I'm busy applying for jobs. Well, this one company wants to interview me on Friday . . . at two o'clock. It's probably going to take about an hour or so. But since the bus leaves at one and my interview is at two . . .

M2: Yeah. I see your point . . . Is there any way that you can postpone the interview? Or maybe you could go there on Thursday?

M1: I already asked. They said no. And this is a job I really want. So I have to go to the interview. I'm really sorry about this, Coach.

M2: Hold on. I'm not giving up yet. You don't have a car, right? So you can't drive yourself to the tournament. Am I correct?

M1: Yes, sir. I don't have my car here on campus. It's back home at my parents' house.

M2: Well, in that case, I'll just have one of my assistant coaches drive you as soon as you're done with the interview.

M1: You can do that?

M2: Of course I can. You're one of my starters, Jim. I'm counting on you to have a big tournament. Now, let me know the address where you're going to be. I'll have someone waiting for you outside the building. Once the interview is over, you two can drive to the tournament together.

1 [Gist-Content Question]

The student tells his coach, "I need to talk to you about the tournament. I, uh . . . I don't think I'll be able to go to it."

2 [Detail Question]

The student says, "Well, this one company wants to interview me on Friday . . . at two o'clock."

3 [Detail Question]

To solve the student's problem, the coach says, "I'll just have one of my assistant coaches drive you as soon as you're done with the interview."

4 [Understanding Attitude Question]

The coach states, "You're one of my starters, Jim. I'm counting on you to have a big tournament." He clearly believes that the student is a valuable member of the team.

5 [Making Inferences Question]

Because the coach will have someone drive the student to the tournament, it can be inferred that the student will be able to participate in the tournament.

p.154

1	B	2	B	3	D	4	D
5	A	6	B	7	E	8	D
9	A	10	F	11	B	12	C

Part C

Experiencing the TOEFL iBT
Actual Tests

Actual Test | **01**   p.156

1 D	2 B	3 B	4 C	5 A
6 D	7 A, C	8 A	9 D	10 B	11 B
12 A	13 B	14 D	15 C	16 C	17 A

[Questions 1–5]

Script 03-03

M Student: Hello, Professor Owens. I hate to bother you, but I have a question.

W Professor: You're not bothering me, Rick. What do you need to know?

M: Well, uh, it's about Professor Jackson. I've been looking for him all day long. But I haven't been able to find him. I know your office is right next to his. So, uh, do you happen to know where he is right now?

W: Sorry, Rick. I haven't seen him all day long either.

M: That's too bad. I really need to find him.

W: Ah, hold on a second . . . I remember talking to him yesterday. He told me that he won't be back at school until Monday.

M: Monday? You mean, like, next week?

W: Yes. I'm afraid so. He went to a conference in, uh . . . Chicago, I think. He's presenting a paper there. It's a pretty big deal for him.

M: Well, that's great for him. But it's not so great for me. I can't believe this.

W: What's the problem, Rick? The semester is only two weeks old. So you can't have any serious assignments in his class yet, can you?

M: Actually, I'm not even enrolled in his class. I was hoping to sign up for it though. But today is the last day we're allowed to sign up for new classes. And, well, if he's not here . . .

W: Yeah, I see what you mean. Only a professor can sign a slip for a student to add a class. Out of curiosity . . . Which of his two classes were you hoping to add this semester?

M: The one on medieval history. I don't have to take it of course. My focus is on modern American history.

However, the class looks pretty interesting. And I've always been fascinated by the Middle Ages. I guess I'll have to wait until next semester now.

W: You know . . . You might not have to do that.

M: Huh? How so?

W: [5]Did you know that I'm also teaching a class on medieval history this semester?

M: Yeah. It meets on Tuesday and Thursday from one to two thirty, right? **I just assumed that your class was already full.** It is, isn't it?

W: Not quite yet. I happen to have room for some new students who want to enroll in the class. So I could sign you up . . . if you want.

M: I want. I definitely want. Can you sign an add slip for me? I've got one right here.

W: I sure can. Let me grab a pen from my office. Then you can go to the Registrar's office and turn the form in. Welcome to History 342, Rick. It's good to have you as a student again.

1 [Gist-Purpose Question]

The student goes to Professor Owens and says, "Well, uh, it's about Professor Jackson. I've been looking for him all day long. But I haven't been able to find him. I know your office is right next to his. So, uh, do you happen to know where he is right now?" So he is looking for another professor.

2 [Detail Question]

The student wants to sign up for a class on medieval history that Professor Jackson is teaching.

3 [Understanding Attitude Question]

Throughout the conversation, the professor is very polite to the student. Her tone of voice also indicates that she is kind, so she is considerate toward him.

4 [Making Inferences Question]

At the end of the conversation, the professor tells the student, "It's good to have you as a student again." By saying that, she implies that the student took a class with her in the past.

5 [Understanding Function Question]

The student says, "I just assumed that your class was already full." Professors that are popular usually have full classes. The student assumes that her class is full, so he is implying that she is popular with students.

M1 Professor: We're almost out of time for the day. However, we do have enough time to cover one more topic. Everyone, please look up here on the screen . . . Can anybody tell me what this is . . . ? Ah, I see lots of hands raised. How about . . . Stephanie, what is that?

W Student: That's a picture of a mosquito.

M: Correct. Tell me . . . What do you know about mosquitoes?

W: [11]They really like to bite me every summer. I can't stand that. And I know they carry diseases. But, uh, I'm not sure which ones. Malaria maybe?

M: **That was a good guess.** And yes, you're correct. Mosquitoes do carry diseases and also like biting me and probably everyone else in this room.

But before I discuss that, let me give you a few facts about them. There are more than 3,000 species of mosquitoes. They live around the world. But they're especially prevalent in places with warm or hot climates. Mosquitoes breed in stagnant water. Uh, that means water which isn't moving. So they won't lay their eggs in rivers or streams. But ponds, lakes, swamps, marshes, and even puddles can be breeding areas for them. That's why you can commonly see them—and experience being bitten by them—at the lake near the school. So be careful if you go fishing or even else just walking there.

Interestingly, females are the only mosquitoes that bite people and suck their blood. Mosquitoes have a tubelike extension called a proboscis. That's spelled P-R-O-B-O-S-C-I-S in case you don't know. Females have a strong one while males have one that is weaker. The proboscis actually has two tubes. One sucks blood from the victim. The other injects an enzyme that causes the blood in the victim to clot. That, uh, keeps the victim from bleeding too much after being bitten. Now can someone tell me why only females drink blood . . . ? Mark, what do you think?

M2 Student: Hmm . . . Males don't drink blood. So the blood can't be used for nourishment. Or both males and females would drink blood. So, uh, I guess females drink blood for their eggs. That seems logical.

M1: Well reasoned, Mark. And correct. The blood provides protein for the mosquitoes' eggs.

Now, since females are the ones that drink blood, that means they're also the ones that transmit diseases. They do that when some of their saliva enters their victims as they feed. Most of the time, mosquito bites are just annoying. Sure, they might cause a bit of pain. They sometimes cause rashes as well. But they aren't deadly.

However, there are three mosquitoes that can spread very deadly diseases. The anopheles mosquito carries malaria and encephalitis. The aedes mosquito carries dengue fever, encephalitis, and yellow fever. And the culex mosquito carries encephalitis and the West Nile virus. Those diseases can be extremely deadly. In fact, the mosquito is the deadliest animal on the planet. Really. It's true. Crocodiles, sharks, and hippos kill a relatively small number of people each year. But mosquitoes may kill anywhere between 800,000 and 3,000,000 people every single year.

M2: That many people? Are you serious? Why don't we ever hear about this?

M1: Well, deaths here in the United States are somewhat uncommon. Most of the deaths take place in Africa. There are also many deaths in South America and Asia, uh, especially in Southeast Asia. So we basically just don't see many deaths happening. As a result, most people don't realize what's going on.

There are, however, some actions we can take. They can reduce the number of annual deaths. First, vaccines are available for some of the diseases spread by mosquitoes. Let's see . . . There's a vaccine for yellow fever. There's one for Japanese encephalitis, too. There's a fairly new vaccine for malaria. It was just approved recently. And that's a good thing because malaria is a huge killer.

People can also take steps to prevent mosquitoes from breeding. Remember that I said mosquitoes breed in stagnant water. Well, removing sources of stagnant water keeps them from breeding. Simply spraying insecticide in areas where they breed kills them, too. Now, uh, some people oppose using insecticides to kill mosquitoes. But they really are the most effective way to get rid of huge numbers of them.

6 [Gist-Content Question]

The professor mainly discusses the harm that mosquitoes cause people.

7 [Detail Question]

The professor tells the class, "The proboscis actually has two tubes. One sucks blood from the victim. The other injects an enzyme that causes the blood in the victim to clot. That, uh, keeps the victim from bleeding too much after being bitten."

8 [Detail Question]

The professor notes, "The blood provides protein for the mosquitoes' eggs."

9 [Connecting Content Question]

The professor talks about what diseases each mosquito spreads.

10 [Understanding Attitude Question]

The professor says, "There's a fairly new vaccine for malaria. It was just approved recently. And that's a good thing because malaria is a huge killer," so he is pleased that the malaria vaccine was approved.

11 [Understanding Function Question]

When the professor says, "That was a good guess," he is indicating that the student's statement is correct.

[Questions 12–17]

Script 03-05

W Professor: During the mid-1800s, photography was invented. Many artists began utilizing it to help them with their paintings. This was the beginning of the school of art called Naturalism. For your information, some people refer to it as Realism. There's some debate on which term is correct. It doesn't matter to me which term you use. But I'm going to use the term Naturalism in this class. All right . . . ? Good.

Naturalism seeks to show the realities of life. Naturalist artists wanted to paint people as they appeared in nature. Their subjects were common people in everyday situations. [16]Cameras and photographs were tools that Naturalists used. They were sort of, uh, I guess you could say memory aids. They helped painters see and then reproduce natural settings. **I suppose they were like writers taking notes to help them as they create a story.**

Excuse me . . . Naturalism originated in France in the 1840s. At that time, the major school of art was Romanticism. As you can probably guess, Romantic artists depicted highly idealized visions of man. They made man heroic, and the world was a place where man triumphed. Naturalism was a rebellion against this. No longer was man heroic. Instead, man was just, well, man. There was nothing special about him.

The first two major Naturalist artists were Jean-Francois Millet and Gustave Courbet. Millet was famous for his landscapes of Normandy. [17]He also painted many rural scenes of common folk. His most famous work is on page 59 in your books. It's called *The Gleaners*. **Take a look at it . . .** It shows some poor women gathering the remains of wheat from a field after the harvest. Back then, this was a common activity. The poor would pick through, or glean, the fields for any small remaining bits of wheat. Notice the stooped labor of the women . . . the small bits of grain they are gathering . . . the colors of the field. This is what Naturalism is all about: common people doing common things. Interestingly, despite Millet's fame today, his work was not well accepted by either art critics or the public during his life. Doesn't that seem like it's always the case?

The same was true of Gustave Courbet's work. His most famous painting is *A Burial at Ornans*. It's up here on the screen . . . It's a large canvas that shows the funeral of Courbet's uncle. The painting was criticized for its lack of religious themes. Its scale was also considered too large for such an, uh, an unimportant event. Notice too how no one seems particularly sad in the painting. Interestingly, Courbet used the actual people who attended the funeral as his models. When he exhibited this work in Paris in 1850, there was, alas, a strong negative reaction to it.

Over time, however, tastes changed. By the 1870s, Naturalism was widely accepted as an art form. Perhaps the artist at that time who came the closest to capturing real life on canvas was Jules Bastien-Lepage. At times, his works almost resemble photographs. Here. You be the judge. This . . . is called *The Haymakers* . . . The workers are in the field resting after a day of hard work. Next . . . is *The Fisherman's Children*. They're playing on some rocks on the beach. Notice how realistic it appears. I mean, uh, you can almost imagine that this was made by someone with a camera. Now, here . . . is his famous painting of Joan of Arc. In it, she's standing outside a small house and appears to be hearing the word of God.

Sadly for the world of art, Bastien-Lepage died of cancer in 1884 when he was only thirty-eight. Despite his short life, he produced more than 200 works of art. He greatly influenced Naturalism all around the world. Both the public and critics in France praised him. Others in Europe and across the Atlantic in the U.S. praised him as well. His paintings were considered real art as opposed to the works produced by the Impressionists, the, uh, the newest artists to come on the scene. Well . . . I think that does it for today. We'll continue next time by discussing the Impressionists and why they made such a bad, uh, impression when they first began painting.

12 [Gist-Content Question]

In her lecture, the professor names and then describes several important works by major Naturalist artists.

13 [Understanding Organization Question]

At the beginning of the lecture, the professor says, "This was the beginning of the school of art called Naturalism. For your information, some people refer to it as Realism." She mentions that Realism is another term for Naturalism.

14 [Detail Question]

The professor tells the students, "The same was true of Gustave Courbet's work. His most famous painting is *A Burial at Ornans*."

15 [Making Inferences Question]

The professor states, "I think that does it for today. We'll continue next time by discussing the Impressionists and why they made such a bad, uh, impression when they first began painting." When she says, "That does it for today," she means that the class is finished, so she is going to dismiss the students next.

16 [Understanding Function Question]

When the professor notes, "I suppose they were like writers," she is making a comparison.

17 [Understanding Attitude Question]

The professor tells the students about a picture on page 59 in their books. She then says, "Take a look at it." She clearly expects the students to have their textbooks with them in class.

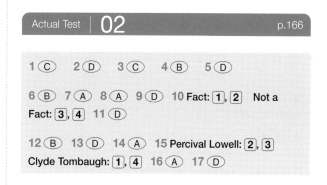

Actual Test | 02   p.166

1 Ⓒ   2 Ⓓ   3 Ⓒ   4 Ⓑ   5 Ⓓ

6 Ⓑ   7 Ⓐ   8 Ⓐ   9 Ⓓ   10 Fact: 1, 2   Not a Fact: 3, 4   11 Ⓓ

12 Ⓑ   13 Ⓓ   14 Ⓐ   15 Percival Lowell: 2, 3 Clyde Tombaugh: 1, 4   16 Ⓐ   17 Ⓓ

[Questions 1–5]

Script 03-08

W Student Activities Office Employee: Good morning. Welcome to the student activities office. How can I help you today?

M Student: Hello. I'm here about the homecoming parade.

W: Ah, sure. The homecoming parade will be held three weeks from now. It will take place on Friday, October 11. It will start at 3:00 in the afternoon. And it should last for slightly more than an hour.

M: Er . . . I'm sorry. I wasn't very clear. I'm actually helping build one of the floats for the parade.

W: I see. Then, um, what exactly do you need assistance with?

M: My team has to purchase some materials for the float we're making. Mr. Roberts—he's the guy in charge of the parade—told me you could order whatever I ask for.

W: Okay. Do you have a list of the items you want?

M: Yes, I do. I've got it right here . . . Uh, here you are. As you can see, it has exactly what we require and the estimated price of each item.

W: ⁵Hold on a moment. Let me take a look, please . . . Um, you're requesting that we spend quite a bit of money. **We do have a budget for this event.**

M: But, uh, Mr. Roberts already looked at everything on the list. He told me this request should be fine. I didn't expect there to be any problems.

W: He said that? He must not have looked at the prices very carefully.

M: So . . . can I get everything? We won't be able to make our float without all of that stuff.

W: Actually, now that I'm looking more closely . . . Hmm . . . You know, you don't have to order the majority of the items on the list. We should already have nearly everything you need.

M: No kidding? How do I get it?

W: You have to speak with someone at B&G. Uh, that's Building and Grounds. The person you should talk to is Mark McNeil. He works in Goddard Hall. His phone number is 546-9863. Give him a call.

M: Okay. But, uh . . . Which items on the list can he help me get?

W: Okay . . . let me give you a hand. I'll give him a call in a moment. I'll tell him that you're going to visit him in his office and that he should help you. You show him the list. Then, he'll get you whatever he can.

M: That sounds perfect. But what if he doesn't have something on the list?

W: Then come back here. I'll order anything else you need. Then you'll be able to get your float for the parade done. How about that?

M: I can't thank you enough.

1 [Gist-Purpose Question]

The student tells the woman, "My team has to purchase some materials for the float we're making. Mr. Roberts—he's the guy in charge of the parade—told me you could order whatever I ask for."

2 [Detail Question]

When the woman asks the student if he has a list of what he needs, the student says, "Here you are," and gives it to her.

3 [Detail Question]

When the student asks the woman how he can get some of the things on his list, she responds, "You have to speak with someone at B&G. Uh, that's Building and Grounds. The person you should talk to is Mark McNeil."

4 [Understand Attitude Question]

At the end of the conversation, the student tells the woman, "I can't thank you enough." So he appreciates her assistance very much.

5 [Understanding Function Question]

When the woman says, "We do have a budget for this event," she is implying that the student wants to spend too much money, so she cannot order everything that he wants.

[Questions 6–11]

Script 03-09

M Professor: We often believe that the people who lived in the past were isolated from one another. Well, uh, that's true in many cases. However, people in many ancient civilizations were aware of one another. They frequently even engaged in trade. Sure, it took a long time for that trade to take place. After all, there were no oceangoing freighters or airplanes 2,000 years ago. Nevertheless, the ancient world had trade routes which merchants used to transport goods from place to place. One of the most famous trade routes was the Silk Road. Have any of you heard of it . . . ? Okay. I see some heads nodding.

So, uh, what was the Silk Road? Where did it begin and end? It pretty much began at the Mediterranean Sea and ended in China. Oh, China is where the name "Silk Road" comes from. During ancient times, only the Chinese possessed the secret to making silk, which was highly valued back then. As a result, silk was commonly traded from the East to the West. Obviously, the Chinese link was an important aspect of the Silk Road. So that's how the route got its name. In addition, uh, it's a fairly new name. It wasn't used until the nineteenth century.

Okay. Back to the route the Silk Road followed . . . First, keep in mind that it wasn't a single road. There were no highways or interstates spanning entire continents centuries ago. Instead, the Silk Road was a series of trails, roads, paths, and even, uh, coastal shipping routes. Basically, it ran from China to India and then went across Asia through the Middle East to the Mediterranean Sea. From there, ships transported trade goods to Rome and other parts of Europe. As for the route itself, in Asia, parts of the Silk Road were well marked. This made it easy to follow. However, in other places, there was nothing except for open land. Travelers just knew to go in a certain direction.

For the most part, the Silk Road followed the best routes. Here's an example. [11]At one place in China, the Silk Road divided into northern and southern routes. How come . . . ? Well, going straight ahead would have taken merchants straight through a desert in western China. **By going north or south, merchants could avoid the desert and, most likely, a fatal trip.** What else . . . ? The Silk Road required travelers to cross mountains . . . to go across small deserts . . . and to traverse wide-open grasslands. It went through populated and unpopulated areas. In short, the trip from China to the Middle East required many long, tiring months of traveling.

W Student: Who traveled on the Silk Road? I mean, uh, did individual travelers go on it? Or was it mostly large groups?

M: There were occasional lone travelers. Yet they were rare. Instead, huge caravans laden with goods most frequently used the Silk Road. Why were these caravans more common than individual travelers? Well, there was safety in numbers. Today, most people don't think twice about traveling alone. In the past, this definitely wasn't the case. Regrettably, gangs of thieves regularly attacked lone travelers and even large groups on the Silk Road. Therefore, caravans and merchants always took guards with them. The guards battled the thieves and brigands when they attacked. Some caravans were overwhelmed and destroyed. Yet the majority reached their destinations. Once the merchants made it to the Middle East, their Chinese silks, Indian spices, and other luxurious goods were sent elsewhere. Where? Mostly to Rome, Egypt, Greece, and other places in the West.

W: When did the Silk Road trade begin?

M: It began at different times in different places. The first trade routes in Asia began around 3,000 B.C. The donkey, the camel, and the horse had all been domesticated by that time. Oh, yeah, uh, using

animals to transport goods means you can, well, carry more goods with you. That makes trade more profitable. But the Silk Road didn't come into existence in 3,000 B.C. Please don't misunderstand. I'd say that by, oh, 300 B.C., the overland route was pretty well established. This was thanks primarily to Alexander the Great. He conquered much of western Asia until his death in 323 B.C., which helped open more trade routes throughout Asia.

6 [Gist-Content Question]

Throughout his lecture, the professor mostly talks about which routes the Silk Road followed in various parts of Asia.

7 [Gist-Purpose Question]

About the origins of the Silk Road's name, the professor notes, "Oh, China is where the name 'Silk Road' comes from. During ancient times, only the Chinese possessed the secret to making silk, which was highly valued back then. As a result, silk was commonly traded from east to west. Obviously, the Chinese link was an important aspect of the Silk Road. So that's how the route got its name." By stating this, he is stressing the road's connection with China.

8 [Understanding Attitude Question]

The professor mentions that the Silk Road was dangerous because of gangs of thieves. He explains that they attacked lone travelers. So he feels that the Silk Road was unsafe for lone travelers.

9 [Making Inferences Question]

The professor first talks about silk going from China to the west. The professor also states, "Once the merchants made it to the Middle East, their Chinese silks, Indian spices, and other luxurious goods were sent elsewhere. Where? Mostly to Rome, Egypt, Greece, and other places in the West." He does not talk about trade goods going from the West to the East. So he implies that more trade goods went to the West than to the East.

10 [Detail Question]

According to the lecture, it is a fact that the Silk Road went from the Mediterranean Sea to China. The professor also mentions that sometimes the Silk Road went over mountains. However, lone travelers sometimes went on the Silk Road, so it is not a fact that only caravans were permitted to travel on it. In addition, Alexander the Great did not order the Silk Road to be constructed. It was already in existence before Alexander the Great lived.

11 [Understanding Function Question]

When the professor mentions that going across the desert could be a "fatal trip," he means that it was dangerous—and possibly deadly—for merchants to cross the desert.

[Questions 12–17]

Script 03-10

> **W Professor**: That's enough about the major planets in the solar system. [16]Now, let's examine the dwarf planets. You remember how they're different from the major planets, right . . . ? Okay. **I'm glad I don't have to cover that again.** Remember also that Pluto is no longer a major planet. Nowadays, astronomers consider it a dwarf planet.
>
> **M Student**: Professor Kimble, I have a question. Why did people consider Pluto a major planet to begin with?
>
> **W**: Hmm . . . Well, it's related to a couple of things. The first is connected with how Pluto was discovered. The second concerns how little we knew about it for decades.
>
> I suppose this is a good time to discuss the discovery of Pluto. Let's begin . . . Pluto was discovered in 1930. For many years before that, astronomers believed an unknown planet existed somewhere beyond both Neptune and Uranus. Neptune had been discovered in 1845. The reason people had searched for it was that changes in Uranus's orbit made astronomers believe that another planet's gravity was affecting it. They were right, and, thus, Neptune was discovered.
>
> So when Neptune's orbit underwent the same changes, people naturally assumed there was a, uh, another planet affecting it. Some astronomers began calling it Planet X. Percival Lowell led the hunt for Pluto. He was a wealthy man who came to astronomy late in his life. He was mostly interested in Mars. Lowell, however, became captivated by the notion of finding an unknown planet. He established a project to find Planet X. Unfortunately for him, he died in 1916 before Pluto was discovered.
>
> Nevertheless, Lowell left money to continue the quest, and others took up the cause. By making mathematical calculations, astronomers had a, uh, a general idea of where Planet X should be. They actually discovered it by taking photographs. The planet was too small to tell it apart from the stars in the background. The astronomers needed to see movement. So they took photos of the area every two weeks. Finally, in early 1930, they confirmed the existence of the mysterious Planet X. Later, of course, it was named Pluto. Yes? Another question?
>
> **M**: Yes. Um, why did it take them so long to find Pluto?
>
> **W**: Two reasons: the equipment they used and a lack of money. The astronomers then didn't have the excellent telescopes and cameras we possess today. So observing such small faraway objects was difficult for them. In fact, they later determined that they'd captured Pluto on film back in 1915. But no one had realized it at that time. In addition, the money . . . Well, Lowell left money for the project, but his wife wanted it back after he died. So there were legal issues that took until 1929 to sort out.
>
> Then, a year later, a young astronomer named Clyde Tombaugh made the big discovery. He examined some photographs taken two weeks apart in January 1930. He used a special machine. It could show small changes in photographs that the human eye might easily miss. Tombaugh noticed that one object had clearly changed positions. He realized that it had to be Planet X. Today, Tombaugh is officially credited with discovering Pluto. But Percival Lowell played a major role in its discovery.
>
> As you can imagine, Pluto is far from Earth. Even with powerful telescopes, it's almost impossible to see much of anything on Pluto. That's why it was first classified as a major planet. Pluto's mass was initially calculated based on its influence on Neptune, not by making any real observations. For instance, at first, Pluto was thought to be the same size as Earth. Later, it was considered to be a smaller Mars-sized planet. [17]Then, even later, in 1978, astronomers discovered that Pluto had a moon. But, uh, the moon was almost the same size as Pluto. It seemed like they were binary planets . . . **uh, you know, twins.** Eventually, Pluto's mass was more accurately calculated. And the final result . . . ? Today, Pluto is believed to be smaller than the moon. Earth's moon, that is. This contributed greatly to Pluto being considered a dwarf planet and not a major planet. Okay, so, uh, how about looking at some of the other dwarf planets now?

12 [Detail Question]

The professor states, "So when Neptune's orbit underwent the same changes, people naturally assumed there was a, uh, another planet affecting it. Some astronomers began calling it Planet X." This was why people began to search for Pluto.

13 [Understanding Attitude Question]

A student asks why it took so long to find Pluto. The professor answers, "Two reasons: the equipment they used and a lack of money." So she implies that if the astronomers had possessed better equipment, they could have found Pluto faster.

14 [Understanding Organization Question]

During her lecture, the professor talks about the events leading to the discovery of Pluto in chronological order.

15 [Connecting Content Question]

According to the lecture, Percival Lowell provided money to help find Pluto. He was also interested in Mars before he started to search for Pluto. As for Clyde Tombaugh, he actually discovered Pluto. To do this, he used a special machine that analyzed photographs taken of the sky.

16 [Making Inferences Question]

When the professor says, "I'm glad I don't have to cover that again," while mentioning dwarf planets, she implies that she has already discussed dwarf planets in a previous lecture.

17 [Understanding Function Question]

The professor states that Pluto and its moon are like binary planets. Then, she tells the students, "Uh, you know, twins." When she says that, she is clarifying the term that she just used.

MEMO

MEMO

MEMO

MEMO

TOEFL®
MAP New TOEFL® Edition
Listening

Basic